The sexual relationship

An object relations view of sex and the family

David E. Scharff, M.D.

Tavistock/Routledge
London and New York

First published in 1982
by Routledge
11 New Fetter Lane, London EC4P 4EE
Reprinted as a new paperback in 1988
Reprinted 1990

Simultaneously published in the USA and Canada
by Routledge
a division of Routledge, Chapman and Hall Inc.
29 West 35th Street, New York, NY 10001

Set in 10 on 12 pt Press Roman by
Donald Typesetting, Bristol
Printed in Great Britain by
T.J. Press (Padstow) Ltd, Padstow, Cornwall

Library of Congress Cataloging in Publication Data

Scharff, David E., 1941 –

The sexual relationship
(The International library of group
psychotherapy and group process)
Includes bibliographical references and
index.
1. Sex (Psychology) 2. Children and sex.
3. Parent and child. 4. Marriage – Psychological
aspects. 5. Sexual disorders. I. Title.
II. Series. [DNLM: 1. Family. 2. Object
attachment. 3. Sex behaviour. 4. Sex disorders –
Etiology. 5. Psychosexual development.
WM 460.5.S83 S311s]
BF692.S265   616.6′9   82-7477

ISBN 0-415-00081-5   AACR2

For Jill

Contents

Illustrations

Tables

Preface and acknowledgments

The recent revolution in knowledge about the sexual response and its treatment has at times led to an almost exclusive focus on the behavioral and mechanistic aspects of sexual interaction. But as the field of sex therapy has grown, the difficulty of the work has become more apparent, and the need for further study of the place of sexuality in human relationships has emerged.

Psychoanalytic object relations theory, which has already proved useful in the study and treatment of marriages, can be readily extended to the study of the sexual relationship. In turn, knowledge gained about physical aspects of sexual interaction through the specific focus of sex therapy can illuminate the understanding of the inner object relationships. This book is an attempt to combine this dual focus, and is the result of my efforts to synthesize knowledge and experience from the fields of sex therapy, psychoanalysis, especially object relations theory, marital studies, and family therapy.

On the way to this point I was influenced by many valued teachers and colleagues in Boston, as well as more recently in Washington, D.C., and London, England. Here I want to mention those whose influence on the writing of this book is more direct. In my year at the Tavistock Centre in 1972-3, there were many of the staff who introduced me to British object relations theory. Arthur Hyatt Williams, the late Dugmore Hunter, and Isca Wittenberg of the Adolescent Department, taught me to use the work of Melanie Klein in particular. Robert Gosling and Pierre Turquet taught me something about the application of object relations theory to group process and Fred Balfour about its application to adolescent development. I had the good fortune to spend time with the late Henry Dicks whose book *Marital Tensions* is the starting place for my work, and with John Bowlby by whom I have been greatly influenced. I am especially grateful to John Hill for guiding me through my first clinical research which resulted in our collaborating in the volume *Between Two Worlds: Aspects of the Transition from School to Work* (London: Careers Consultants, 1976). Although the subject is superficially unrelated, I could not have completed the current work without the many lessons I learned from him in that collaboration.

In Washington, D.C., I owe a great deal to my supervisors, teachers, and colleagues in the Washington Psychoanalytic Institute and at Children's Hospital. Roger Shapiro and Vamik Volkan have helped me integrate object relations theory with other aspects of psychoanalysis, and Jean Yacoubian has provided thoughtful discussion of child development. The faculty and students of the Psychodynamic Family Therapy Program of the Washington School of Psychiatry have been invaluable in the testing of ideas and have collaborated in thinking about the use of object relations theory in family and marital therapy.

My clinical work developed in collaboration at the Sex Therapy Program at Preterm of Washington, D.C. I owe much to that organization for supporting our program and to my colleagues there who include currently Elise de Vries, Pat Harding, Benjamin Ellis, and formerly Sally Bowie and James Lieberman. We were helped in 1974 to launch our program by consultation from Michael Evans, with the generous support of Judy Jones, then Director of Preterm of Washington, D.C., and Harry Levin, the first Chairman of the Board.

Elise de Vries, Benjamin Ellis, and Wells Goodrich were gracious in reading the manuscript and making many helpful comments. Charles Schwarzbeck contributed substantially to my thinking on the relevance of early mother–infant interaction to the sexual relationship, and reviewed several parts of the manuscript in depth. Susan Williamson, with an extraordinary ability to decipher my writing while remaining cheerful, provided a thoroughly professional secretarial service for the several drafts and final copy. Elaine Mariggio supplied additional secretarial support as did Brenda White through Preterm.

I especially want to thank two people without whom I could not have completed this task. Earl Hopper gave many hours to careful reading and thoughtful commentary, guiding me through to publication. Jill, as my wife, encouraged me to begin and to continue writing, managing the family needs during my preoccupation, and, as my colleague, contributed ideas and major editorial assistance.

Finally, I am grateful to my patients who have taught me what I have learned about the sexual relationship.

My thanks to Hospital Publications, publishers of *Medical Aspects of Human Sexuality*, and Human Sciences Press, publishers of the *Journal of Sex and Marital Therapy*, for permission to draw upon articles of mine previously published therein; and to Jason Aronson, Inc., for permission to use a figure from *Female Sexuality and the Oedipus Complex* by Humberto Nagera. Material from Canto I of *The Inferno* by Dante Alighieri, translated by John Ciardi, copyright © 1954 John Ciardi, is reprinted by arrangement with The New American Library, Inc., New York.

Foreword.

by A.C. Robin Skynner

This book is, I believe, the first satisfactory treatment of sexual love within its natural context of parenthood, the family and the developmental life cycle. It celebrates a conceptual marriage of many approaches not previously brought into fruitful relationship, uniting psychoanalytic with behavioural methods; family-systems approaches with individual-based developmental ideas; classical psychoanalytic concepts with the more recent British object-relations derivatives; historical understanding of the inner world with its outer manifestation in the 'here and now' of transference interaction.

Few discoveries have had more profound implications than Freud's recognition of the central importance of sexual attraction and jealousy among parents and their children, and of the numerous defences erected to preserve the family against harmful aspects of these emotions. That the act of sex should arouse intense feelings in us, even when it enters our head merely as a thought, is scarcely surprising. That act is the source of our being, the moment of origin of each of us as a separate individual. It not only draws our parents together to couple and conceive us; it also forms a crucial bond which can stabilise their relationship – the source of our security – if it works well, or can powerfully disrupt it if it fails. And the oedipal sexual bond between parents and children together with its frustration and consequent jealousy, despite or even due to its pain, is also a major source of growth and change which propels children into the wider world to couple, form new families of their own and continue the species.

In a lifetime of work as a psychotherapist, with families and couples as well as individuals and groups, it has become more and more evident to me that most of us fear the extremes of pleasure, joy and love far more than hate, anxiety and despair. The negative emotions close us in upon ourselves, tether us safely to the ground, help us to feel clearly defined. They are familiar, repetitive, known, while the most positive emotions encourage us to abandon ourselves and threaten change and growth, even perhaps surrender to others or to causes greater than our petty selves.

Small wonder, then, that we spend so much of our time preoccupied with sexual experience (whether in fantasy of our own or through curiosity or gossip about others) or defending ourselves from its disturbing and troubling impressions. The defences are legion, as Freud discovered. Any other activity, emotion or other preoccupation can be used to hide it, deny it or reduce it to manageable 'ordinary' experience. Chief among these defences is the splitting of the total experience of sexual love into fragments and keeping these apart – 'physical', 'emotional', 'spiritual', 'mother love', 'genital sex', etc. In another split we seek protection from its power in 'sex' without 'affection' (as in pornography) or in its mirror-image 'affection' without 'sex' (as in much romantic fiction).

Freud experienced these defences in practice not only in his patients and his own self-analysis, but also in the intense negative reaction of medical colleagues and the general public. He also encountered the same resistance in the defection of many of his pupils; the major splits in the psychoanalytic movement have at root centred around this issue of the fundamental, universal importance of the oedipal conflict. Less often recognized is the fact that these defensive splits extend to professional choice, adoption of theoretical positions, and institutional structures. Partisan, polarized positions are taken up between 'individual' and 'group' psychotherapy; between 'systems' and 'psychodynamic' family therapy; between 'behavioural' and 'psychoanalytic' orientations; between 'biological' and 'psychological' psychiatrists, etc. All such extreme, irrational polarizations are irrelevant, indeed meaningless, except in so far as their object is to prevent 'mother' and 'father', which the two poles in each case represent, from getting together and doing something even more interesting than either of them can do apart.

Given the power of this group dynamic, it is not surprising that progress in integrating these polarized orientations has been slow. Nevertheless, there have been great advances in recent years. There has been a burgeoning of marital and family therapy knowledge and technique. Kinsey and his colleagues made the general public as well as the helping professions aware that sexual difficulties were endemic. Masters and Johnson studied the physiological responses directly and applied behavioural principles to make possible remedies for these ills sufficiently rapid and widely applicable to match the scale of the problem. Their early successes were not always repeated on different populations, but Helen Singer Kaplan next demonstrated that psychoanalytic and behavioural methods could be combined and could facilitate each other. It has remained for someone to bring all this earlier work together in systematic fashion, and also to link it with family dynamics and the knowledge of life-span developmental psychology now available.

This task David Scharff has performed brilliantly, using as a major resource the British object-relations theorists, including the work of Dicks on marital pathology and on psychoanalytic conjoint marital therapy.

In this volume he has provided us with a marvellous integration of all these seemingly diverse ideas, in a masterly presentation which is clearly thought out and structured and written in such a simple, clear, readable style that it is a delight to read and easy to absorb. The many excellent examples illustrating the concepts show more than anything else all the care and skill that underlie the whole volume; they are concise and clear, yet contain all the detail needed to convey their point and each one portrays vividly the dynamic in question. These merits will make the book equally understandable and valuable to family and marital therapists of all orientations. However, it will also become a vital reference for psychoanalysts, students of human development and others interested in psychodynamic approaches whether or not they have a special interest in family, marital or sexual therapy.

Chapter 1
Introduction

A sexual relationship offers a vehicle for building links to another person, and at the same time, it is pleasurable proof of those links. It can function either constructively or maladaptively — and often does some of both. In much of life, but especially for an adult couple, sexuality also serves as the physical aspect of integration between a person and those who are important to him. It does this because a physical sexual relationship draws, for better and worse, on the internalized aspects of past relationships, giving them new life and providing an opportunity for reworking these old relationships in the context of the present ones.

Adult sexual ties thereby unite the images and memories of the past family with the experience of the current family, revising and preserving the past in the new context. Sexual life thus offers a symbolic opportunity for the repair of what was previously felt to be lacking and for continuation of what was previously valued in past relationships, an opportunity the couple is impelled toward by the hopes for the immediate pleasures and comforts of their sexual encounters. In this way, current sexual pleasure supports a couple's efforts to provide for their future (and indirectly for that of their children), just as the failure to achieve sexual pleasure undermines these efforts. This central importance of sexual experience accounts for its richness and for its vulnerability.

The lifelong phenomena of sexuality have been at the center of theories of personality development and psychopathology since Freud's early psychoanalytic researches.[1] His revolutionary discovery of the world of infantile sexuality through his reconstructions from adult analyses were later supplemented by findings from the psychoanalysis of young children.[2] More recently direct observation of infants and

1

young children clarified the dynamic aspects of psychosexual development. Crucial aspects of adult sexual functioning, however, were still
unknown until Masters and Johnson's research revolutionized our
knowledge of sexual physiology, highlighted by the publication of
Human Sexual Response in 1966.[3] This led to a new comprehensive
form of treatment for sexual disorders pioneered by them and by Helen
Singer Kaplan which yielded further clinical information about adult
sexual experience.[4] Integrating our theories of psychosexual development and new information on sexual functioning with understanding
of child and family growth is the remaining task.

This book attempts to extend our understanding of the functions
and failures of sexuality in the growth of the family and its individual
members. It draws on the diverse resources of psychoanalytic object
relations theory, child development, sexual physiology and therapy,
family therapy, and group analysis. It is necessary to range widely
because the complexity of human personality and interaction insures
that no single theory can explain the panoply of experiences.[5] Theories
which seem logically inconsistent or are held to be mutually exclusive
by their adherents may still inform students of complex behavior.
Here no attempt will be made to validate any single theory or therapeutic approach. Instead, theories will be drawn upon when they
seem to extend our understanding. It is hoped, however, that a theoretical integration will emerge concerning the nature and mutual influence
of family and individual contributions to sexual development.

As theoretical ideas which illuminate or extend the basic psychoanalytic orientation are used, they will be explained in and integrated
with the text. All of them are subsumed by the object relations theory
which is the fundamental theoretical basis of this book's conceptualization of sexual interaction. This theory holds that the individual's
personality development is determined by the need for and availability
of relationships to primary figures in early life, rather than by aggressive
or sexual drives seeking an outlet. These relationships are mentally
represented within the psyche as 'inner objects' which, if they were
unsatisfyingly need-exciting or need-frustrating are defended against by
repression and split off from conscious control. They operate out of
awareness, influencing current relationships to conform to the model of
the inner object relationship situation.

For the reader who wishes to pursue the theoretical underpinnings and
is unfamiliar with this point of view, appendix I outlines object relations
theory and its application to the study of relationships in families.

Much of the clinical material to be presented has been drawn from experience with patients in sex therapy. The model used by the author and his colleagues resembles that described by Helen Singer Kaplan who combined a behavioral treatment format with a psychodynamic approach.[6] Again, for the reader unfamiliar with this format, appendix II describes the techniques and rationale of this method. The references to the appendices provide a guide to further reading.

The organization of the book

Specific difficulties in sexual life are fundamentally disorders of inner object life given expression in bodily sexuality. It is this aspect of sexual development and sexual disorder which is the arena of this book, offering a view of sexual disorders applicable to a variety of therapeutic approaches to the individual, the couple and the family. These therapies are the subject of a second volume and are not addressed here; but therapeutic principles are demonstrated *pari passu* throughout this volume, since the progressive discovery of the ties to people in the current and past family and their reflection in a treatment transference is the foundation for all psychodynamic therapy.

The next chapter introduces a number of concepts about sexuality and object relations. Taken with the two appendices, it lays the theoretical foundation for the book. The chapters that follow move sequentially through the life cycle beginning with the infant and his family and proceeding through old age, with separate, concluding discussions of extra-marital sex and sexual maturity. But the straightline development of this sequence is deceptive in that personal and sexual development accrue like a rolling snowball, layer by layer, so that in a sense every stage depends on what comes before. And beyond that, the issues of adult life affect the infant in his beginning. To meet this complex situation, each chapter will attempt to highlight both the developmental issues and the sexual disorders which tend to be in focus at that stage — and thus to a considerable extent each chapter can be considered independently.

Chapter 2
The sexual relationship

There are thus good reasons why a child sucking at his mother's breast has become the prototype of every relation of love. The finding of an object is in fact a refinding of it.

Sigmund Freud, 'Three essays on
the theory of sexuality'*

Sexuality forms a bridge between the deeper needs of the individual and the buffeting of everyday life. In an adult, a major thrust of personal development has led to the walling off of childhood needs, channeling them so that gratification comes increasingly in vicarious and symbolic ways. Sexuality renews the old bond between the physical and the symbolic levels of gratification, reviving the childhood developmental conflicts of the individual and transiently permitting more direct gratification. The urgency of this physical aspect of a couple's intimacy is often so compelling that it can only be readily compared to the physical interaction between child and mother in the first years and months of life, the other time in the life cycle when intense physicality is a major characteristic of the interaction of people who are each other's primary love objects.

The infant relates to his mother through using his body and hers. She relates similarly to him, and within this physical context their mutual feelings of attachment, concern, and pleasure grow. In this process, the nursing couple develops a reciprocal psychosomatic partnership.[1] The neurological capacities of the infant mature in the context of this support from mother and family which is required if he is to learn the uses of his body, interpret his bodily feelings, and to understand the meaning of his body in experience with the environment. (I use the word 'mother' here and throughout as a shorthand

4

term to mean the mothering person or people − those who perform the mothering functions no matter who the actual persons are. Usually it will be the actual mother, but in other societies, and increasingly in our changing times, this will not always be true.)

Adult couples need a similar psychosomatic partnership to interpret their own sexual urges and functioning − the psychological signals and potentials which mean nothing until given an interpersonal environment. They need each other to fulfill individual potential. In the interaction of meeting the physical needs, a bridge is formed not only between their two object worlds, but also between the soma and psyche inside each of them. This bridge provides each person new opportunities to rework old issues which, for many people, are rekindled most vividly within their sexual life. The sexual life of the parents is a source for strengthening bonds within themselves and the larger family, but it is also an area which will reflect any difficulty in those wider family bonds.

The importance of the body in experience and relationship

Those aspects of relating which include the body have a special poignance which any non-bodily relationship lacks. It is not just the orgasm which makes it so, although orgasm has a special place.[2] Right from the beginning, the infant and his mother share bodily contact and the experience of building a mutual give-and-take which synchronizes their bodily rhythms to a degree that research is only now beginning to appreciate.[3] Then, as the infant takes the first step toward separation, it is his own body (mouth, fingers, toes, skin) and mother's body (her breast, mouth, hands) which become the first toys and objects of pleasure. Later, masturbation in childhood and adolescence is associated with the most important fantasies of linking oneself to parents fantasies which are so compelling because they are tied to the body.[4] And in adulthood, some of the most profound and earliest hopes and fears, loves and disappointments are awakened by bodily experience or by its frustration. Because of the tangible re-enactment of the past, this interlocking force of physical and psychological urges in adult physical intimacy is as powerful as anything in the realm of human relationships.

Individual development and sexual functioning

Freud described how individual personality formed in its progression through a sequence of steps linked to sexual development. These steps were triggered by the biological maturation of certain erotic zones and the drive for tension release through them.[5] Since then, others have emphasized that the individual's growth is so completely dependent on the context of mother and family that it cannot be understood without reference to them.[6] Here a psychoanalytic theory of object relations – the study of the internalization of experience with the primary figures or love 'objects' – is of help in the exploration of mutual influence and interaction between the individual and his family.[7] Henry Dicks and Robin Skynner have begun the process of applying object relations theory to marital and family interaction.[8] In what follows, we will be extending the object relations view to the sphere of sexual interaction. In the object relations view, there are three components of inner objects: need-satisfying or ideal object; need-frustrating or anti-libidinal object; and need-exciting or libidinal object. The corresponding part of the self – the central ego, the anti-libidinal ego, and the libidinal ego – invests in its counterpart object structure. These six structures of self and object can be seen to be psychologically active in the sexual life of the individual and the couple.[9] This is seen in the sexual situation when people act as though relating to parts of primary figures from their past. An understanding of how this occurs requires first, an awareness of several, unique aspects of sexuality, and later a detailed study derived from clinical situations of the interaction of these unique phenomena and the couple's inner object life.

Sexual development unfolds as a series of biological events which both trigger and form the context for psychological growth.[10] As it does so, specific aspects of sexuality interact with family life. In each stage of individual and family development, sex has a unique role in being the bodily focus of pleasurable emotions. A few functions of sexuality will be important in the examination of several stages of life. They are illustrated most easily in the sexuality of an adult couple.

The erotic zone as projection screen

The genitalia and the woman's breasts are the physical parts of the body most often chosen by an adult couple or individual to be the physical locus of the conflicts both with internalized objects (for instance, the internalized parents) and with current primary figures. The penis and vagina, those rather small organs, became a battlefront for personal and interpersonal conflict. Issues of enormous complexity have to be psychologically factored (added, subtracted, or multiplied like vector forces) and then distilled in order to fit in these small areas. Massive conflicts barely remembered or long surrendered to the unconscious are projected in condensed form on the body screen of the genitalia. These screens are too small to allow the showing of a whole picture, so the outcome is, by necessity, simplified and condensed, seen only as through the wrong end of a telescope. Important details can no longer be differentiated, and one conflict is superimposed on another, one internalized relationship fused with others, much in the same way that the ego of the dreamer condenses and distorts events in the process of creating a brief dream which may nevertheless express worlds of meaning and feeling.

Although the resulting mixture of feelings is about many people, about old relationships and current ones, it still must be expressed along the final common pathway of physicality in a relatively simplified and direct way. For instance, there either is, or is not, sexual activity and responsiveness in a given situation. There are complications of varying degrees of openness, withholding, sexual failure, or aggression, but the sexual encounter either feels good or it does not.

Earlier in development, the precursor erotic zones carry a similarly condensed power of expression, uniting and speaking most forcefully for many aspects of interpersonal interaction and individual issues. Later, we shall see how this is so in turn for the oral and anal zones which precede genital dominance. For most adults the genital zone incorporates the experience of these earlier zones when it takes the predominant role.

As development proceeds, conflicts from earlier history are subsumed in each succeeding phase. For instance, those contained in the adolescent masturbation fantasy must later be carried into adult sexual life. We can see, therefore, how condensed the genital projection screen for this multiplicity of fantasies must be. We can begin to see the fate that may befall such issues if we look at the sexual functioning of a couple, and then try to understand the connection between the literal and fantasy levels of their sexuality. Even looking at a superficial difficulty in communication gives a hint at the complexity of meeting deeper needs, as in the following example. (The couple described below was seen in sex therapy of the sort described in appendix II. Here, as in all other examples, fictitious names and alteration of circumstances are employed in order to protect patients' anonymity.)

Bob, the husband in a couple in sex therapy, reported entering into a sexual encounter with some ambivalence. He wished to give and to get caring, physically and emotionally, but he noted that he felt some reluctance, fear, and unexpressed anger that seemed to stem from his day at work. Nevertheless, on balance, Bob would have liked to be held, cared for, and allowed sexual expression. His wife, Sally, responded to his initiative, and then had to decide how to deal with Bob's subtle irritability which he denied at the time. Sally did not know the source or meaning of Bob's irritability and when she asked him if everything was well, he reassured her, but in such a manner that she grew uneasy. She was then dealing with condensed contradictory messages: an invitation to love accompanied by a subtle anger. In looking back at this episode, Sally was able to understand that the mixed message triggered her old fears of being rejected by parents and boyfriends and the intolerable anger and hurt that she felt then, as well as an uneasiness with Bob's behavior at this moment of the invitation to make love. Although she was also wishing for physical and psychological closeness, she began to feel rejected. The moment of coming together heightened the vulnerability to rejection because of the exposing of her own desires. On this occasion, Sally's mixture of longing and fear of rejection was expressed as clitoral irritation when Bob touched her. As a result, she withdrew and Bob in turn felt rejected. (This episode corresponds approximately to figure A.3 in appendix I in which libidinal egos seeking exciting objects instead meet the frustrating, anti-libidinal objects.)

The details of sex therapy sessions tell us that such signs of ambivalence are not subtle. They are easily divined through tangible signs. The signal may be an immediate turning away of the head, a difficulty in kissing, a distaste for a part of the other's body, an unusually hurried approach, or a clear manner of rejection. When Sally noticed Bob's irritability, she grew wary. Other women in such circumstances might lie still or experience a headache. Bob, unaware of the contribution of his own ambivalence, although he was dimly aware of its existence, was puzzled and hurt. He summed up the experience by saying 'Sometimes I feel I'm just the victim of a frigid wife.' Such a statement rekindled Sally's repressed identification of herself as a reincarnation of her own distant and rejecting mother. Typically, things began to deteriorate for them at this point as they both felt rejected and angry. However, in the therapy now, Bob was able to associate this image of Sally with that of his own mother whom he had experienced as rejecting of his boyish longings for her love and approval. Once he could own his tendency to provoke rejection by his expectation of repetition, he felt less victimized by Sally and more confident of his own sexual wishes.

The symbolic function of sex

This description of the link between inner issues and the surface fate of sexuality can be used to explore the symbolic reverberation of physical sexuality.[11] Sex is partly a physical interaction in the real external world. But when it expresses the aliveness of the emotional link between two people, it is also a sign of the link between each person and his internal objects. And when its failure voices the severing of that link, it recalls the internal relationship to the bad object. Over time, sex becomes the sign symbolizing the internal sense of well-being. Like mythological symbols, this personal symbol has the characteristics of ambiguity and paradox. For instance, in the couple we have just considered, when the sexual failure was unremitting, that sexual failure paradoxically provided the living bond between Bob and Sally and even between them and their children. Fighting and squabbling used to accompany their repeated sexual failures, and the arguments themselves became partially invested in an emotional bond between them – one they seemed to treasure deeply. They were, in a sense, fond enemies. Their successful sexual encounters, although rare, remained as a vehicle and sign of overcoming the distance and difficulty that they ordinarily experienced. In other couples, when sex helps the partners to renew their bond, it allows them to tolerate the distance experienced at times of stress because the sexual success symbolizes the capacity for reparation to the injured internal objects.

What, then, does the symbol of sex stand for? Among many possibilities, a few seem to be universally important:

1   It stands for the struggle to hold onto the memory of the giving, loving parent, to have an image of him or her inside, and to care

for him or her while being cared for.

2   At the same time, it also stands for the struggle to overcome the image of the withholding parent, the one who does not seem to care. It encompasses tolerating and forgiving even this withholding parent figure because of the opportunity he paradoxically provides to come together.

3   Most important, it symbolizes the attempt to synthesize and repair these two images, to make whole a sense of being cared for by allowing each person to feel loved while giving love — in the context of overcoming distance and the ever-present threat of destruction of closeness.

If we again, briefly, consider the metaphor of the reversed telescopic condensation of libidinal and anti-libidinal issues onto the genitalia then we can understand the nature of symbolic repair to mean the provision of caring and the act of caring in such a way that the effects are showered and redistributed along those same tangled skeins that originally contributed to the moment of impossible condensation. Successful sexual performance constitutes both an actual and a symbolic reparation, a reinfusion of loving from the body to the multiple sources of physical and emotional needs. In contrast, failed sex restimulates the feeling of need and deprivation without relief.

If we postulate this potential for sexual life, then just how good does it have to be to serve in the symbolic and actual areas as an integrating force? For any marriage to survive, the forces that divide the couple must be overcome. These divisive forces become especially prominent after the breakdown of the early phases of the marriage or relationship when the romantic idealization falls away, and when the couple must struggle with their competition with each other, their mutual envy, with the discovery that at times the partner looks more like the hated, frustrating parts of the parents than was previously acknowledged.

Good-enough sex

With this in mind, let us consider what comprises 'good-enough sex.' This expression is a rephrasing of Winnicott's term *the good-enough mother*, by which he means that the ordinary mother provides an adequate environment which the infant, with his multipotentiality, transforms into one that is just right.[12] It is not necessary for the mother to be 'perfect' — that is, neither does she have to provide unerringly and intuitively a flawless environment, nor does any mother constantly have to be on her guard for some crucial error that will mark her child forever. Most children, with the ability to struggle with the particular vicissitudes of their own lives, will not be marred by conflict. They will have their share of neurotic conflict like the rest of us, but will have had, from the beginning, the experience of coping with it, being at *some times* given exactly what they need and want. And equally important, there will be inevitable lapses in their being given what they want. During these lapses they will develop the capacity to tolerate temporary frustration.

Similarly reasonable goals for sexuality are that it be a useful, and on the whole enjoyable part of a marriage or relationship that is capable of containing and facilitating the average amount of conflict and frustration, giving at *some times* exactly what is needed and wished for. This is the physical expression of a psychological stage described by Klein as 'the depressive position' — which refers to the ability to tolerate good and bad experience while maintaining an integrated view of the good and bad aspects of the caretaker.[13] In the context of the needs of the larger family, the couple's sexual life should be adequate to allow them to feel sufficiently loved by each other that they, as parents, can give to their children.

The sex life of the parents is therefore closely related to the adequacy of the nurturing environment given to the child and adolescent. The ways in which this is true are often startlingly direct. In some families characterized by poor boundaries between parent and child, direct incestuous advances are made by a 'frustrated parent' to one of the children. But even in much better integrated families, the relationship between the sex life of the parents and the environment surrounding the child is quite direct. The complexities and subtleties of these matters are the subject of this volume.

The bodily locus of object relationships

In sex therapy, the assignment of graded, behaviorally designed exercises in bodily interaction help to isolate the parts of the body which are connected to specific aspects of internal object life.[14] These examples may be specifically sexual or they may involve the use of other parts of the body. Both genital and non-genital body parts may be used in the service of symbolic representation, speaking, as do dreams, the concrete language of emotional experience.

Mr and Mrs H came for the treatment of his secondary impotence, but Mrs H had difficulty from the first day of 'the sensate focus' exercises even though she had no demonstrable dysfunction. She could massage her husband's front, but found his back distasteful, fixing on one mole she described as repugnant. Her spontaneous association however led her to remember that she always felt that 'her father had turned his back on her' when she became adolescent. Now in the exercises, she projected this experience onto her husband and rejected him for his back. It later turned out *she* was in the process of turning her back on him and leaving the marriage.

In this case, a minute part of the spouse's body became a symbolic focus and was rejected in retribution as well as in identification with the father. The psychological mechanism in use is projective identification, described by Melanie Klein (see appendix I) in which Mrs H saw a part of her husband as if it were a repudiated part of herself.

The second example is specifically genital and demonstrates the way the genitals and breasts contain and compartmentalize the problem with the internal object which is repressed while the overall relatedness of the couple is exceedingly good.

Freda suffered from pelvic pains during intercourse which were originally thought to result from post-operative adhesions. But even in preparatory psychotherapeutic work, which is often recommended to patients with unstable ego structures, she could identify the pelvic pains with a childhood feeling of congestion following sporadic episodes in which her father, naked and drunk, came into her room and manipulated her vulva. (At other times he had largely ignored her, and joined her mother in being a quite rejecting, neglectful parent.) After a good deal of prior therapy, she fearfully decided to attempt sex therapy. Despite her husband's completely unthreatening demeanor, she was frequently fearful and essentially phobic of the exercises. When her husband was to touch her breasts, she was initially reminded of the times her father held them, ostensibly to express concern over their dissymmetry. And when she was supposed to touch her husband's genitals, she finally told me that her most abhorrent memory was her father forcing her to place her hand on his wet penis as he touched her genitals. While there had been no intercourse with father, she had feared it on many occasions. And finally, once Freda could herself tolerate handling her husband's penis, she experienced a sudden feeling of nausea which reminded her that she had felt both aroused and nauseated in the episodes of touching her father's penis. The previously repressed memory of his ejaculating into her hand flooded back as though he were in the room. She recalled that her three-year-old daughter had once told her that 'women get pregnant by swallowing daddy's seed.' We were then able to ascertain that her nausea represented partly the wish and partly the fear of having her father's baby.

There are many more subtle examples of this kind of experience, but Freda's illustrates the full range, from conscious memories associated with an exciting and rejecting parent, to ones which are conscious but withheld, to ones which are active psychologically but completely unknown. The memories of the internal object projected onto the body of her husband and interred in her own body come to life again as she attempts to resume growth. Before therapy, by rejecting sexual feelings, she avoided the threatening aspects of men, of fathers, and of her own self. The feelings were compartmentalized, split off and kept far apart from the loving feelings for her husband.

Sexual disjunctions: The pathology of sexual interaction

In the last decade, most adult sexual difficulty has been given the name 'sexual dysfunction' — a general term for sexual failure in some or all situations. It follows from what has been said so far that the view taken in the current exploration is that many of these disorders consist primarily of object relationship *disjunctions*. In these sexual malfunctions there is a problem in object relationship which may be either of recent origin or more profound. Even the cases caused by inexperience or physical disability stir up disjunctional elements or threaten the positive aspects of internal and external relationships. The term 'sexual disjunction' which will be used in this volume is meant to underscore the understanding of the disability as caused largely by a disconnection of personal bonds. Its 'pathology' resides in the vicissitudes of internalized object life.

Chapter 3

The relevance of infancy for sexuality I:
The child's attachment to its mother

In the primitive sensory exchanges taking place between mother and infant one could see the precursor of adult sexuality.

Heinz Lichtenstein,
'Identity and sexuality'*

A whole family centers itself on the relationship of the parental couple. Other relationships take their direction with reference to this central one, and their strengths or weaknesses echo vicissitudes of the central bond. Yet the ability of parents to form a bond is in large part determined by their own earlier experience. This chapter turns to the beginnings of that experience, the infant's life with its mother.

The mother–child bond

A child's life depends on having a mother. Rene Spitz showed that children raised in infancy in orphanages do poorly because of the absence of a single committed mothering person, while those raised in equally poor environmental circumstances, but with their own mothers present, do virtually as well as more advantaged children.[1] In his classic study comparing infants raised in an orphanage in a relatively good physical environment but with several caretakers to those raised in the sparse physical surroundings of a prison by their own incarcerated mothers, Spitz demonstrated that the orphanage infants failed to thrive in every respect, showing extremely slow development emotionally and physically, and suffering staggering rates of morbidity and mortality. But the infants of the imprisoned mothers grew and thrived normally during the first year.

The environment that matters to the infant for the first two years is the environment that the mother provides and, essentially, nothing else. The horizon of the baby extends at first a few inches, and later only a few feet from his body. Its adequacy is determined by the very restricted exchange between mother and child — nutrition, body care, and the group of responses we have began to explore which, for want of a better word, might be called 'emotional conversations.' It is now known that these exchanges are made up of essentially non-verbal, physical interchanges unique to an infant's *and* mother's synchronous rise and fall of arousal with accompanying self-quieting. The overall pattern stimulates the rhythmic bodily homeostasis necessary for the infant's survival.[2] Spitz found that in both the orphanage and the prison, nutrition and body care functions were essentially adequate. If anything, they were better in the orphanage. But the emotional conversation was inadequate in the orphanage not only because it was too infrequent, but mainly because it was not carried out by a single mothering person (or even a small, constant group) primarily interested in *that* infant. They were deprived of a 'good-enough' mother even though they were fed and clothed. During the first year of life, the interest of the prisoner-mother was all that was required to make up for an inadequate environment. They were good-enough mothers.

Anecdotal and clinical experience also tells us of families that provide adequate environmental support, but in which the mother is unable to supply the emotional feeding and caring. These are the 'poor little rich boys and girls' whose truly impoverished inner life is expressed by a spoiled, depressed, or detached behavior, by an impairment in the ability to relate to others.

Recently, Selma Fraiberg and her colleagues investigated infants who were doing poorly within the first three to six months of life. In the poignant paper 'Ghosts in the Nursery,'[3] they were able to demonstrate how the mother's own early history of impoverishment and abuse began to be relived with her child, who then failed to develop just as did Spitz's orphaned children. For example, one mother's pervasive depression and threat of eruptions of uncontrollable violence removed her from meaningful functioning with her infant. Therapy was carried out with the mother by a worker who helped her understand her own childhood deprivation and its relevance to her inhibition in mothering. The inability of the mother to engage with and provide for her infant could be linked to her own inner difficulty, her inner life and the experience that haunted her, peopling the nursery with 'ghosts' who then haunted the infant's development. The link between the infant and the past object life *had* to be made before the mother could begin to function. She could not even be taught until some of the ghosts were exhumed, identified, and mourned. Once this comprehensive therapeutic effort was accomplished, she was less driven to repeat her earlier experience. When such an early major failure is not reversed, the children are so severely damaged that subsequent sexual difficulties pale in comparison to widespread difficulties with object relationships and ego functioning.[4]

For patients who are sexually disabled, similar ghosts haunt the marriage bed and from there have life in the family at large – more subtle, not individually life-threatening – but haunting and lethal to marital and family life nevertheless. The sexual derivatives of these issues which originate early between mother and infant are part of patterns which are lived out within the broader family context for the next 10, 15, or even 30 years. It will not only be mother, but father, siblings, substitute parents, and their emotional replacements who contribute, modify, exacerbate, or give solace for early and continuing deficits. These issues have a particular poignance because they *begin* early and have an archaic heritage and tend to persist unconsciously without modification. If they go wrong, the uncorrected reverberations of early issues continue to strike notes of discord in adolescent and adult life.

The sexual development of the child occurs in the larger context of the relationship to mother and family, and it is therefore to the relationship primarily to the mother that we now turn. By 'mother' is again meant the person or persons who share the mothering functions of holding, feeding, and caretaking. The use of the word 'mother' recognizes that while the function may be shared, in practice the principal caretaker is usually the literal mother.

In his studies of the fundamental role of the attachment of infant to mother, John Bowlby describes behaviors of the infant which contribute to initial attachment behavior: *crying, calling, babbling,* and *smiling* tend to bring mother to the baby and keep her close by; *clinging* brings the infant to the mother as does visual and locomotor *following*; and *non-nutritive sucking* keeps the baby attached and is therefore to be differentiated from the nutritive sucking with its separate goal. It can be seen that these behaviors function either to signal the mother to approach, or to facilitate and maintain the child's contact with her.[5] The attachment is not secondary to the need for nutrition, but is primary and instinctually built into the infant. The maintenance of attachment to primary figures is a normal condition throughout life. (This is so even when the infant begins to separate from his mother, as described in the next chapter.) In infancy and early childhood a hierarchy of successful attachment can already be described.[6]

Secure attachment

When the infant is strongly attached to the mother he uses her as a base from which to explore the world, being willing to separate from her for brief periods. The infant (and the older person he becomes) has an 'unthinking confidence in the unfailing accessibility and support of attachment figures.'[7]

Anxious attachment or insecure attachment

A 'clinging' or 'overdependent' person is actually one who is anxious about the reliability of his attachment figures. He lacks confidence that they will be available and responsive to his needs. Consequently, he adopts a strategy of staying close to them to maximize their reliability. The actual experiences of an inconsistent, anxious, or unreliable attachment figure, early object loss, and overt or covert *threats* of abandonment (e.g., parental quarrels in which the child perceives such a threat) all contribute significantly to anxiety and insecurity about attachment.[8]

Detachment

Detachment or turning away from mother is a normal response by a child separated from the attachment figure. Its severity and duration correlate to the length of separation and is a more regular response to the return of an absent mother than to a returning father. Chronically repeated separations can also result in detached behavior. Detachment arises out of defensive processes set in motion by the experience of loss and if sustained frequently or long enough can result in a characterologic impairment in the person's willingness or ability to form attachments.

Defenses are also constructed against the 'loss' experienced by the infant if he is in effect mismatched temperamentally with his mother and they fail to establish a shared rhythmic connection. While major early failures are catastrophic as previously discussed, more minor ones may be carried forward as variants in development and are more likely to be the kind seen in patients who present with sexual symptomatology.[9]

The relevance of the infant's earliest attachments to sexual development is demonstrated in a classical series of ethological experiments performed by Harry Harlowe and his colleagues at the Wisconsin Primate Center. Infant rhesus monkeys were reared without their mothers.[10] Terrycloth-covered 'dummy' mothers were available without food, as were wire dummies with a 'lactating' nipple. Cloth dummy mothers, who did not offer milk, were preferred by the infant monkeys over the wire mothers who did. In a choice situation, the monkey would spend most of his time clinging to the cloth substitute, only going to the wire mother's nipple for food. If possible, he would lean from the security of the cloth mother to nurse on the wire one. In addition, the cloth mothers gave an infant much more security in fear-arousing situations.

This experiment points out that skin-like contact took precedence over food in giving the baby a sense of security and in decreasing fear, an emotional effect we will be concerned about in discussing sexual contact. But there was something far more striking: none of the monkeys raised without live mothers could perform sexually as adolescents or adults. The males were completely unable to perform intercourse even though provided with plenty of chance to learn by observation. And the females would collapse helplessly on the floor, subject sometimes to a rape-like penetration by a competent male monkey, but never able to act cooperatively. And finally, to complete the cycle, those motherless females who did become pregnant (by artificial insemination) were helpless to mother their young, forming a group of 'motherless mothers,' who were frightened by the persistent attempts of their infants to make contact. The mothers were unable to learn how to negotiate the mutual relationship necessary in their infant's survival because they had not learned it in their own infancy. Some were abusive to their infants before the infants could be removed. Thus began a cycle of emotional deprivation. In their inability to respond to their own normal infants, the motherless monkeys carried over the effects of their own missing mothers. The initially normal monkeys could now be expected to carry the experience of privation within them in a similar manner.

One other aspect reported by McKinney is worthy of our attention:

> This story is not complete, however, for if one impregnates these motherless mothers a *second* time, a modified tale emerges. The mothers who were indifferent, though not abusive, to their first infant often proved to be very effective mothers with their second infant. *This change in their maternal behavior may be related to the sustained efforts of the artificially fed first infants to establish contact*. On the other hand, there was a tendency for the mothers who were *overly abusive* to their first infants to continue this pattern, although their behaviors sometimes modified with subsequent infants.[11] [Emphasis mine, D.E.S.]

These mothers who improved with their second infants can be likened to Fraiberg's mothers whose treatment depended on the presence of their baby as the context for their own growth. The baby in these situations acts as a surrogate mother to its own deprived mother, forming a context in which the mother can grow and providing a dramatic example of symbolic reparation made to its mother. This example is of interest later in this book when a partner in a sexual context can form a similarly reparative context to someone with relative early privation.

In many ways, this experimental series speaks for itself. Deprivation in infancy leads to social development which is so impoverished that a repertoire for any sexual behavior and interaction never develops even when the monkey can see other sexually competent monkeys. Why this is so, and why the related phenomena of sexual disjunctions would develop in humans may be clarified by the next section which examines mother-infant bonds more closely.

Gaze interaction

Gaze interaction is one physical function for which we can draw a developmental line from infancy to adulthood that illuminates the concepts of· growth in object relations and sexuality. Although in practice it is part of the larger context of holding, handling, and vocalizing, it can be separated out for purposes of study and illustration. Current research tells us that meaningful 'conversations' between child and mother begin at just a few weeks, perhaps as early as three weeks.[12] Typically, the infant initiates the search for and 'seduces' his mother's response by looking for her eyes, smiling, vocalizing, and altering his physical posture. If she responds, looks at him, smiles, and coos, they have an interaction sequence which has a pattern of beginning, being sustained, and being ended when the infant turns his eyes away. If, however, the mother fails to respond, the infant will at first increase his effort to draw her in, and only then lose interest, assume a posture which looks 'beaten,' and even fall limp. Looking at an infant whose mother has been instructed to look at him but to keep an impassive, unresponsive face is a painful experience for the viewer, evoking responses from observers much like those upon seeing a child beaten. After a failure, typically the child will again try to initiate the gaze and voice sequence, and will become more and more lifeless looking if consistently not responded to. A similar result can also follow an out-of-phase interaction. The 'defeated' picture of the infant occurs if the mother tries to respond but she and the infant continuously miss each other.[13]

Henry Massie has studied home movies of children subsequently documented as autistic.[14] He suggests that the repeated failure of the sequence of attempts to get a visual conversation going without relief may be crucial in the genesis of autism — the most severe and earliest form of psychotic non-relatedness. He also notes, importantly, that it is not *per se* the mother's failure to respond to the baby's attempt to have gaze interaction, but *the shared inability of the mother–infant dyad to establish a bond*. The gaze failure is a crucial part of this. It can come about because of (1) an incapacity of the baby; (2) the inability of the mother; or (3) a combination of the two in failing to achieve a match. Autism, then, represents the crucial *early failure of the bond* — whether because of the child's incapacity, the mother's, or both. Symptoms of detachment are already present by 4 to 6 months in some of these children.

Studies of blind infants document the tortuous use of alternate pathways required to accomplish the parts of bonding and growth which are ordinarily contributed by the exchange of gaze with mothers.[15] These relatively normal infants with a single handicap employ all the alternative routes available, such as increased tactile and vocal communication, to assist in their development, but they are delayed in development despite the use of detours.

Looking at some of the specific ways in which mothers and their

infants interact may allow us to translate the language of early responses into that of adult physical and emotional life and later to trace
the specific *aspects* of sexual failure which originate in early childhood. It is useful to borrow the term 'mirroring' from D. W. Winnicott,
referring to *the child first seeing himself reflected in his mother's
eyes*, and gaining a first sense of self in the process.[16] This concept
emphasizes the requirement of a mothering relationship for the growth
of knowledge of oneself as a person. Central aspects of the ego, the
rudiments of a core of self, come through this process. As the child
grows, the mirror of the mother presents a 'true' picture if the mother
responds to the child's needs and moods without unduly distorting
them in the process. That is to say, if the child is happy, she *acknowledges* this, 'reflects the smile,' and equally, if the child is sad or angry,
she can both *tolerate* and *reflect* these states without taking them on
herself. Indeed, it becomes increasingly important with growth and
differentiation that she contain these feeling states for the child who
can then hold them as his own. The *containing* and *transforming* aspect
of the mother, as Bion has termed this function, is spoken about by
Loewald as the role of the mother in leading the child to progressively
higher levels of organization.[17] Thus, while the mother–infant interaction is reciprocal, it is still the mother who leads toward a more
organized experience and binds anxiety, sensing what it is the infant
is trying to become but also holding in mind a vision of the child's
potential development which is beyond his own awareness of it. This
discussion of gaze and mirroring can now be reconnected to the whole
pattern of mother–infant interaction by recalling a passage of Heinz
Lichtenstein.

Mirroring experiences are intimately linked with the emergence of
both body and image and 'sense of identity.' I feel that the term
'mirror' overemphasizes the visual element of the experience. It
would seem that the primitive modalities of 'somatic recognition'
between mother and infant . . . constitute a kind of mirroring
experience, but the 'image' of oneself that the mirror conveys is
at this early stage a stage 'before images are formed' – outlined in
terms of sensory responsiveness, not as visual perception . . . More-
over, these responses as well as the primitive stimuli that elicit them
form a continuous interchange of need creation and need satisfaction between the two partners of the symbiotic world. While the
mother satisfies the infant's needs, in fact creates certain specific

needs which she delights in satisfying, the infant is transformed into an organ or an instrument for the satisfaction of the mother's unconscious needs. It is at this point I see a link between sexuality and the emergence of identity in man. An interaction between two partners where each partner experiences himself as uniquely and specifically capable of serving as the instrument of the other's sensory gratification, such a partnership can be called a partnership of sensual involvement. I believe that this type of relationship is, in the adult, established in the sexual involvement of two individuals. In the primitive sensory exchanges taking place between mother and infant one could see the precursor of adult sexuality. . . . The primitive modalities of stimulation occurring between mother and infant in the earliest phases of life are a primitive, pregenital form of adult sexuality.[18]

A developmental line of gaze interaction

When the mother looks at her infant before he can see her, and later when she responds to his looks and smiles, the infant begins a line of development which extends beyond the first needs of attachment. Their exchange of gazes contributes significantly to sexual and emotional life. The first long-awaited smiles trigger a sudden new process between the infant and parents of getting to know each other and finding themselves in each other. This also gives the infant its first experiences of mastery as it 'enjoys the success' of attuning mother to its level of bodily comfort and excitement. The baby's range of expression grows within these relationships so that within a few months he can play hide-and-seek gleefully. Later he can look and smile coquettishly, or frown disapprovingly. By age 3, a whole range of complex expressions surround every glance, constituting virtually the same visual signals which later accompany adolescent and adult courting and sexual life. This extensive range of feelings is born, like other developments, in the space between mother and infant. Its creative use continues for the rest of the infant's life.

The reflection of true and false self

The 'false self' is described by Winnicott as a situation in which the child develops an external personality in order to please the mother, at the expense of his true inner self.[19] Aspects of a hollow compliance and falsification characterize such adults. We can trace such development to a failure of the mother to reflect the infant's true emotional state, overriding it with an insistence that the infant comply almost exclusively with her needs. For instance, when depressed mothers such as those described by Fraiberg can only reflect a joyless lifelessness and are unable to mirror other feelings, the infant may develop a false self which is depressed in compliance to the mother. Any sign of joy or liveliness is suppressed to keep from overwhelming or upsetting the mother. Whether the mother contradicts the child's experience or demands an emotional response to compensate for her own inability, the distortions implant a need to present a 'false self' to and for her, since presenting certain aspects of the true self is met with rejection and is felt to harm or alienate the mother.

It is the object-seeking qualities of the infant and child that stimulate the development of the 'false self' and the hiding of the 'true self.' The fate of the 'true self' in this situation is varied, depending on the profundity of its rejection by the mother, the capacity of the child to survive intact, and the availability of other substitute primary objects. But if a true–false self dichotomy is carried forward in growth, the 'true self,' close to the resurgent inner signals of the child himself, will remain hidden but alive – carefully shielded from the mother out of fear of losing or hurting her. In later growth, the child may appear to be sunny, neat, or compliant, a person who hides an angry or depressed core not only from the world, but also from intimates, friends, lovers, and spouse. In Fairbairn's terms, it is now the Central Ego and its Ideal Object which are repressed while the Libidinal Ego and Object usurp their executive function. When such adults form long-term relationships, the 'true self' core sooner or later cries out for recognition, often through a symptom of sexual difficulty in which it is the sex which speaks for the buried but central lost self. There may or may not be a sense of falseness or shallowness in someone with a significant false self. Or the split in the person between true and false elements may speak by contradictory yearnings which seem puzzling to the person himself. But sex, connected as it is by bodily ties to the central core of feelings, is a frequent avenue of expression for the ambivalent derivatives of such problems, even when there is nothing else symptomatic to draw our attention to false self problems.

A woman's sexual difficulty illustrating problems in mirroring, true–false self, and exclusive (detached) need to care for her own body

The adult needs for kissing, smiling, and physical caring or love-making have their origins in the shared gaze, touch, holding, and vocal 'conversations' of infant and mother. The response of each partner to the other is required for a sense of well-being. Failures of mirroring in infancy leading to false self problems make it difficult to recreate the mirroring experience in adult sexual life. Without a capacity for mutual mirroring sexual exchange is severely hampered as in the following example.

> Penelope S was a reserved, 40-year-old mother of three who was fond of her husband and her family. She could masturbate to orgasm, but 'felt no arousal' in sexual relationships with Richard, her husband. 'I don't feel any warmth from him, he just can't get it across to me,' she said on repeated occasions. Using behavioral techniques of sex therapy, she was able to progress to the point of experiencing orgasm in Richard's presence by clitoral stimulation, but she could not bear for him to watch her do so. She also began to complain *more* bitterly that 'he gave off no warmth.' Richard was also reserved but as treatment progressed he was increasingly able to express warmth for Penelope. She had originally chosen him largely because he did not threaten an intolerable amount of closeness. The larger part of the failure was Penelope's inability to react to his warmth and caring 'glance,' and to reflect it herself, either to him or to herself. She contended that the coldness came solely from his inability to feel and reflect warmth. Richard, however, experienced dejection when he felt warmly and felt rejected by Penelope.
>
> Penelope remembered her parents as distant and cold beyond the norm of the reserved Vermont culture she came from. She specifically recalled that her parents repeatedly quashed any expression of hurt, sadness, or anger on her part with the insistent rejoinder 'Nonsense! You don't feel angry. You feel fine.' Or, 'Don't cry! It doesn't hurt!' Penelope was able to describe, after some time, withdrawing from her parents in order to quietly preserve any sense of what she actually did feel.

In this case, the failure to engage sexually is due partly to a propensity for difficulty in emotional exchange in both partners, but the more severe disability is in the wife, who is similar to the child who has its own barrier to acknowledging warm glances from its mother, its own defects which inhibit mother–infant reciprocity. Mothers can overcome this by working harder at it while standing the inherent frustration, but there is a limit beyond which it will not work, as there is in a sexual relationship. Penelope seems to have had parents who themselves had difficulty in responding to her, and she picked a husband who also had some of this difficulty. But despite Richard's reserve, he had tried to express warmth, infuriating Penelope all the more. In the process of reversing the role she had in childhood, Penelope denied and distorted the reflection of affectionate feelings of her spouse, as her mother apparently had distorted and denied hers (as well as spurning the more direct bids for affection). Richard and she were each left with the feeling that the need each had for warmth was not reflected.

Penelope has grown to feel that she *did* feel a number of negative emotions and would not be *made* to feel good just because her parents told her that she should. It would have been a denial of her 'true self' core to have done so and she developed a significant false self. In reaction to this 'true versus false self' conflict, she refused to respond to Richard and limited her sexual life to private masturbation to orgasm. These mechanisms relate to the early modes of primary object relationship we have been examining. They are attempts to preserve self from the object, to avoid being overwhelmed by it, and therefore are set up against being given to by the other person. With this forceful detachment, a strong defense against attachment, there can be no adult mutuality.

Penelope's difficulty in being able to relate to Richard, then, represents a dead-end in one line of development. She walled off the use of her body for emotional connectedness. She could, for instance, give to her children and could apparently adequately mirror and contain anxieties about potentially difficult experiences *for them*, but her barrier was firm in the area of responding to Richard physically and allowing the vulnerabilities to exist with him. She balked here because it was here that her true self took refuge from a terror that anyone else might tell her how she felt. Responding to Richard meant, to her defended 'true self' that he would not only be telling her how to feel, but *making* her feel it, invalidating her as the person who received the sensations from her body and allowing him to take over at the core. She felt she had to fight against this so centrally that she would rather have been abandoned by him (as a maternal transference projection) than risk loss of herself in being replaced by the false self which was dedicated to pleasing both him and historically her mother. For Penelope, the sexual interaction with Richard directly tapped her anti-libidinal mother–child experience, which had been unmodified since childhood.

This example illustrates (1) a lack of mirroring; (2) the induction of a false self; (3) the defensive detachment from the husband as a transference primary object; and (4) Penelope's premature and inflexible need to take care of herself emotionally and her body physically to avoid echoes of an interactive somatic responsiveness. She could not risk revealing her longing to be cared for for herself in case it should be denied and she be annihilated emotionally.

Chapter 4

The relevance of infancy for sexuality II:
Separation and individuation

The role of the father in attachment and separation

The gradual movement of the child from complete attachment to the mother to the separate-but-attached state begins in infancy. Mahler notes that the father is someone the child is aware of from early on, 'not fully outside the symbiotic union, neither is he ever fully a part of it.' She observes that the infant seems to perceive from very early the special relationship between mother and father, but that we know very little about it.[1]

An investigation by Brazleton and his co-workers[2] compared infant–mother and infant–father interactions filmed over a timed period in the same manner of the study reported in chapter 3. Tentatively, they concluded that the early interactions seem to have different characteristic patterns than those between mother and infants, and perhaps therefore indicate differing developmental functions. Characteristically, in father–infant interactions the pattern was one of quicker arousal, a shorter plateau of intense arousal, and sometimes a briefer deceleration phase. This was somewhat similar to the infant's pattern with a total stranger, lending support to the notion of the father as a partial outsider.[3]

The father during the pre-oedipal phase has been seen as an important, but usually secondary, caretaker who is mainly a substitute mother or a special outsider, his role being *similar to the mother's in attachment function*, but differentiated by its *secondary nature* in comparison to the mother's.

But beyond this back-up role the father has a more important two-fold function. First, he is there to secure the original attachment process. In shoring up and pinch-hitting for mother, he also provides a 'container' for her and the infant which protects them from the demands of the wider world. Then mother, feeling safe about the outside world, looks inward on the infant with a safety that allows her 'primary maternal preoccupation' to proceed undisturbed.[4] And secondly, from the beginning the father is a force to draw the child out of the symbiosis with mother. By providing support from his position of being half in and half out from the beginning, he is ready to encourage the baby out of its autistic and symbiotic shell toward him and the outer reality. As the mother at first allows an autistic focus, and then helps the baby to hatch out of it through a protected symbiosis with her, so the father allows the two of them to be an almost exclusive pair, and then operates to pull them both back to the wider world. Brazleton's findings that the baby is more excitable in interaction with the father suggests that the father is, from early on, less a part of the background of the infant's life, more of a special focus and a new-found object which the infant must become familiar with, while mother remains more in the role of providing the context of the baby's existence. It is not only when genital oedipal development occurs that the father is seen as a treasured outsider, although that heightens the process. The father is a kind of gentle 'fifth columnist' from the early days, and he also begins early both to fortify the walls and to encourage two-way traffic beyond the walls of maternal attachment into the wider world.

In Bion's terms, one can envisage a series of 'containers-within-containers.' The infant (who contains the nipple in his mouth) is contained by mother, and the mother–child unit is contained by father. In each case, the container operates to transform the contained into a more mature form ready for separation. (It should be said that the father is here considered in his pre-oedipal role, and that oedipal functions will be considered later.)

The child's separation and individuation from its mother

The whole movement for the child out of the earliest attachments to mother and toward separateness has been studied over the last two decades by Margaret Mahler and her colleagues.[5] Its vicissitudes are also the focus of John Bowlby's second volume in his *Attachment and Loss* trilogy.[6] Knowledge of these developments is also crucial for understanding sexual attachment because the ability to come together sexually requires the ability to separate from the object and to remain separate for periods of time. If there is no gap to cross, there can be no coming together.

The separation–individuation process begins after the initial attachment has developed from what has been thought of as an unknowing merged union into a symbiotic mother–child bond. (Actually, as demonstrated in chapter 2, a great deal of cognitive and emotional exchange has already been going on.) Mahler describes two early phases which cover the material of the previous chapter. The normal autistic phase (birth to 3 or 4 months), and the symbiotic phase (beginning at 2 months, peaking at 4 or 5 months). Although attachment is not completed by this time, the process of separation already begins. She groups the separation–individuation process into four overlapping subphases:

Separation–individuation subphases

1   Differentiation and the development of body image (hatching), 5 to 9 months
2   Practicing (movement away from mother, locomotion), 9 to 14 months. 'The world as the junior toddler's oyster.'
3   Rapprochement, 15 to 24 months. (Shadowing and darting from and to mother, beginning a wider world, splitting of objects.)
4   Consolidation of individuality and the beginnings of emotional object constancy, 24 to 36 months and beyond.

It is useful to consider the whole process as an overlapping one, with the traces of subphases of development usually not clearly defined from each other. We can therefore draw on the whole process of separation–individuation in attempting to understand why some couples cling together symbiotically, some use deviant methods (e.g., sado-masochistic) to force a separation they cannot otherwise tolerate, while others go back and forth in what seems to be an endless reliving of rapprochement as though they either cannot remain individuals if the spouse gets too close or takes over, or they cannot let go for fear of loss of the object and of themselves as well. Much of the process of defense can be understood around the anxieties of the failure to make a secure attachment and the fears of separation from and loss of the attachment figure. Later in life, when defenses interfere with sexual life, they will also be speaking for these early anxieties concerning loss of the love object.

The beginnings of mourning in infancy

The period of separation–individuation also introduces the first responses to prolonged or frequent separation from mother. Once the infant has firmly identified the mother as his own mother, an event traditionally dated by the appearance of the 8-month 'stranger anxiety,' he begins to treat her prolonged absence in a characteristic way.[7] A sequence is set in motion which begins with the infant's *protest* at the absence of the mother (crying and angry responses). Continuation of her absence leads to the infant's *despair*, and if the separation is prolonged, his *detachment* from her. While the details of this model are of great interest, they are beyond the scope of this presentation. However, it can be noted that a microscopic early form of this sequence can already be seen in the studies reported in chapter 3. When the mother fails to respond in the face-to-face interaction, the infant tries harder, then looks despairing, and if this sequence predominates over time, detaches not only from the mother, but from the object itself. (While angry protest is not itself demonstrated in this model, it can be assumed that the cry of the newborn expresses the need for its mother among other things.)

The importance of this early sequence of protest–despair–detachment is two-fold. It provides a model for the growth of the capacity to mourn losses, a painful emotional process which Bowlby has likened to the necessary but often painful process of wound healing. And it helps conceptualize the development of psychological defenses as forms of detachment from aspects of the lost object. In the case of 'Bill,' described at the end of this chapter, defensive detachment and attempts to control the object are a response to the early loss due to premature separation from mother.

Through childhood the maturation of a capacity to mourn is enhanced by the continuing presence of a stable attachment figure. While there is much controversy about exactly when the child becomes capable of mourning, here we are interested in the similarity of the mature process of mourning to the infantile paradigm of protest despair, and detachment.[8] Adult mourning consists of four phases which overlap and exist with differing emphasis:

1   A phase of *numbing*, usually lasting from hours to a week. Out bursts of intense anger and/or distress may erupt. Aspects of denial and anger may persist over a longer time.

2   A phase of yearning and searching for the lost person over months
     or even years.
3   A phase of disorganization and despair.
4   A phase of greater or lesser reorganization.[9]

This model and the vicissitudes of an incapacity to mourn are taken
up in later chapters. Here we can note that the child's continuing
capacity to grow and his parents' capacity to let him grow require that
they each possess an appropriate level of the capacity to mourn what is
lost between them at every stage of major change. This notion of the
mourning implicit in growth is implicit in the conceptualization of life
as an unending series of 'psychosocial transitions' which involve progressive separation from the original primary objects even as the
individual makes attachments to new objects.[10] Thus, the capacity to
mourn becomes a cornerstone of successful growth and differentiation.
In the presentation of adult couples with sexual difficulty, the sexual
symptom can often be understood as embodying a failure to mourn
an early aspect of separation from parental figures.

Transitional objects and transitional phenomena

The *transitional object*, first described by Winnicott, is the piece of
infantile accoutrement which the child drags everywhere with him,
uses to hold onto, suck, chew, and as a solace when getting to sleep.[11]
It is born in the space that grows between mother and child in the
process of separation and it symbolically represents the original interface between mother and child. It is treated by the infant as though it
were a piece of the mother which is under his total control and is
therefore crucially unlike the mother herself who can be withdrawn
when the child wishes she were there. It therefore also stands for the
loss of the experience of being at one with mother. The concrete
material object (blanket, stuffed animal, pacifier, or anything the
child chooses) comes on the scene later than *transitional phenomena*
(stroking the mother's face) which begin as early as 5 or 6 months, and
is well in evidence by the age of 2 in many children. Transitional
objects and phenomena may last until late childhood, or the feelings
for them may be shifted onto other objects, such as collections of coins
or baseball cards, a favorite doll or even, as in one case, old tires!
The 'fate' and uses of transitional objects and phenomena tell us a good

deal about the child's growth in personal relationships. Mahler has observed a variety of transitional phenomena whereby the child could control symbolic access to mother during rapprochement.[12]

It is in the potential space between the mother and infant that the transitional phenomena occur - a space that expands as separation proceeds. This widening gap between the child and his mother - and later between him and each of his primary objects - always retains the inheritance of the original closeness. Winnicott calls this gap between the child and his object the 'locus of cultural experience,' signifying that all creativity occurs out of the tensions of attachment and separation in this gap.[13] The gap we are considering is not only the actual external one, but also the derivative inner, mental gap between ego and internal object.

Winnicott widened the concept of transitional object to include many transitional phenomena which play important normal and abnormal roles in adolescence and adulthood. Adolescents often hang onto each other more like transitional blankets than real persons, using someone or a whole peer group outside the family to provide a kind of substitute mothering. The concept can be usefully extended beyond Winnicott's application of it to refer to the phenomena of sexual interaction. Sexual encounters occur across this same transitional interface, involving the same issues which were originally handled by the use of the transitional object - all of them having to do with the relationship of self to object. Therefore, the control of the object and its threatened loss are frequently at stake in sexual life. The degree of flexibility and security, of alternating closeness and distance in the original mother-infant bond is echoed in the transitional phenomena of adult sexual life.

A frequent example is in the joint use by a sexual couple of the penis as a 'third person in bed,' friendly to both and under their shared control. Here a part of one of them becomes a jointly externalized 'friend' and giver of care, in a way closely analogous to the transitional 'blanket.' A man's use of the woman's breasts is often similar, a wish and love for a part of the woman which is felt to be more directly under his control than the overall woman can ever be, either as a transferential mother or as a real person.

These parts of the body are used as part-objects, as though they were the whole loved person giving the pleasure and love, or denying it and becoming the hated person. Developmentally, from the infantile period on into adolescence, masturbation relies on a kind of bodily splitting to enable one part of the body to give pleasure to another, in the control of the single person without the threat of mother's withdrawal. That use of body parts as transitional objects becomes even more important when they are invested with keeping control from being taken by the other person, just as the original transitional phenomena were invested with keeping the power of withdrawal away from the withdrawing mother by holding onto oneself. This transitional difficulty occurs in various forms of sexual difficulty. Premature ejaculation may be traceable to the need to hold onto the penis and keep it in the man's control. Disinterest in being genitally aroused may represent for a woman withholding of the genitals so they are in her control. While both these symptoms involve an aspect of splitting of the ego, they do so in concert with a splitting of the body to give concrete representation to the split of ego (and the implied split of internal object). If withholding becomes the predominant mode of sexual exchange, the transitional area has now become a struggle *against* connectedness used in the service of separation from the primary object. This may occur out of simultaneous fear of and longing for merger with the object. The use of the withdrawn genitalia for transitional disconnectedness leaves it as an empty fortress or an impotent sword. When the experience of withdrawal can be integrated with the transferential mother's again being available within a reasonable time, the need to split off the transitional area and keep it rigorously to oneself may become less severe and may enable the person to share control more easily. This was not the case in the following example.

John B felt unsure of his wife Silva's love unless they had sex daily. Whenever more than a day passed without it, he began to sulk, and rage. He barely tolerated abstinence during Silva's menses or illness. He even resorted to assaultive behavior such as giving her a sleeping pill and cutting off her pants to reach her genitals. Only in actual, frequent genital contact could he feel cared about, and no argument to the contrary dented his conviction that he had a right to unlimited access to his wife's genitals.

John used his penis as a pipeline to the transitional part-object, a kind of umbilical cord to the sought-after mother – a mother whose genitals counted for everything. His use of the transitional object was remarkable and pathological. He insisted on having an actual part of the maternal object instead of developing any substitute which could be withdrawn from her, allowing an actual separation. His failure in the separation process and in the creation of transitional phenomena represents an extreme in the use of a sexual part-object to shore up an anxious attachment to the internal mother.

The psychosomatic partnership and separation

As we have seen, it is the psychosomatic partnership – the union of bodily responsiveness between mother and child – which gives birth to transitional objects which bridge the ever-widening gap between them. The baby's ability to become competent in mastery of bodily skills, mobility, and emotion all derive from the mother's early physical and emotional handling of him, from her sharing of this responsibility with the child in which she turns it over to him in gradual steps. He is initially the instrument for the fulfillment of his mother's unconscious needs, while she helps him make sense of his inner rhythms and disorganized world. Through being engaged in a bodily reciprocity, she leads him toward levels of higher organization.[14] In this process, she needs to impart a sense that the child cannot only take care of his body, but can use it to master skills and enjoy bodily pleasure. Through an ability to mourn the losses of symbiotic elements, she is able to enjoy her baby's separateness as she returns to her own separateness. In the beginning this involves her in responding to him while not overriding his own direction in their interaction. Later it is the holding and care of his body that is handed over to the child in steps so slow that it is not really finished psychologically until adolescence.[15]

While this fosters real growth and independence, it also serves as a vehicle of communication between child and parent, giving pleasure to both. By summing up the qualities of these ways of bodily relating, we can develop a continuum of experience from the infantile interaction of the bodily and emotional partnerships to the adult stage of genital intimacy. In adulthood, however, when one or both partners in a sexual encounter may not be able to have a psychosomatic partnership, a symptomatic picture develops as in the following example.

An example of difficulty in the psychosomatic partnership and issues of the rapprochement subphase

Bill and Diane were young adults who each hoped the other would take care of his or her needs. Diane, independent and well able

to manage when on her own, fell into the trap of feeling she needed
to take care of Bill, give in to him, in disregard of any of her own
independent wishes. In identifying with his longing to be taken
care of, she handled her own dependent longings by taking care of
him. She had no difficulty sexually as long as this worked. On the
other hand, while Bill wanted her to take care of him, at the same
time he feared it. He had some difficulty with premature
ejaculation at age 22, before meeting Diane, and it continued to
crop up from time to time, even though he had successfully overcome it as a regular problem. It returned when he was most
frightened she would take over. His longing for her to take care
of his body stemmed from the times his mother was unavailable
to him because when he was 3, she suddenly began working all
day. When Bill was 7, he had taken to the ritual of arranging his
clothes in his room in perfect position every night. In adulthood,
he could still remember the brand name of the clothes which had
become like transitional objects. He also said ritual prayers, asking
God to protect each member of his large family. He thereby replaced
with obsessional rituals the care he wished his mother would have
taken of him. This kind of wish, transferred to Diane in his young
adulthood, alternated with the fear that she too would become
unavailable. The compromise was that his wish to have her take
care of him was stunted; when frightened or angry, he held out on
her via premature ejaculation to avoid being taken in, controlled,
and then abandoned, a defense which contained a strong element
of detachment.

Bill's childhood pattern with his parents had been one of compliance to his parents' wishes, coupled with the rituals which stood
as a condensed symbol for his anger at them for leaving him alone
with his care left to others and himself. He developed a premature
ability to take care of his own body and its extensions by rituals
rather than reason. The rituals neutralized the anger he bore his
parents for abandoning him. He always 'fixed things perfectly'
when he really wished to leave them an angry mess. The premature
ejaculation was a transient but recurring symptom which also
expressed both his anger at his wife and a fear of hurting her, making
sure that only he was in control of what happened to their bodies
as a defense against the longing that she would take care of him,
and then the subsequent fear that his own wishes would trap him
into her control.

Bill's difficulty illustrates two of the concepts discussed in this chapter. He has difficulty in the psychosomatic partnership which leads at some times of stress to the withdrawal of or partial detachment from the bodily partnership. His disability can be described in terms of difficulty in the rapprochement level of issues in his relationship to Diane. His anger at his mother for withdrawing from him at about age 3 disrupted his attachment to her as a reasonably securely loving object. He was thrown back to an earlier level of experiencing his attachment to her, namely, as an object split into alternating good and bad parts. He then attempted to keep control of access to the good part of her. Now, when he feels secure, Bill operates at a higher level. When stressed, either by too much closeness or by the threat of loss, the bodily partnership falls victim to his fear that he will not be able to refind his integrated view of his mother and to his anger at the internal mother. His sense of himself collapses, and he withdraws his penis from 'her' control, keeping it as a transitional object under his own control.

This example illustrates the vicissitudes of the child's relatively immature capacity to mourn the prematurely absent mother. Traces of anger, fear, and longing are encapsulated in his character development, in his ritualized defenses, and his sexual symptom. To further understand the contribution of a child's growth at the state during which Bill's mother became less available, it is necessary to inquire about specifically sexual development at that time. This will be considered in the next chapter.

Chapter 5
The beginnings of sexual relatedness in infancy and childhood

To begin with, sexual activity attaches itself to functions serving
the purpose of self-preservation and does not become independent
of them until later.

Sigmund Freud, 'Three essays on
the theory of sexuality'*

The successes and failures of adult sexuality both rest on the foundation of mother–infant and family–child interaction. In the previous
chapters, we have discussed ways in which sex in adult life carries
forward the physical part of emotional primary bonds as the physical
contact between mother and infant does for the infant. Having reviewed
aspects of the family and child development, I want now to consider
development specifically in the sexual area.

The sexual life of the infant

Major deficits in the general development of the infant lead to the
profound failure to thrive which makes specific sexual development
clinically irrelevant. However, the totality of the experience of being
mothered also contributes to the infant's specific sexual life. In the
beginning, being held and looked on, the infant sucks from the breast,
at first seemingly mechanically and without awareness. But by 5 or 6
months, the baby plays with the breast with his fingers, holds it, and
tooths on it. At times, he seems to lust after his mother and her breast.
He also has found ways of moulding around the mother as she responds
to him. At other times, the baby takes in parts of himself and parts
of his mother with his mouth, chewing on his fingers or her face while

37

appearing pleasantly excited. He is more excitedly interested in her face than in his own hand or a pacifier which offers use as a more calming object. While mother may calm him in holding, she is also, intermittently, the exciting object. Another way of saying this would be that *while mother is often the reassuring context for his own activities and growth, she is also the focus of his early attention, and later of his love*. From the early undifferentiated reciprocity of holding and loving, the interactions become more coquettish. Hide-and-seek games which underly separation–individuation are exciting because the baby is playing and experimenting with losing and refinding the loved object. From here, gaze interactions and smiles, frowns, teasing, or sad looks develop into the complex facial expressions which we see again years later in courtship and love-making – expressions of finding and signalling to the lover.

The infant does not relate to the mother solely for the purpose of the satisfaction of a particular nutritive need, or exclusively through the oral, anal, or genital zones. The relationship between instinctual attachment behavior and what Freud described as the primacy of the erotic zones is that need satisfaction, in the broadest possible sense, including the infant's need for an attachment, is the area for the stimulation and expression of sexual excitation.

Freud noted in 1905 that sexual excitation arises 'as a reproduction of satisfaction experienced in connection with other organic processes' as well as through direct stimulation of erotogenic zones. The erotogenic regions of skin 'merely show a special intensification of a kind of susceptibility to stimulus which is possessed in a certain degree by the whole cutaneous surface.' Other, general stimuli such as thermal stimulation, rhythmic agitation of the body, muscular activity itself, and all intense emotional processes, including terrifying ones, thus contribute to sexual excitation.[1]

The oral zone, then, is the first *focus* of initial infantile sexuality, but this specific heightening occurs in the *context* of the infant's overall tie to and experience with his mother. While the development of attachment behavior is a crucial organizing step, once it is relatively in place, the attachment then becomes the context for *all* subsequent development and within that embracing context the sexual focus organizes and gives form to the attachment. The emotional exchange in the erotic zone is mainly a pleasurably charged one which draws in all aspects of the attachment and which in turn is reflected in all those same aspects. When separation begins in the second half of the first year, a more active, broadened oral zone and later the anal zone serve the same functions, as does the final organization under phallic zone dominance. Throughout early development, then, attachment and the developmental move toward separation from the attachment figure form the context in which the sexual focus develops.

While the sexual life of the infant is not at first mainly genital, it ordinarily includes a genital element from the beginning. The parents focus on the genital with great feeling, even at birth, because of its role as a signifier of gender. They may feel love and approval if they are satisfied with the gender of the child, or dissatisfaction if not. Even if they are initially disappointed, the genital has a role in helping them mourn the loss of the gender they had wished for.

One mother was bitterly disappointed to have a third daughter because she had felt this was her last chance for a son. But as her infant girl won her over with love, this mother began to feel that her daughter's genital was indeed lovable. The loss, mourning, and restitution focused on her feeling about the baby's vulva.

Genital activity is already a feature in infancy. Genital touching begins during accidental exploration or in imitation of the mother's handling the genitals during cleaning. The baby repeats the manipulations from time to time because they are pleasurable, later often making at least a few attempts to get his mother to manipulate him. If overall care is satisfactory and if the genital is not overvalued, this genital activity remains occasional and unfocused. In the first 18 months, genital play does not yet have the characteristics of masturbation, but at 18 months or later, a more organized, rhythmic activity begins which can be called masturbation.[2] Rene Spitz found that infants ordinarily begin to touch themselves in the first year and that the absence of autoerotic activity related to the absence or inadequacy of mothering.[3] Good-enough mothering consists of adequate amounts of the mixture of holding, handling, and caring which forms a climate in which the infant learns the earliest precursors of caretaking and pleasure-giving for himself. But various elements of deprivation or overstimulation often lead to an overreliance on genital manipulation as a source of solace in a lonely or anxious world.

Debbie presented at age 5 with the symptom of compulsive masturbation, mostly in the presence of her parents but sometimes even in public. Her mother was struggling with a complete inability to respond to her husband sexually and had been herself a child who used sexualized approaches to adults in an atmosphere of severely negligent parenting. Debbie's mother, however, had cared deeply about Debbie, but in anxiously turning to her daughter as a libidinal object, she had stirred up such diffuse anxiety that Debbie now used masturbation as a kind of catch-all mechanism. It served to solve her loneliness, to organize chaotic, threatening feelings, and to build a protective enclave into which she could retreat to escape her anxiously engulfing mother. Here in a precocious usage, the genital had already come to serve the purpose of mediating the interaction between Debbie and her mother.

Even though some genital manipulation begins in the first 12 to 18 months, the infant's sexual activities normally continue to focus primarily on other zones during the second year. The change in focus from mouth and skin to a focus on the anal and urethral zones comes as the child and mother interact now in a way that may use the functions of those areas to serve the heightened (and therefore sexualized) aspects of their interaction. This interaction may be alternately teasing, oppositional, or cooperative. It may be specifically focused by the pair on the bodily zones, or it may proceed without much to call them to attention.

The shift in focus from one zone to another happens partly because of progressive physical maturation, especially of the central nervous system. It is also triggered by the maturing cognitive capacity of the infant and the change in mode of interaction brought about because he becomes a more competent partner. For instance, the shift from oral to anal mode dominance occurs when the toddler can contribute to decisions about what he is going to do with his own body, with his waste products, and in his interactions. He now is not only in possession of a temperament which directs him. He also has a will of his own which includes a cognitive component even before words are fully available. The anal zone becomes prominent partly because it is the body area which most readily expresses this new function of the child and the new mode of interaction with his mother.

The same confluence of zone and mode of behavior applies in the third year when the genital first achieves prominence for both boys and girls. This may begin with an interest in being naked or rubbing against parents and an interest in the parent's sexual equipment, often with the child growing intrusive if they attempt to remain modest. Then something startling happens around the third birthday in a girl, a bit later in boys. The developing capacity to see the difference between men and women and to make something of it suddenly erupts into a kind of crisis. A child may have known intellectually about genital differences, but now he or she notices with a new intensity.

At 2¾ years, Clara went to nursery school for the first time. Suddenly she began sitting backwards on the toilet in imitation of the boys who stood up. She announced that boys had 'wiggly bottoms.' She asked her father if he had a wiggly bottom, and when he admitted he did, Clara said soulfully, 'I wish I had one.' Soon after this she 'did not love her mother anymore,' a phrase previously used only for people who had been away from her or shown favor to her baby sister. She said she only loved daddy. She began asking for Band-Aids for imaginary wounds, up to a dozen a day. And she fell several times, actually hurting herself although previously she was rarely awkward. She was only reconciled to loving her mother a few days later when mother bought her some coveted, gaily-colored sandals, called 'flip-flops.' She then said, 'I do love you mommy *because* you bought me my "flippies." '

Another 3-year-old girl told her father 'I do have a penis inside my pee-pee. It's sleeping and when it wakes up, it will come out.' And 4-year-old Nan said to her mother, 'Would you mind getting divorced and leaving daddy with me?' (To the credit of latency development, her 8-year-old sister said to her, 'Don't say that, Nan. It's okay to think it, but you mustn't say it.') Nan's drawings of this period also pictured a close and sexualized relationship with father (plates 1 and 2).

The boy, in possession of the treasured penis, gets very anxious at the threat of castration so vividly implied in seeing the girl's 'castrated' situation. He also wears Band-Aids everywhere. He may coquettishly approach mother with his penis, asking her to touch it, while boasting of how he will best his father. A typical story of this period comes from a father who heard his little boy singing 'I love mommy. I'll marry her someday.' He called out, 'What's that you're singing, son?' His son promptly replied, with an offended air, 'Don't worry, daddy. It's *just* a song!'[4]

Recently, emphasis has been made of the fact that a phallic stage and aspect of development comes before and can be differentiated from the later genital–oedipal stage.[5] The phallic stage is more dyadic and focuses more on the issues of the relationship of the child to each of his parents individually, while the oedipal stage focuses more on the triangular issues of the child's wish to have a sexualized relationship with one parent (primarily of the opposite sex) and his resultant fears of retribution from the other parent. While noting this difference between phallic and oedipal stages, it is also worth recalling that there are triangular aspects to earlier stages and that the British School would describe oral and anal phases of early oedipal development.[6]

While latency development is setting in as the child attempts to cover the more obvious genital and object-directed aspects of oedipal life, there are the doctor games and the outbursts of sexual material. Latency is a time when the child tries to keep down his sexual life or to contain it within bounds, but there are the many breakthroughs which betray its active presence. For girls, jump rope rhymes often contain active sexual concerns, while channelling sexual themes into the bodily excitement of the exercise activity, a sublimated derivative of masturbation:

> Cinderella
> Dressed in yella
> Went upstairs
> To kiss her fella
> By mistake
> She kissed a snake
> How many doctors did it take?
> One–two–three–four etc.[7]

The latency child is far from asexual, even on the surface of his life.[8] Sexual concerns are continually breaking through. Turmoil is often not far away, especially in the children who make up a clinical population. In the next chapter, we will see the earliest examples of overt sexual symptomatology in the young children whose latency development is not fully possible because of the continued sexualization of their anxiety. Indeed, a large proportion of the clinical population in child psychiatry is made up of those children who cannot keep effective ego control over sexual material so that energies can be channeled into new learning of skills. Even in normal growth, there are frequent breakthroughs of sexual material signalling that sexual material is never very far beneath the surface.

Chapter 6
Sexual symptomatology in childhood and adolescence

What constitutes sexual difficulty *per se* in children is not an easy question. The baby's sexual functioning is not well differentiated from the total relationship to its mother. The behaviors which prefigure what are later seen as specifically sexual also mark the beginning of other non-sexual trends. The shared origins are of great interest. Later chapters will explore the way specifically sexual symptoms including adult sexual dysfunctions are intertwined with other aspects of growth and relationships.

Nevertheless, a number of specific sexual symptoms can be seen in childhood. This brief sampling will consider family contributions to and consequences of sexual symptoms.

Childhood sleeping disorders as a symptom

The mother of a 2-year-old boy, Sam, and a 3½-year-old girl, Sheila, asked for a consultation because Sheila cried frequently, refused to go to school, and woke several times at night, asking to come into the parents' bed. Sometimes they turned her down, but often they acquiesced for part of the night. The morning after such a night Sheila frequently clung to her mother and refused to go to school. Mother felt increasingly trapped as Sheila's anxiety mounted.

Sheila's nighttime travels had begun at the time mother was breastfeeding Sam who therefore, as an infant, was able to spend a part of each night in bed with her. Much of Sheila's jealousy of Sam was translated into this specific request. But in addition, the parents' sexual life was held in abeyance by mother's aversion to sex. While mother was conscious that Sheila's presence kept father sexually at bay, she denied that as a motive for allowing Sheila into their bed.

This girl's oedipal development was hampered by a generally anxious attachment to her mother. The anxiety was given a spur by her jealousy and by her feeling excluded at the brother's arrival. The symptom began during the vicissitudes of the early phases of separation–individuation at approximately 18 months, but during the oedipal phase it was sexualized. The resulting 'symptom' of the nighttime wakings put her in the middle of her parents' sexual difficulty. From her mother's side, an ambivalent regressive attachment to her own internal mother was reawakened by her relationship to Sheila, instead of the appropriate level of attachment to her husband as successor to the internalized father. And finally, Sheila's father was called on, and colluded in taking a desexualized maternal role himself. Instead of acting to pull his wife out of an anxious symbiosis, he supported mother and daughter in the prolonged maintenance of the symptom, becoming a substitute mother to both of them.

For father, the failure to confront his wife over the use of Sheila as an excuse for the sexual withdrawal stemmed at least partly from his own relationship to his mother. Feeling partially rejected by her, he felt incapable of an oedipal victory and allowed his wife to play the role of the internal rejecting mother, whom he could then reparatively mother.

Thus, collusion existed at all levels in this family: the parents' sexual disjunction represented a collusive symptom between father and mother; and the child's sleep pattern represented both her own issues and the unconscious cooperation of her parents since here intrusion had the effect of letting them both off the hook.

Childhood masturbation

Excessive masturbation is an early sexual symptom for which children are sometimes referred for evaluation. This example draws on the previous discussion of the developmental role of masturbation in chapter 5 to illustrate exemplary family contributions to a symptomatic presentation of a child.

Debbie, the 4-year-old described previously, was brought by her mother because of a diffusely anxious picture which included frequent masturbation in the form of manual rhythmic stimulation of her genitals, often under a blanket. This had been going on for at least a year. When the parents noticed the masturbation but said nothing, Debbie was said to 'look guilty but rub even harder.' Whether the parents asked her to stop or yelled at her, she was frequently unable to do so. The genital manipulation took on a compulsive, driven quality. Holding Debbie gently on either parent's lap often did help her stop.

Debbie had been left in the care of a single caring babysitter all day from her early months as both parents worked, but after the age of 2½ had been placed in extended day care. The masturbation seemed to have the quality of filling in for an absent parent. This aspect persisted into her latency years. She was unable to refrain from compulsively masturbating at school, causing peers to tease her. This was one factor contributing to a massive depression with increasingly frequent threats that she would run away or kill herself.

Some of the parental history sheds light on Debbie's difficulty. Her mother was unable to respond sexually to father, treating him as the reincarnation of her own sexually threatening father. In addition, mother's own mother was so neglectful of her as a child, that now Debbie's mother tried to overcompensate to ensure Debbie would never feel neglected (despite going to work in a full-time job from the time Debbie was a few months old). The result was an ambivalent overinvestment of the mother–daughter relationship while father was in essence locked out. He angrily resented this and made it openly known to both of them. Finally, Debbie's mother had a brief extra-marital liaison when Debbie was 2 years old. Mother then promptly gave up this relationship and began therapy. There she discovered that the affair had represented an attempt to get caring from a man she had made into a part object. Unconsciously she saw him as a sexually-exciting father figure who would symbolically rescue her from her neglectful mother and her abusive, raging (although sexually stimulating) father. Her unconscious view of her husband had assigned the anti-libidinal (or 'bad') elements to him while splitting the libidinal ('exciting' or so-called 'good') elements onto the man with whom she launched the affair. The affair partly also represented a fear that Debbie would be valued by the husband in her place, so an alternative sexual and parental object had to be sought.

Masturbation was Debbie's way, then, of dealing with her many sources of anxiety. It was a sexualized attempt to get parental caring. As such, it was adopted in unconscious identification with her mother. It also expressed concern about her own bond to her parents. Masturbating brought her parents' attention, calmed her from expressing anger at them for excluding her from their relationship, and gave her a self-induced bodily excitement which substituted for the holding and handling she missed. The compulsive masturbation became, in sum, an exaggerated transitional phenomenon which muted anxiety and brought multiple sources of anxiety under Debbie's control. It was a tenuous solution for many problems, in both her external and internal object worlds.

Effeminate behavior and enuresis in a 5-year-old boy

The next case represents a picture of the formation of a homosexual tendency *in statu nascendi*. The similarity is striking when this picture of a young child is compared to the adult case of homosexuality described later.

> Jackie was 5 when he was brought to the clinic because he was wetting his bed and refusing to go to kindergarten. But much more striking during the examination was his effeminate style, his fearfulness, and his preference for dolls and tea parties.
>
> Jackie's father was a fireman who was alcoholic and who escaped home whenever possible. His mother was an overbearing woman of 26 who kept Jackie closely tied to her. She came from a long line of matriarchs who always got rid of their men in one way or another, and who belittled them before they left. Although Jackie was her prize, she feared his growing up would make him like his no-good father.
>
> In play therapy, Jackie was teasing and coy, afraid to express anger. He treated me as he did his mother, serving tea and playing doll family. As he was more able to be angry and to form an affectionate bond and identification with me as a man, he began to play with circus animals who fell and broke their legs, acting out his castration fear. He provocatively made such a terrific mess in the playroom that I knew he was daring me to swat him. At home as he began to dare the outspokenness of a little boy, his mother had

great difficulty tolerating his new-found aggression. Repeated
efforts had to be made in the mother's therapy to ensure she did
not act to discourage the development of a masculine identification
by helping her develop a capacity to enjoy him as a little man.

Jackie's history can remind us that enuresis is often an essentially
sexual symptom. For him, it was one of the few ways he could covertly
indicate that he was a functioning male with a penis, identified with
his father the fireman and with his firehose. The effect of the enuresis,
however, was to involve his mother in pregenitally caring for him and
to increase his own passivity. This symptom, a manifestation of deviant
sexual development, is also often intertwined in a compulsively repeated
mother–child interaction which betrays strain in the early attachment
to mother and the difficulty in becoming separate from her without
risking losing her altogether.

Cross-dressing in a 10-year-old boy

Tom, a 10-year-old boy, presented a variation of this picture at a
somewhat later age. He had been sporadically dressing as a girl to
gain recognition from his mother and to reassure her. She had
clearly feared men since both her own father and Tom's father,
her first husband, had abandoned her. Tom was not brought to
treatment for the cross-dressing but for a threat to jump out of a
second-story window. On that occasion, his mother went to the
window, raised the sash, and dared him to jump.
   In family treatment, mother was helped to see the way Tom
had inhibited a masculine identification as an appeal to her. She
could then encourage Tom to identify with her new husband in a
masculine way. As she did this, she was able to feel less inadequate
and threatened herself and Tom gave up the symptomatic cross-
dressing.

The mother's earlier choice of a punitive man who abandoned her
and her three children had left her in isolation as her own family of
origin had been when her father left. The boy accommodated to her
fear of men by developing a sexual deviation that had the effect of
making her more available to him, at the same time that it gave her
someone to be close to without fear. Here again parent and child

colluded unconsciously as their shared need for affection and fear of closeness was represented by the sexual symptom. The early anxieties about attachment were gratified through a sexualized bond. Although the early anxiety about the bond to mother was still not settled, the sexualization of the bond served to skew Tom's developing identity and prevent oedipal development.

Sibling incest

In the next case, I want briefly to summarize a complex reconstituted family in which several children, including an adolescent, were involved in sexual activity.

> Mr and Mrs B brought Mr B's two sons, Mike, 13, and Dick, 5, and Mrs B's daughter, Sandy, 8, for family evaluation because they had been involved in sibling incest. Mr B's first wife, mother of the two boys, had been intermittently psychotic and committed suicide three years earlier. Dick, then aged 3, was present when she was discovered. Less than a year later, Mr B met the second Mrs B who had then been divorced for two years from an abusive and alcoholic man for whom, however, she still cared. Despite her longing for her first husband, the Bs married six months after meeting, partly because Mr B felt so much in need of help. Within a matter of weeks, Mike, aged 12, was forcing Sandy, aged 7, into intercourse, sometimes while Dick watched. This went on over several months until Dick dropped such clear hints to the parents that they could not fail to notice and sought help.
>
> In family therapy it became clear that Sandy shared her mother's masochism. Mrs B's first marriage had been a sado-masochistic one, and Sandy's role in the incestuous step-family had the effect of keeping a version of her father alive. For Mike it had been an opportunity to punish a female who represented the rejecting aspect of his dead mother with whom he had an ambivalent relationship. It also symbolically punished the mother for dying and leaving him, and at the same time it sexually represented the tie to her. But for 5-year-old Dick, the experience furthered the difficulties he was already having in moving through oedipal development. He remained excitable and impulsive, shouting sexual words in therapy or regressing to sitting on his father's lap like a 3-year-old.

He idolized Mike although Mike teased him relentlessly, calling him 'punk' or 'fag.' In individual play therapy, sexual material sent Dick into a chaotic excitement. When he finally could settle, he made large exploding structures in which a phallic object like a rocket destroyed the building which contained it. At the end of such play, he would crow 'I'm the greatest,' indicating that if he were in control of the rocket, it would not turn on him but on something or someone else.

Premature pregnancy

Although adolescence is discussed extensively in a later chapter, a brief example here illustrates the similar way in which the sexual symptomatology of adolescents and children embodies the relationship to their parents.

Tanya's pregnancy at age 15 represented both her own and her mother's wishes to have a baby, while avoiding the sexual difficulties her mother apparently encountered with her own husband. Tanya's relationship turned out to be with a younger male 'friend' of her mother, a man who represented a 'good' father to both of them, and an extension of her mother to Tanya. This choice fitted the shared wish of the girl and her mother for good parenting, which they hoped to get also by identification with the new baby.

Sexual and personal identification comes alive in Tanya's adolescent behavior which literally and symbolically ties mother and daughter together even as it also comes between them and puts them in potentially explosive conflict. The sexual activity gives Tanya two new persons, the man and the baby, expressing her ambivalent struggle for autonomy. It also identifies her more closely with her mother, brings her and her mother literally closer around the new baby, and offers Tanya a chance to be cared for as a child in what now poses as an adult way, but which actually again speaks for an internalized sense of deficiency in the attachment to and differentiation from her mother.

With these few cases, we can see a range of symptomatology from the diffuse picture in Debbie in which the masturbation was one of several indicators of difficulty, to the gender symptoms in Tom, to the extremely specific nature of the incestuous sexual material in the B family and in Tanya. In all these cases, the disturbance in the family spread beyond the sexual nature of the disturbance. *A sexual symptom became the leading edge of an attempt to rework fundamental aspects of attachment, separation, and loss.* In addition, however, there had already been a *sexual aspect to the family-wide difficulty* in each case. As we shall see in the later chapters, the sexual symptom in the child usually represents the struggle between both the internalized aspects of the parents and the actual current relationship with those same parents.

It also expresses something on behalf of the parents through a collusive process involving their identification with the child. In this process, the child represents a repressed part of the parent. Debbie, for instance, represents her mother's internal exciting object, a child-in-need-of-care, and mother responds to Debbie mainly through her libidinal ego – that is, she over-indulges her for fear Debbie will otherwise become the rejecting object.

In another kind of example, the mothers of Jackie and Tom begin by treating these boys as threatening objects – that is, projective identification equates the boys with the mothers' internal anti-libidinal objects. Then the boys act to undo this projection by altering themselves and their behavior to secure a link with mother by becoming what they feel is her idea of a safe libidinal object. In so doing, they simultaneously express and deny their understanding of the mothers' fear and rejection of them, and they also manage to express some hostility back about it.

Finally, in a third form of shared identification, Tanya manages to be like her mother and to express her mother's partially hidden and denied sexual wishes for Tanya. This process was described in 1942 by Adelaide Johnson and her colleagues when they noted that adolescent delinquent behavior frequently expressed unconscious 'superego lacunae' of the parents.[1] This meant that while the parent professed one morality, the adolescent sensed that the parent unknowingly sanctioned the delinquency through a 'lacuna' in the dictates of the parent's superego. This phenomenon is also explained by the concepts of projective and introjective identification of repressed ego structures.

Some of these children's symptoms were relatively specifically transmitted from family-wide sexual issues as in the cases of Tanya and the B family. Others develop via the more diffuse channel of the spread of uncontained anxiety and the failure to shape developmentally-based impulses as in the example of Debbie. The specific relationship of sexual symptomatology to the currents of family life is taken up more extensively in the next three chapters.

Chapter 7
The childhood origins of sexual difficulty I:
The effect of early experiences with parents

I have learned to look upon unconscious love relations like this
(which are marked by their abnormal consequences) – between a
father and a daughter, or between a mother and a son – as a revival
of germs of feeling in infancy. I have shown at length elsewhere at
what an early age sexual attraction makes itself felt between parents
and children, and I have explained that the legend of Oedipus is
probably to be regarded as a poetical rendering of what is typical
in these relations.

Sigmund Freud, 'Fragment of an
analysis of a case of hysteria' *

The object-related transmission of social and cultural values

Sexual difficulty in adults represents a complex inheritance of factors
which are in addition to the family experience. In particular, Masters
and Johnson focus extensively on the cultural and religious contributions in the etiology of sexual dysfunctions. For instance, in
discussing primary impotence they state:

Severe religious orthodoxy may indoctrinate the teenager with
the concept that any form of overt sexual activity prior to marriage
not only is totally unacceptable but is personally destructive, de-
moralizing, degrading, dehumanizing and injurious to one's physical
and/or mental health. Perhaps even more unfortunate, the psycho-
social expectations, if any, for the sexual relationship in marriage
are given no honorable factual support. . . . It is fortunate that more
virginal males of similar background, failing in their tension-filled

51

initial exposures to the physical verities of marital sexual functioning, do not succumb to the pressures of these frightening initial episodes of failure by developing the relevant symptoms of primary impotence.[1]

Although Masters and Johnson note that certain patients are made more vulnerable to the strictures of religious orthology, for instance the male who has been subjected to unopposed dominance of either parent, the mechanism of influence by the religions or cultural factors is not taken up.[2]

Cultural and religious factors are transmitted by the primary figures who constitute the models for internal objects. When religion or culture has influence, it does so through the interpersonal context in which it is taken in, and which is revived in the current setting. It is this inter-personal context which allows an understanding of the mechanism of action. The following is a relatively benign example.

John and Mary Santini, she 56, he 62, shared a common heritage of strict Italian-American Catholic families in which their parents had immigrated to the United States. They had been married three years and were deeply in love when they presented for sexual difficulty. Each had been devoted throughout almost three decades to original marriages in which sex had been infrequent and unsatisfying. Presumably these first unhappy marriages had lasted so long partly because of internalized attitudes about divorces. John's first wife had died before he met Mary. She was separated from her husband, but he did not die until after an affair had begun between the two. This was a source of considerable guilt for Mary despite her clear wish to be with John.

John and Mary shared two cultural and family values: strict religiosity and a compelling commitment to take care of their family – mothers, brothers and sisters, husband and wife, and children. Neither voiced any ethic about enjoyment of oneself – only guilt about the idea of putting self before others. Since they shared this value, they were able to do for each other so that neither was in any danger of 'going without.' This extreme selflessness did not seem to infringe on their life, except sexually.

Mary was orgasmic and loved sex with her husband. Although he was initially sexually functional, John now began to experience increasingly frequent secondary impotence, paralyzing their sexual life. When they began intercourse, he would be thinking immediately of whether he was offering Mary enough pleasure. She could achieve reliable orgasm only in the female-superior position, a factor he believed firmly to be his fault. As he tried harder, his erection became less reliable and within a year of their marriage, he had become functionally impotent.

In the brief sex therapy in which they were seen by a co-therapy team, interesting things happened. Both were unable initially to enjoy anything for themselves. When active in massaging, each would report getting far more pleasure from the other's response – and if cut off from hearing about it because the therapists asked for silence between them, they grew bored and restless. In receiving pleasuring, they were anxious and guilty. With help from the therapists, and with authoritative sanction, they pushed past this. But in doing so, the apparently tangential material which came forth, especially from Mary, illustrated the power of religious sanctions concerning sex.

Mary spoke about the care she took of her aging mother for years, the guilt about finally placing her in a nursing home, and now about the wish to take care of her own children. She remembered the kind and understanding priest who gave her permission to have a hysterectomy after three children when her life was in danger, and she reached further back to the childhood experiences with her loving but guilt-instilling, selfless parents and the nuns who had taught her. It was not just that she had been taught that sex was wrong – because it had been sanctioned in marriage. But in all her early objects, there was no model for enjoying oneself, only for selfless efforts prodded always by the threat of guilt.

In a final confrontation with this archaic demon, Mary told the therapists of trying to pleasure herself by masturbating (as they had told her to do) only to look up on her bedroom wall and see a statuette of 'The Virgin Mother' looking down at her – a symbol of sexless self-sacrifice after whom she had been named! She had, not surprisingly, been unable to continue. With a few days more work, however, she was able to move the statuette and the accompanying feeling out of the bedroom and to talk with her grown daughters about paying attention to one's own needs too. Responding warmly, her daughters praised her, and in turn she gave one of her adoring but similarly guilt-ridden daughters the books she had found so helpful in learning to accept pleasure for herself.

Intrapsychic life is a major factor in sexual difficulty, not only because it is involved in the mediation of these social and religious values, but because in the clinical population, it is a factor in more unique ways in the patients who have most difficulty. Things are complicated when two people, over the long time span of most marriages, are confronted with the heritage of their combined experiences during childhood in their families of origin and in the most intimate surroundings of the families. The list of people whose influence ranks close to that of family members is limited to a few substitute parent figures (relatives, teachers, nurses, nuns, priests, etc.) and to peers in adolescence. These early complex influences become unconsciously linked to adult sexuality in either normally functioning or dysfunctional sexual life. When sex is normal, we can assume the present relationship is predominantly benign, consisting of reparative feelings on balance rather than destructive or fearful ones. It is worth keeping in mind those cases in which the parents' values support a liberal sexuality but the child, when grown, is too anxious to enjoy that heritage and acts as if the parents were the strictest puritans. These cases make the point dramatically that culture is only one factor in a complex field.

The assessment of the internal object life

Childhood experiences, general or traumatic, do not *alone* cause a dysfunction which is a symptom determined by many factors, including the vulnerability of the sexual system typical of psychosomatic diseases.[3] But in couples who do present with sexual disorders, it is always worth investigating the internal family and its contribution to the current impasse. While this is sometimes useful to the patient or couple even in an initial interview, often it can only be made useful with much longer exploration. Even a brief introductory history can be used to locate the probable origin of symptoms and to estimate the kind of treatment required to improve the patient's sexual functioning.

This information is available from two main sources: the literal verbal history given by the patient, and less obvious, the reliving of the parental relationship present in the transference to the spouse and to the therapists as the patient discusses the sexual difficulty. In briefer encounters a rapid transference assessment offers us an early opportunity to experience what the couple and the family live with constantly. The sexual symptom may be the leading edge of a chronic difficulty, the clue that a seeming immunity to a chronic situation is far from perfect as in the following case.

Tamara's husband Roy insisted on an evaluation about their sexual life 'when her excuses finally ran out.' Both were 38 and they had been married 4½ years. During the marriage they had had no sex which had been pleasurable to her, although it had been fully gratifying before their marriage. When she had first felt fully committed to Roy, the sex became vulnerable and finally unpleasant.

She became pregnant on the honeymoon and pregnant again as soon as she stopped nursing the first baby. Only when a year had elapsed after nursing the second child and still she feared sex, did she agree to seek help.

In the initial interview with the therapists, Tamara was guarded and anxious. She felt she should seek help because she valued her marriage and felt she owed it to Roy. She expressed both relief at finally being able to talk, and a sense of threat. In subsequent evaluation sessions she talked easily but remained vague, especially about her parents who were idealized. But when the woman therapist made a tentative comment that she might have mixed feelings about her mother, Tamara erupted into a rage, screaming that 'she couldn't stand being treated like that!' and that she felt criticized by the therapist. She quickly recovered herself, however, and said that this kind of rage was extremely unusual for her except that she had many angry outbursts at Roy and her children – eruptions she did not understand. Why did she only rage at those people she loved most? This interview concluded amicably soon after and in a subsequent interview with the male co-therapist Tamara was not only more reasonable, but generally more insightful.

The therapists guessed on the basis of this event that Tamara felt misunderstood and criticized and badly treated by her mother. The interview with the woman, and especially a comment questioning her feelings about mother presumably tapped feelings which Tamara could not begin to look at in the evaluation. That her relationship with father was more benign was supported by the wholly different feeling in her interview with a man. The therapists guessed that it was the maternal 'bad object' at which she raged in her children and husband. When psychoanalysis was recommended, a male analyst was suggested because of her early transference difficulty with women.

It was only months later in the analysis that Tamara was first able to acknowledge that her mother was critical in a subtle but persistent way and to get even a glimmer of her resentment. It came then in a series of dreams in which houses represented her inner world. After a few dreams in which the rooms and furniture were enlarging (as analysis made more of her inner world available), she reported the following dream:

> 'It was at home, pushing furniture against the walls of the living room to make more space, trying to arrange a table like our neighbors have done in a way I like. Mother was there. She said either, "that looks terrible" or "you should put it back the way it was." I remember being really angry she said that. When I woke, it occurred to me my mother is always there in my house telling me how to rearrange it. If the house signified my mind, then she's there too!'

This dream about the critical mother was also about mother's condemnation of Tamara's childhood masturbation. It told us that her mother (and she as well) could not admire her genitals and her body (her 'living room'). The anti-libidinal internal mother is the one who forbids sex. In confirmation of this new understanding (which was not mentioned at the time) Tamara began to masturbate after years of abstinence, and tenuously initiated sex with Roy a few days later.

The clue in the early transference situation provided information of which the patient herself was unaware. In fact, because of the nature of her defense of 'not wanting to know' about the resentment of the internalized critical mother, she denied not only any resentment of her mother, but the existence of the situation. So the therapists could only infer that the presence of this reaction betrayed a hidden internalization which was relevant to Tamara's sexual withdrawal too. Confirmation and modification had to wait to unfold.

A framework for considering the childhood experiences of sexually dysfunctional patients

As we have seen, childhood experiences with parents largely organize themselves around memories and unconsciously-carried internalizations of events which bear a fundamental relationship to parents. In this chapter, I want to consider two groupings of these internalizations, and later I will consider an additional two:

I   the quality of the bond to the parents of the same and opposite sex;
II the quality of the bond between the parents themselves at different stages;
III the adequacy of the parents' functioning *as parents*; and
IV the peer and substitute-parent experiences of later childhood and adolescence (memories which carry forward and modify the themes of earlier parenting) - this area will be considered in the section on adolescence.

In all four, some general themes are important to the quality of the sexual bond and experience in adulthood; threats or actual experiences of abandonment; the amount and direction of anger and hate; the ease of feeling loved and cared for. These will surface repeatedly in the discussion and cases which follow.

I   The quality of the bond with parents

This experience falls into two groups:

1   Pre-oedipal development, including the earliest bonding of the infant (boy or girl) to his or her mother.
2   Oedipal development, different for boys and girls, including both positive and negative oedipal development, that is:

The positive oedipal picture: identification with the parent of the same sex - boy with his father; girl with her mother; and the sexualized bond of approval and attractiveness to the parent of the opposite sex.
The negative oedipal picture: the sexualized bond to the parent of the same sex.

1   Primary mother–infant experiences

As we have discussed, these first experiences involve intense physical exchanges as the medium for building the bulwark of trust for true mutual attachment and concern. Disruption here is crucial to personality development, only one aspect of which may be the development of sexual difficulties which, under these circumstances, are closely related to and overshadowed by more profound psychological troubles. Since sex may be used in an attempt to gain mothering, many patients with early and chronic disruptions in mothering are acting out sexually long before reaching adulthood. Others with only moderate early damage can function sexually better than in some other spheres.

Judy Green, at age 14, had experienced severe abuses of sexuality in her young life. Her mother was ambivalent about her from the first, focusing many of her doubts about herself on her relationship with Judy as an infant (something her 3-year-older brother had escaped since her mother had not identified so many negative aspects of herself with a son).

Mother had regretted the marriage itself even before Judy was born. She was depressed during Judy's first years and treated Judy with alternating neglect and resentment. Attention came in spurts of guilty overcompensation. On at least one occasion when Judy was 4, mother forced her to nurse at the breast. This may have indicated, as was suspected, that mother preferred the intimacy of infantile relationships and encouraged regressive and dependent but sexualized behavior. The demands of a growing child apparently were too much for her. Judy's relationship to her father was also marked by seduction on both sides. He called her 'Judy-babe' and enjoyed her coquettishly playing up to him. Presumably, he wished for gratification from her which he missed in the unhappy marriage, just as Judy wished to receive care from him to make up for what was missing with mother.

Her plight was therefore deepened when he developed cancer when she was 4 and died when she was 5. (She had one early memory of father picking her up joyfully, and another of being completely alone.) Mother was especially guilty because she had been having an affair at the time her husband's illness was discovered. The level of depression in the mother and chaos in the family improved somewhat when the mother remarried two years later, but not enough to make up for the early inadequate parenting to Judy. She engaged in incestuous sexual activity regularly with her brother for a year when she was 9 and her brother 11. This was discovered and stopped, but by age 13, Judy was severely depressed, consumed with guilt, and began using sex as a way of acting out. She had intercourse with a variety of boys quickly while her mother was out of the house. Soon a pregnancy scare occasioned by a late menstrual period became confused with a memory of accidental death of an infant which she had witnessed a year earlier, and she became severely depressed. She was admitted to the hospital finally after taking 100 aspirins.

For Judy, the stage for sexual acting out was set by the deficit in early mothering both in the primary experience with mother in which mother's depression led to emotional absence, and in the withdrawal of mother when she felt Judy to be unmanageable. The loss of father meant the loss of what compensation she had been able to obtain. Nothing interrupted her depressed mother's projection of poor self-esteem onto her daughter, a situation which had pertained from the beginning of Judy's life onward. What ensued was the enactment of many of the other elements of poor parent-child relationships focused in the sexual sphere. Judy's childhood and adolescent attempts to get mothering were determined by the earliest deficits in experience with her mother as exacerbated and continued by additional later deprivations and by an identification with the mother's own sexualized attempt (the affair) to obtain relief when Judy was 4.

Many of the most basic deficits are not verbally documentable by patients for two reasons. First, if they are particularly severe, the disturbances in behavior begin early in childhood and permeate the child's growing personality, extending far beyond the sexual sphere. Second, the fundamentals of the mother–child relationship are laid down before language and cognitive memory, at a time as we have noted when thought is concrete and body-centered, born in the cradle of physical parent–infant exchanges. Patients with these early defects recall Harlow's motherless monkeys (chapter 3) for they too have experienced their mothers psychologically as stiff, wire imitations of live mothers. Like the dummy wire or terrycloth monkey 'mothers,' their human mothers failed to convey warmth through holding, handling, and reflection. Since sexual relating - as opposed to mechanical functioning - requires an internalization of a whole, live experience from the beginning, these patients were seriously handicapped. On the other hand, some of the less severe human examples surface as a continued but less thorough difficulty between mother and child. As in Judy's case, derivatives of the earliest difficulty are then interwoven with the next phases of growth.

2   *Oedipal development in males: The bond and identification with parents*

Between the ages of 3 and 5, the boy ordinarily moves from valuing his mother as an attachment figure and caretaker to valuing her as the object of his genital sexual and libidinal interest, and he first recognizes the threatening rivalry this brings on with father. Although at first he uses an exhibitionistic appeal to both parents during what can be called the 'phallic–narcissistic phase,'[4] he later comes to envy and fear his father as a rival, wishing at times to destroy him and imagining father might retaliate by destroying him or his penis for his angry wishes. At the same time, he continues to love and identify with his father despite the envy, anger, and fear. This constellation makes up the positive oedipal complex shown in box A of figure 7.1.[5]

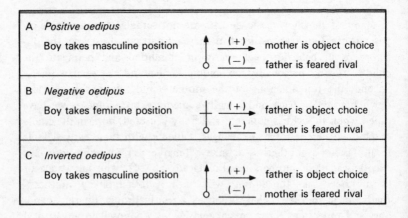

Figure 7.1 The oedipal situation in the boy

However, part of the boy's interest shifts to imagining himself as a girl (identified with mother) whom father could love sexually (figure 7.1, box B). Then he would not have to worry about father's retaliation against his penis. This *negative oedipal complex* is also an expression of the boy's fundamental bisexuality.

Confusion often arises between the terms '*negative*' and '*inverted*' *oedipus* (see figure 7.1, box C). *In the 'negative oedipus,' the boy takes a feminine position with father as his object. He acts passively, or figuratively, like a girl and loves father. In the 'inverted oedipus' he acts like a boy (that is, he is active) and loves father.* In the inverted oedipus then there is no change from the more active and masculine position, only a change of object choice. The inverted oedipus situation stems from the normal phallic–narcissistic phase preceding full oedipal development. In this earlier phase, the boy exhibits his masculinity to father in the same way he does to his mother – in the interests of gaining father's approval and love.[6] Later, when the boy is oedipally drawn to mother, the inverted elements of the oedipal situation continue to play a role as he tries to work out a situation in which he loves both parents and yet has a sexual identity as a boy. If father is absent or provides a weak figure for identification while mother is dominant, an exaggerated positive oedipal situation may develop. But if the boy turns to father to make up for mothering he felt to be deficient, aspects of a negative or inverted picture may ensue.

The fact that there are these three basic ways (and many combinations of them) for the boy to negotiate the oedipal situation underscores the relevance of intra-psychic object relations. Two boys, viewed from outside, may both seem to be acting like little men loving their fathers. Yet one of them may intrapsychically be heavily identified with mother, acting like a female loving a man. And the other may be primarily identified as a boy and be in the process of working out an identification with his father.

The positive oedipal constellation and its role in the origin of sexual disorders is highlighted in the next example.

A case example of exaggerated positive oedipal development

Henry de F came at 41 because his wife, Claire, was non-orgasmic and uninterested in sex and was frequently depressed. It was soon revealed that he had significant premature ejaculation. He never lasted more than 30 to 60 seconds on any occasion, including in pre-marital and occasional extra-marital forays with prostitutes. Additionally, when his wife used sex therapy to become orgasmic, more enthusiastic sexually, and less depressed, he began to have long periods of loss of all sexual interest and of significant depression.

Henry's family history was interesting regarding both parents. His mother was a formidable and dominating woman who had married a pharmacist in Idaho who was her childhood sweetheart. He was loving and supportive of Henry, but was apparently a bland character. When Henry was 5, mother left the pharmacist to marry a brilliant French aristocrat, Mr de F, who, it turned out, was Henry's real father. Mr de F was, however, extremely depressed and demanding. Henry's mother spent all her time taking care of him. She was required to closet herself with her new husband and ignore Henry while the new-found father looked angrily on Henry as a rival and a burden. His mother had to be constantly on tap for father's sexual demands and if she was not, he occasionally threatened suicide.

Henry's struggles with his father cannot escape our notice, but his feeling of involvement with his mother was more intense. It was his mother's preoccupation with the two men which fixed his attention, leading him to avoid domination by a mother. He picked a woman who was not sexually responsive. He knew this before deciding to marry her and he had had adequate prior sexual experience with other women for comparison. Once married, he tried to court and subdue her into responsiveness. At the same time his premature ejaculation contained the nidus of holding out against her. The refusal to be dominated by her protected him from anxiety of being controlled *by* her just as he longed *to* control her. When Claire became responsive, his retreat became more obvious and massive. The full-blown sexual withdrawal from his wife represented the need to protect himself from both the libidinal engulfing mother and the anti-libidinal one who had left him for both his fathers.

Henry's loss of the loved first father who was vanquished during the oedipal period was a significant part of his serious depression. The sexual disorder (including the premature ejaculation, the later loss of interest, and the choice of his unresponsive wife) represents an iden- tification with this lost object, fueled by his own guilty longing for and

fear of his mother. There were undoubtedly issues in the early relationship with her that contributed to his difficulty, but it was during the
oedipal phase that his difficulty seemed to have begun in earnest.
While the sex therapy was effective in the matters of Claire's dysfunctions and Henry's premature ejaculation, the unmasking of his
sexual disjunction and the depression which went with it required
referral for intensive psychotherapy and for a trial of anti-depressant
therapy.

A case with negative and inverted oedipal development

The following case illustrates how the negative and inverted oedipal
elements developed to cope with a conflict with a father (here augmented by a libidinally inverted grandfather) to produce sexual symptomatology. Little information became available about mother directly
during treatment, but the indirect evidence demonstrated an attitude
of deficiency and fearful retreat from her.

> Bob talked at length about his father who had high hopes for him
> while his mother was presented as a vague and unsupportive figure.
> Willing to do anything to be close to father, Bob feared that he
> would be forced into submission by him. As a child, he had refused
> to wear pajamas because he thought his father wanted him to. Later
> the pajamas became a fetish-like object which he found sexually
> exciting. He would masturbate while wearing them. In therapy, he
> connected the pajamas to the long underwear of his grandfather, a
> man he loved and with whom he frequently shared a bed.
> Ambivalence felt about the pajamas was also expressed in his inability
> to sustain an erection long enough for penetration with his girl-
> friend; for he would think immediately that his father would be
> wanting him to have intercourse and his penis would promptly wilt.
> Bob's progress in tolerating the anxiety ran concurrent with his
> increasing ability to modify his view of his father as someone who
> would not take over his autonomy if Bob began to identify with
> him as an active male. He came progressively to see that the
> ambivalence represented some of his father's own doubts about his
> own personal potency and a longing for a closer relationship with
> Bob that had, for Bob, a homosexual tint parallel to his own feelings
> for his grandfather. The feelings for father had seemed to require
> him to passively submit. In a paradoxical way, he was standing up
> for himself by refusing to have an erection. At the same time, he

had, in an active way, wished to reach out to his grandfather. The same paradox developed in the transference to the male therapist. Bob would resist getting into a sexually threatening situation as if it were only for the therapist that he would have intercourse, and at the same time he actively wished to succeed and to please the therapist.

There are issues involved for Bob which share common ground with men who become homosexual. An identification with father is confused with a longing to turn to him as a libidinal object (seen by Bob in the grandfather). This in turn is overshadowed by the anti-libidinal object seen in the father threatening castration and turning him into a woman. Presumably, women are also seen as anti-libidinal and threatening, although confirming verbal material about mother was not available. His withdrawal from women and fear of their domination seemed to indicate a similar fear of his mother.

Bob does not have a homosexual identification and has slowly been able to identify with his male therapist and from there, move toward more effective relationships with women. For him, positive feelings toward father threatened castration which he defended against. An attempt to identify with father by having intercourse was so confused with submitting to father as a girl that he withdrew his penis to save it. Issues of the *inverted oedipal constellation* are suggested here: of Bob's tie *as a boy* to his father. These could not be fully differentiated in his limited treatment and the predominant understanding remained that of his fear of a negative oedipal situation.

3   Oedipal development in women: The bond and identification with parents

It is generally held that the path of growth for girls is more complex than that for boys, because the girl must move from a primary attachment to the mother to one with father.[7] Two recent contributions to our understanding of female sexual development have taken alternate paths, although both are by workers whose names are closely associated with the Hampstead Clinic in London. We will consider first that of Humberto Nagera, which extends the exploration of Freud's original view that the little girl originally acts like a boy, while the second by Rose Edgcumbe and Marion Burgner adopts a new view - that a 'phallic-narcissistic phase' marks a transitional zone between dyadic pre-oedipal and triadic oedipal development.

Nagera's formulation of the female oedipal development can be understood with reference to figure 7.2.[8] He states that before the age of 2½ to 3, the pre-oedipal girl acts and identifies much like a little boy. In the normal *first* phase of her oedipal period she acts as though she were a boy and takes mother as the object of her love (box A, figure 7.2). At about 2½ to 3 years of age, she adopts a more receptive mode and shifts to a feminine position, now with father as the principal recipient of her love (box C). However, during each of these periods there is a *negative* oedipal position. Before age 3, when the girl is predominantly acting like a boy, the negative picture (present in a covert way normally) is that she is a girl seeking father (box B). These are the little girls who prematurely turn to father under the pressure of an unavailable mother. After the age of 3, the *negative* picture is now that the girl acts like a *boy* seeking mother (box D).

First stage PHALLIC − OEDIPAL		Second stage OEDIPAL	
A Positive ▲ MOTHER +++ ○ FATHER −−−	B Negative │ FATHER + ○ MOTHER −	C Positive │ FATHER +++ ○ MOTHER −−−	D Negative ▲ MOTHER +++ ○ FATHER −−−
E Inverted ▲ │ FATHER + ○ MOTHER −		F Inverted │ ▲ MOTHER + ○ FATHER −	

Figure 7.2 Oedipal positions of the girl (modified from Nagera, 1975, p. 11)

The situation is actually far more complex, however. There are in addition two *inverted* versions of the phases (see boxes E and F). In the first stage the girl with an *inverted* oedipal picture acts like a *boy* but the libidinal object is *father*. That is, she is still the phallic-oedipal 'boy' who chooses father over mother. In the second later inverted phase, she has made the shift to acting like the *girl* of the normal second stage, but her libidinal object is *mother* instead of father. These represent ways of conceptualizing the fact that with the girl's inherent bisexuality and her shift of dominant mode, all permutations are possible in a clinical picture. It is necessary to think about a complexity of factors, whether the attachment is first or second phase, whether it is positive, negative, or inverted. (Nagera's thorough and thoughtful consideration of the vicissitudes of these phases and their contribution to female sexuality goes beyond our scope here. But his schema is invaluable in looking at the contribution of the oedipus complex to sexual disorder in female patients.)

We can see that the boy is spared most of the vicissitudes of this complex staging because (1) although he had an early passive stage, pre-oedipal development has already brought him into activity and his normal dominant mode; and (2) he does not have to change libidinal objects in the normal situation. He only has to make room for a secondary one (father) with whom he can identify. (Here Henry de F had difficulty.) But the girl has to *identify with her mother even as she is pushed to give her up as a libidinal object*.

Nagera's explanation extends Freud's idea which many find objectionable, that the little girl is acting 'like a boy' and that masculinity is assumed to be primary. While his formulations are clinically useful (some women *do* unconsciously act as if they were boys), a corrective is called for concerning this aspect of his formulation.

This corrective may be provided by the second study of Edgcumbe and Burgner.[9] On the basis of observation and analysis of boys and girls, they described a pre-oedipal stage of development which they termed the phallic–narcissistic phase. During this stage, when the genital first becomes a source of pleasure and focus, there is little difference between boy and girl. Both engage in auto-erotic stimulation and wish for genital stimulation from the object with little differentiation between self and object or between father and mother. Exhibitionism and scoptophilia characterize the approach to the object. The child says 'Look at me and what I can do!' and is intensely curious about seeing both parents. There is a first castration anxiety which is not as severe in boys as in girls. The boy becomes aware of the comparative small size of his penis, while the girl begins the process of coming to terms with living without one. The girl's envy for the missing penis is based on the greater narcissistic blow the girl feels, and fits in with her envy of other things. But in the presence of an adequate model of femininity, the girl still has no trouble with feminine identification. It is only after the successful negotiation of this phase that the child begins oedipal development proper. For a boy, the situation is relatively uncomplicated since the mother who was his primary pre-oedipal object becomes his primary oedipal object. But the girl must shift from mother to father, and from the activity of the phallic–narcissistic phase to the receptive mode of her positive oedipal development.[10] Presumably, if theory concerning negative (or first stage) oedipal development is correct, there should be many cases of the girl's 'negative oedipal development' in which the girl acts like an active or boyish person pursuing mother. Yet Edgcumbe and her colleagues report that in investigating well-documented analyses of girls[11] they could not substantiate evidence for a normal negative oedipal *phase* preceding positive oedipal development, even though in full oedipal development, negative oedipal material might be prominent. This supported the earlier observations that girls ordinarily seemed to have a feminine identification well in hand before the age of 3 when they behave similarly to boys in the phallic–narcissistic phase. That is to say they behave actively and exhibitionistically, but as girls, not 'like boys.' Later, their oedipal pursuit of father is not 'passive receptive' as had been held, but is actively pursued.

Edgcumbe and Burgner thus supply a view of the phallic–narcissistic (or first phase oedipal) girl as being not 'like a boy.' Rather, it is that both boy and girl are like each other in being relatively genitally undifferentiated, *relatively* undifferentiated in terms of self and object, and both active. Both are primarily interested in dyadic relationships and are on the verge of the new horizon of triadic issues and the complications that their new recognition of genital differentiation will bring.

However, Nagera's contribution remains relevant, because we do see patients who have a partial sexual identity contrary to their actual gender. It may be that the transition from phallic–narcissistic to genital-oedipal organization marks a time when object-mediated aspects of sexual identity are exceptionally vulnerable to challenges that have the potential to induce a substantial identification with the opposite sex.

Another way to look at it is to say that when the little girl realizes she is lacking a penis, she must mourn that sense of deficiency. Her rudimentary capacity to mourn is taxed and she resorts to a primitive defense of denial to compensate. If she later identifies herself partly as a boy, it is the relatively undifferentiated self who was *more* like a boy which she retrospectively remakes into a boy as one way of compensating for her early failure to mourn. Presumably, the less family support she receives for her feminine identification, the more likely is this retrospective falsification to happen. Clinically, these are the negative and inverted oedipal pictures which Nagera's work clarifies.

A phallic–narcissistic or first stage oedipal solution

Mrs L was non-orgasmic and was not even interested in becoming sexually aroused with her husband, an admiral, who had alternating difficulty with premature and retarded ejaculation. She had chosen him as someone steady, reliable, and productive, a corrective to her playboy father who had been helpless to support the family when he lost his money in the depression. But her strongest feelings of ambivalence and anger were for her mother who had clung to her after this family catastrophe. Her mother had been a dancer from South America. She had felt culturally isolated and lonely in North America and therefore clung to Mrs L from her childhood. As she talked more, Mrs L's anger at her mother became more clearly linked with the episodes in which she felt she had to renounce potential lovers during late adolescence. Older, artistic men, who might have reminded her of her departed father whose image excited her had to be given up while she stayed to support her mother. It became clear that the identification with her mother as someone chosen by her father because of her foreign allure and sensuous qualities made the notion of becoming sexual herself dangerous, lest her husband leave, or lest she feel aroused, which felt threatening to her. She had chosen Admiral L for his steadfast and *non-sensuous* qualities, and was terrified to even entertain the notion of his having sexual appeal.

The most difficult part of the feelings about her mother focused on her female therapist. She suddenly developed the notion that the therapist was a woman who meant ill toward her and felt she was a bad person. In fact, the therapist felt no such thing, but did have the concern that the quality of Mrs L's internalized relationship to her mother as an anti-libidinal object was intolerably harsh and angry. As sex therapy proceeded, Mrs L's reluctance grew. Despite professed wishes to become sexually responsive, she appeared to be not at all interested. Finally she exclaimed in an outburst, 'I think you hate me and I think you are a horrible person.' When interpretation of the transference failed to remove this resistance, further work with this therapist could not continue. It also became clear gradually that this feeling ånd the inherited self-image were so inextricably tied to the sexual dysfunction that there was little hope of further progress.

Mrs L had completed, as far as one could tell, an initial shift to cathecting her father as a girl (Nagera's second stage, positive oedipal position). But his exploitative and untrustworthy qualities, coupled with the mother's assault on him, tended to push her back to a first phase oedipal solution: being a boy taking care of her mother (whom she also sees as a 'sensuous' woman). She longs for a 'sensuous' man, but ambivalently overcome by the pull of the anti-libidinal mother, cannot accept one, even in her current husband who would himself have liked to be more actively sexual. The solution she worked out in her early twenties – and to which she now returns in her sexual refusal – is effectively to give up sexuality and to connect to a motherly man. One formulation would be that she had fashioned a phallic-narcissistic or first stage oedipal solution with a partial identification *as a boy* herself, treating her husband as a reincarnation of a good mother who cannot then be allowed to become the threatening man (see figure 7.2, box A).[12] This is the best she can manage since her angry identification with her own mother will not allow her to move to a positive second stage solution – loving a man as a receptive woman. Some of the pre-oedipal solution uses anger as a substitute for sex – a solution which is developmentally even earlier than the phallic-narcissistic one. In both her sexual life with her husband and in the transference to the woman therapist she acts on the angry rejection she still carries for her own mother whom she held responsible for blocking her developmental path. It is worth noting that having sequestered this blocked oedipal development within the sexual disjunction, she is relatively free to relate to her husband as a good object in the rest of her life.

Difficulty with the second stage of oedipal development is demonstrated in the next example. As in many cases, the oedipal configuration is complex.

A positive oedipal solution

Enid, age 28, was married, with a 3-year-old child. She had been warm and friendly while she had an affair with her husband who was married when she met him. But after their marriage, the picture changed. Now she had no interest in sex, and since she had never been orgasmic, she wished she could continue her marriage indefinitely without sex. Sex therapy was not successful, and it was only in psychotherapy which followed that she discovered that her poor identification with and denigration of her mother and her related poor self-image were magnified by an idealization of and devotion to her father. She viewed herself as 'the girl for him,' far more able to make him happy than her mother – and that seems to have been historically largely true. For that reason her guilt for psychologically doing in her mother reinforced her self-hate. When her parents told her at age 12 that they were to be divorced, she reasoned that this loss of her father was in retribution for her shutting out her mother. Even though her parents never did divorce, and in fact improved their relationship in subsequent years, she could not allow herself to 'open up' sexually to her husband since she assumed the same fate awaited her. Unconsciously she felt she deserved it as punishment for emotionally displacing her mother with father.

Enid's excessive interest in and longing for her father with its childhood sexualization was given permanent psychological life as a dread about her own fate. This inhibited use of sex within an intimate adult situation did leave her in fact very much in danger of the same kind of abandonment she felt her mother had suffered. Enid had been able to experience sexual arousal pre-maritally when the illicit circumstance permitted gratification of the wish to lure her father, while disguising this since the relationship was not one of continuing commitment as between her father and mother. On marrying, when the object became legitimate, the disguise failed and so under pressure of guilt, she reverted to a repressed but very active identification with her anti-libidinal mother. She became sexually paralyzed. (Incidentally, later information from the mother convinced Enid that her own mother had been rejecting of her because of a similar oedipal constellation with the mother's own parents.)

Enid had consciously thought of herself as the son her father never had. She was heavily identified with father as 'his boy,' rejecting her mother angrily as ineffective and unimportant. Although she related to her father mostly as a girl, she partly regressed to a fixation in the first oedipal phase - she was a boy whose libidinal object was a maternal father.[13] In later development she retained much of the active, masculine quality sequestered in the symptom of her sexual non-response, while in the rest of her life she was then free to act the little *girl* attracted to father. However, her poor image of herself and a constant valuing of her infant son over her daughter (with whom she had a hated negative identification) were also clues to her continuing oedipal difficulty.

4　A final note on oedipal splitting

In this case again, no formulation of an exclusive, simple, positive oedipal problem is possible. It never is. Our patients' complex inner lives include, in each one, the potential for all possibilities, for a dominance of one pattern and the continued activity of others which are repressed but still active. Denied parts of the self continue to have influence. Fairbairn emphasized an additional aspect of the oedipal situation in saying:

> . . . the oedipus situation is essentially built-up around the internalized figures of the exciting mother and the rejecting mother. However, in his attempt to adjust to two ambivalent relationships at the same time, the child seeks to simplify a complex situation by concentrating on the exciting aspect of one parent and the rejecting aspect of the other, and by modifying the nature of the exciting and the rejecting objects accordingly; and in so doing, the child really constitutes the oedipus situation for himself.[14]

For our patients like Mrs L and Enid, sexual symptomatology is often an unconscious attempt to keep the oedipal split simple - to have all the good in the conscious spouse while maintaining repression of the threatening elements at the expense of their sexual life. But the buried elements strive for expression and thereby speak against our patients' wish to 'simplify' their lives.

II The internalization of the bond between the parents

In 'Fragment of an analysis of a case of hysteria', Freud reported that Dora's symptom of shortness of breath was attributable to her having overheard the breathing of her parents in intercourse.[15] In the 'Three essays' he noted that young children exposed to parental intercourse invariably interpreted it to be a sadistic act.[16] Melanie Klein extended Freud's thinking when she explored the fantasies of even the very young child about parental intercourse, and the vicissitudes of the child's own fantasies about the parental relationship.[17]

She did not, however, pay much attention to the child's actual experience of the parents' relationship. The following example will allow some comments on the interaction of actual experience and the fantasy elaboration by the growing child.

> Emma Smith, aged 33, like Enid, had lost interest in sex within three years of her marriage and had never had an orgasm. Her history was more dramatic. She always had a difficult relationship to her mother. She felt very rejected when mother sent her to board in a convent school between the ages of 5 and 8. But the most problematic issue in her current aversion to intercourse and her non-orgasmic status were memories of the nightly battles between her parents after she returned to live with them. Her father would begin to drink at dinner, and she would sit watching her mother bait him to anger, sometimes trying herself to bait him in the name of protecting and siding with her mother. Each evening at about 10 o'clock he would finally stagger off to bed, swearing profusely, and she would joyfully spend the rest of the evening with her mother, the only time she felt close to her. At other times, her father would lurch naked down the hall in the middle of the night, and she would be in terror lest he would come into her room. He actually did so only once. On more than one occasion, Emma's mother brandished a knife at him when he threatened to beat the mother.
>
> Emma's fantasy life during sex was at first completely blank. She hated the feeling of being penetrated, which she described as a 'veil of numbness.' When, during sex therapy, she was able to lift the 'veil' she had a fantasy of being stabbed as if her husband's penis were a knife. In her own retaliatory fantasy, she felt a murderous rage and saw herself stabbing him back.

Emma's adult fantasies were an all too faithful echo of her internalization of her parents' bond to each other. The amount of aggression in the parental bond, precipitated as it often is by alcohol and catalyzed by Emma's own childhood psychosexual development and fantasy life, mixed her ideas of sexuality and aggression into a tangled muddle. Her longing for her mother, excitement around her father's anger, and the general air of mutual assault in their relationship dominated her adult efforts to achieve sexual intimacy.

For Emma, it was both parents who had to be shut out, because of her frustrated longing for each parent, and because the aggressive nature of the bond between them was her only version of adult intimacy. While on the surface, Emma was calm, polite, and compliant, and loved her husband, the frightened and angry girl inside was awakened in any sexual experience, leading to the fears of murderous invasion and the wishes to retaliate. But retaliation was not her only motive. The aggression was also an unshakeable bond to her parents as internal objects, a way of 'lovingly' identifying and of staying in faithful touch with them.

This case lends itself as an illustration of Melanie Klein's discussion of the child's early oedipal issues. Although Emma's memories of her parents' quarrelling relationship came from her latency and adolescence, the later episodes would have rekindled the early fantasies of the parents locked in intercourse with, as Klein put it, the father's penis being held inside the mother's body.[18] This archaic fantasy, the aggressive cast given to it by the parents' actual hostile relationship, and Emma's childhood envy of even that relationship crystallized her sexual difficulty. It is in similarly complex ways that the memory of the parental relationship is often expressed in sexual disorders.

Concerning the lack of specificity in cause and effect

So far we have considered only the first two items of the framework for understanding the way in which early experience modifies psychological growth and sexual development: the bond between child and parent, and the internalization of the parents' bond to each other. Chapters 8 and 9 take up the third item – the functioning of the parents as parents; and chapter 10 deals with the contribution of adolescent development.

In these matters, as in the ones we have already considered, we cannot make exact links between the specific insult and the specific sexual difficulty. This inability remains because although we examine the effect of family events on the intrapsychic world, *the meaning of those events is always mediated by what is in the child's mind at the time something occurs*. And *this in turn is already a function of previous events and of the fantasies at the time of those earlier events*. Despite the resulting inability to predict, an object relation theory does contribute a consistent way of understanding how the individual has interpreted and organized his experience.

With this in mind, we can now turn to the contribution of parenting functions to sexual development.

Chapter 8
The childhood origins of sexual difficulty II:
The adequacy of the parents' functioning as parents

We see, therefore, that the parents' affection for their child may awaken his sexual instinct prematurely (i.e., before the somatic conditions of puberty are present) to such a degree that the mental excitation breaks through in an unmistakable fashion. If, on the other hand, they are fortunate enough to avoid this, then their affection can perform its task of directing the child in his choice of a sexual object when he reaches maturity.

Sigmund Freud, 'Three essays on the theory of sexuality'*

We now come to consider the functioning of parents in taking care of the child's concerns and his body. Even parents who cherish their children and themselves get along reasonably well may still not function adequately as parents, caretakers, and growth facilitators. What is at stake is the integrity of the child's ability to care for himself and to provide himself with a sense of safety after he graduates from parental care. Here examples of such issues in parenting are illustrated which surfaced retrospectively when patients presented with sexual disorders. These exist along a continuum from faults of omission where safety is not consistently protected to faults of commission in which intrusion on the integrity of the child's body is actually encouraged.

Neglect in taking care of the child and the child's body: Carelessness and intrusiveness

Even mild neglect of the child by careless parenting and a lackadaisical attitude about the care of the child's body itself can have pronounced effect on later psychosomatic functioning. Growth and increased autonomy give the child's body progressively to his own keeping, but the growing child still often behaves as though his body is more his mother's concern than his own.[1] The first two examples illustrate mild parental neglect.

Both parents had gone to work when Bill was 3 (see chapter 4). His obsessional rituals began at age 7 and included frequent prayers for the safety of all his family and a compulsive arranging of his clothes. These were designed to take care of himself in his parents' place, and of them and their safety as well. That Bill was angry at his parents for being absent and so negligent, and that the protection of the ritualistic prayers mostly related to protecting them from himself escaped his attention until well into psychotherapy. It was this dual problem which, in his young adult life, was condensed into the premature ejaculation. He 'protected' the woman he was beginning to care for while punishing her with brief intercourse. And he had to take care of himself out of fear that she would either leave him or would respond to his wish for caretaking by overwhelming and controlling him. These fears were all the stronger because of his wish for her to do so.

In other cases, the parental neglect or a hostile-dependent caretaking has alternated with overprotection.

One young woman had enjoyed the excitement of pre-marital sex with a first fiancé (whose cause had been promoted by the family), as well as with her husband. That she was non-orgasmic did not interfere until after marriage. At that point the sexual relationship with her husband became actively unpleasant. It now became colored by memories of the unfulfilled yearnings she felt when her mother had mirrored her moods and wishes in a distorted way, often denying that the daughter experienced them at all. Now grown, this woman felt unconsciously convinced that her husband would also fail to understand and respond accurately to her. The sexual withdrawal which followed this conviction threatened to destroy her marriage. During sex therapy, this aspect of their relationship was worked on through the specific sexual exercises. Improvement led to and was reinforced by the emergence of sexual pleasure and orgasm. She could now feel satisfied emotionally in her marriage, but other relationships continued to reflect the difficulty of the original dyad.

This case recalls the discussion of mirroring and the infant–mother interactions discussed in chapter 3. However, in this case the difficulty was predominantly enacted after infancy in consciously remembered ways. In the many exchanges around clothing and requests for direction, this woman could remember interchanges in which mother withdrew from a directing role or put her own narcissistic needs first. While this woman's overall intactness made it unlikely that a profound degree of this mirror-distortion was present early on, the sexual withdrawal was testament to a partial failure in mother–infant dyad.

Violations of the child's integrity: Real and symbolic incest

Sexual feelings and fantasies between children and their parents are normal and usual at all stages of development. Oedipal-stage children speak freely of them. The majority of such fantasies on the part of parents are, however, usually unconscious. In contrast, *actual* incest represents a special case of parental failure as parent, whether it happens with siblings, step-siblings, adult relatives such as grandparents or uncles, or, most directly, with the father of a girl. It is very uncommon in actual form between a boy and his mother. It is also worthy of note that incest is more common than was previously suspected, especially in inner-city areas where social conditions contribute to parental inability to set boundaries.[2] It is also a rather common finding among couples referred for sex therapy.[3]

Incest can be graded from mildest, that between siblings, through that between step-parent and child, to the incest between parent and child which has the most severe consequences for the child. There is also a notable difference between symbolically-incestuous events, for instance, the repeated sleeping in the parental bed or with one parent, grandparent, or sibling, without any actual sex, and the actual events of incest. The symbolic or partial kind may create problems, but if this is the only element they are likely to be much less severe than problems encountered in families where incest has occurred. Symbolic incest is more frequently a finding in neurotic or less severe disturbance. There is considerable disagreement about whether even actual father–daughter incest always results in serious psychopathology. The position taken here is that in the clinical population, actual incest increases the chances of faulty ego structure enormously, and the more severe the type or the more repeated the trauma, the more severe the ego deficit one expects to see.[4] In my opinion, *all* victims of *actual* incest will develop a borderline ego structure at best if no psychiatric intervention is offered. Two case illustrations will allow a comparison and a fuller discussion. The first case presents an example of relatively mild symbolic incest. The patient complained only of sexual symptomatology and seemed to have an otherwise secure marriage.

> A patient described a phobic aversion to becoming aroused with her husband while he was awake. She could only become aroused by rubbing her vulva against his thigh while he was asleep. Any waking activity closed off arousal. In treatment she recalled the excitement she had felt when she slept in the same room, between 10 and 13, with her two older brothers. Their heavy regular sleep breathing had accompanied her masturbation. Sexual arousal awakened her own internal incestuous object, allowing her to maintain the excited tie to her brothers. But the memory of this tie was too threatening to allow into full play with her husband.

The incest itself is a severe blow to the child's attempt to maintain his or her boundaries and integrity, and parents who allow such events to proceed, especially over a prolonged period of time, as in this case, are being negligent in a specific and crucial way which fails to provide a 'background of safety.'[5] In those cases in which incest does actually occur, it is the culmination of a clear groundswell of preceding events in which parents are using a child consciously or unconsciously to meet their own needs.[6] In this relatively mild kind of case, the trauma is not so much the single episode as it is a cumulative trauma[7] – the repeated allowing of infringements of the child's protective barriers and mechanisms. The above case illustrates that this woman's fantasy life became too threatening, too close to reality when she was *repeatedly* exposed to the exciting presence of her brothers in a fantasy-inducing situation. She felt too open to assault partly because of her own fantasy wish for it. It would not be difficult to guess that her family may also have been not only sexually provocative, but negligent in support of her individual autonomy, although the history is incomplete in this respect. This woman's mental structure was intact; that is, it was not borderline – but her sexual symptomatology represented a splitting of bodily functions in the object-related situations – the transference recall of the incestuous object.

It is the major failure to protect the child, in a bodily way and psychologically, as seen in cases of actual incest which seems to unfailingly lead to a primitiveness of mental organization. Primitive ego splitting and dissociation are required to keep libidinal and anti-libidinal objects apart when the actual experience has included traumatic, bodily penetration or commingling with a highly charged object who combined exciting and persecuting aspects. Incest represents one of the most fundamental violations of the psychosomatic partnership and the repercussions are severe.

However seductive the child is, she is actually helpless to prevent incest from occurring. In the clinical population, we do not find many examples of children who said, 'No!' and the parent stopped there. The protection of the child – even into young adolescence – rests with the parents. In the case below, the father violated the child's right to bodily protection directly. The mother was not only negligent, but blamed the resulting effects on the child, as though the caring for herself should have always been the child's, with the result that the child swallowed her anger and turned it on herself. The distortion of psychosomatic partnership then showed up years later in a very resistant sexual difficulty. The sexual disorder was actually a subclinical one until a 'chance' reconnection by the onset of apparently unrelated pelvic disease (endometrial adhesions) made the sexual disorder clinically significant.

Freda, a 32-year-old woman (previously discussed in chapter 2), was referred because of pelvic and low abdominal pain on intercourse which she said she otherwise enjoyed. Her extremely complex gynecological picture over the last few years dictated that therapy initially focus on how to live with exacerbations of chronic pain deriving from the adhesions of pelvic surgery for an ectopic pregnancy, and perhaps complications of an intrauterine device. Her dedication to her gynecologist, whom she trusted as an excellent physician, alternated with fears that no doctor would really play it straight with her, and with an unwillingness to talk about herself which even she did not understand, and from which she had every conscious wish to free herself. Try as she would, she usually could not talk to her therapist, except about the everyday trivia of her life. Sometimes something would 'give' and she could begin.

After some months, the story began to change. Freda began to feel that the pain was not necessarily physical, and was related to a secret dread of sex, one which she related to the need to be constantly on guard against sexual intrusions from her father. It was her father who told her about sex and boys, who showed her how to use tampons, and who would on occasion ask about her sex life or walk in while she was undressing. On the other hand, the mother had an extremely negligent attitude – 'let matters take care of themselves as they will' – and she was unapproachable by Freda on these or other matters. Instead, mother criticized Freda as someone who could not take care of herself, and would have accidents – mother predicted frequent automobile accidents when Freda got her driver's license at 16, for instance. On one occasion, cursing Freda's carelessness for falling ill prior to mother's departure on vacation, mother left anyway despite Freda's temperature of 104 degrees. In addition, the parents travelled for her father's business, and a series of maids looked after Freda and her brother. Freda was convinced that her parents did not care much about what happened to her, and then on the other hand, that they, and especially her father, wanted to pry into the core of her experience, especially her body and sexual growth. These issues came to a head at 14 when she and her family were on an evening cruise in the Caribbean. When one of the ship's crew tried to rape her, she was unable to tell her parents the full extent of the assault, fearing their curiosity as much as the likelihood they would not care anyhow and their neglect would be confirmed. She did tell her parents that a sailor had approached her, and found that just as she had feared, they reprimanded her for disturbing their bridge game and never investigated the matter of the crew member. In fact, during the next week a raucous male friend of the family was installed in the other bed in Freda's room for several months.

In therapy, the picture emerged now that the dyspareunia was not just due to the adhesions. It reminded Freda of the diffuse 'pain in her stomach' of her early school-phobic responses. When she was supposed to leave for school in first and second grades, she would have a feeling of nausea mixed with pain. The pain she experienced during intercourse now recalled a longing for care by her mother and anger at its being denied. It also filled her with the fear of sexual intrusion by her husband which was transferred

from the guardedness against seductive invasion by her father,
to whom she wished to turn for substitute caring. Her wish to turn
to her father made her own contribution to the fear of 'penetration'
by him all the greater. The surgery and problems in her body had
reawakened this conflict about the care of her body by her parents.
Sexual caring was now so threatening as not to be permitted.

In the treatment transference the same conflict about parenting
was re-enacted – a longing to be understood by her libidinally
exciting father alternating with mute retreat lest the therapist
invade her for his own purposes. The same conflict kept her in
turmoil about her husband who was, she rationally felt, really
a loyal, kind and lovable man. The concreteness of the bodily fear
was also linked to guilt over her childhood masturbation, remembered
from age 4, which she consciously thought occurred as an attempt
to replace her parents by her own pleasure and which was
heightened in frequency and fervor when she missed them most
intensely. Masturbation now made her feel guilty and lonely. Talking
about it in treatment, she came close to tears, but she could not
then trust herself enough to cry in her husband's presence or in
therapy. Her parents had forbidden crying.

After two years of therapy, Freda wanted to attempt specific
sex therapy. She now admitted that she had always feared sex
which she only performed for her husband's sake. She was actually
phobic, not daring to touch her husband's penis.

When the exercises reached the stage of genital involvement, she
felt she had hit a brick wall. Then the rest of the story tumbled out.
On top of all she had said before, her father had actually come to
her room every few weeks from the time she was 8 years old for
several years. He would be naked and drunk. She would be stiffly
frightened while he manipulated her clitoris. He would urge her
to manipulate his penis to ejaculation – a memory which was
repressed until she began pleasuring her husband's penis in sex
therapy. He never attempted intercourse with her, but holding his
penis, she would feel a combination of nausea and abdominal pain.
The nausea turned out to be a reaction to the memory of father
thrusting his penis into her mouth and ejaculating, giving her also
the feeling she would choke. When Freda recalled her own
daughter's theory at age 3 that babies were made by oral
impregnation, she decided she must have thought she would be
impregnated orally by her father. Memories of the abdominal pain

led her to remember masturbating after father had finally left the room. Masturbation had then, at least consciously, been an attempt to get rid of a tortured sense of abdominal fulness. These episodes finally stopped during early adolescence when Freda felt father's erection while dancing with him, screamed and ran from the room. When father followed her, she told him if he ever entered her room again she would tell her mother. Although a doctor was called who gave her an injection which put her to sleep for three days, father never again approached her sexually.

This case represents more of the typical features of father–daughter incest as an extreme in the failure of both parents as parent. A mother not only fails to provide a protective shield for her child, but frequently unconsciously asks the child to replace her sexually with father. In addition, the mother acts harshly toward this daughter as reincarnation of the mother's own rejecting mother. Finally, the father directly assaults the child's bodily integrity in the name of giving care.[8] It is no wonder that such children once grown cannot let down their own massive bodily shield to allow appropriate penetration physically or emotionally, nor is it surprising that borderline personality organization accompanies such histories. The experiences present an assault too massive to be handled by ordinary repression. Instead, the threatening object (which is seen by the child as both an outside aggressive assault and as the return of the bad aggressive projection of itself) has to be split from the image of a good object. That the bad object is so aggressive while being fused with the exciting object leads to further aspects of confusion about the self. In the resulting confused attempt to divide libidinal and anti-libidinal objects, the ego itself tends to split along with the object, and mental integration is essentially impossible. With the culmination of traumatic infringements on the integrity of both body and ego, the result is severe splitting of the ego.[9]

One further aspect of this confusion is that of fantasy and reality. In the usual course of development, incestuous fantasies are rendered unconscious by repression after the oedipal period. In the victims of incest, the fusion of fantasy and reality obstructs the growth of mental function in the varying degrees which roughly correspond to the degree of incest because the fantasies have been realized.

The depth of the traumatic effect of incest varies, not primarily with the traumatic intensity of the single episode, but with the cumulative trauma over time and the parenting deficit which permits it.[10]

Thus, a well functioning family may mitigate a single episode and a malignant family render a similar episode more harmful. For example, Emma Smith's experience with 'symbolic incest' and Freda's real incest marred each woman sexually. They were similar only in that the trauma reflected parental denial of any effect on the child. However, the degree of neglect, denial, and assault was far more profound for Freda and the effect on her was more devastating. Judy Green's actual brother-sister incest described in chapter 7 also represented a severe breakdown in parental ego functioning and boundary-setting, as well as failure to meet other needs. In this case also, parental preoccupations and confusions about dependency needs and libidinal and aggressive wishes contributed to her 'borderline' development. Other patients have suffered from some assaults presumably without any impairment of sexual functioning, but it is doubtful that many have escaped without significant developmental scarring. For those patients with sexual disorders and a history of incest, study of the object relations factors behind the incest will inform our efforts to intervene. For those other patients who constitute the majority of our work and have experienced incestuous relations only in fantasy, the lessons learned here can help understand the depth of dread and conflict such fantasies arouse.

Chapter 9
The parents' function as parents: Problems in sexual identity

> The mother does not convey a *sense* of identity to the infant but an
> *identity*: The child is the organ, the instrument for the fulfillment
> of the mother's unconscious needs. *Out of the infinite potentialities*
> *within the human infant, the specific stimulus combination*
> *emanating from the individual mother 'releases' one, and only one,*
> *concrete way of being this organ, this instrument.*
>
> Heinz Lichtenstein, 'Identity
> and sexuality' *

This chapter continues the exploration of the adequacy of the parents'
functioning as parents. In focusing on three cases of failure of sexual
identity, we can see the parents' influence on the formation of that
identity. Although these cases all consist of clinical perversions, they
form a useful contrast to patients with neurotic sexual disorders who
exhibit difficulty with sexual identity which is less overt, but for whom
the undercurrent needs to be understood and integrated. In these
patients, such symptoms as latent homosexuality, occasional transvestism, sado-masochistic fantasy life, or the incorporation of a fetish
into heterosexual activities may be connected with conflicting internal
object relations and identifications similar to those in the cases described
below. (For example, see Emma and Bob in chapter 7.)[1]

The patients to be described struggled with problems in sexual and
gender identity as a solution to early experience with both mother
and father. Issues between the parents were focused on the child
instead of being resolved within the couple. In all three, experience
of parents as intrusive and yet deficient was critical to the child's
development.

Two cases of homosexual identification

It is not the intention here to take up a detailed discussion of the origins of homosexuality in men or in women. Controversy exists about the relative importance of the influence of the pre-oedipal mother as compared to the early oedipal attempts to compensate with father. It is safe to say, however, that homosexual identification usually involves *both* mother and father, and the experience of the first two or three years as well as that of the oedipal period.

In homosexuality, as in other perversions, the expression of a remnant of childhood sexuality is a required component of adult sexual expression. The person uses this piece of surviving infantile sexuality to allow displaced expression for other, more feared pre-genital components and object relationships which are only thereby susceptible to repression. (This is known as the Sachs mechanism in the perversions.)[2] Kernberg and Socarides have recently noted that homosexuality may express four basic kinds of internalized object relationships with their corresponding ego organizations:[3]

Oedipal: The patient uses homosexuality to reflect a submission of the infantile self to a domineering parent of the same sex.
Pre-oedipal, higher level: The homosexual object stands partly for self and is partly a representative of the pre-oedipal mother.
Pre-oedipal, lower level: The homosexual object is purely a representative of the grandiose self. Relationships are brief and there is little or no concern for the object as such.
Schizo-homosexuality: There is a coexistence of homosexuality and schizophrenia with a lack of separation of self from object. The psychotic has lost his internal object representations and tries to fill the void through transient, impersonal relationships.[4]

There is also controversy about the constellation of family relationships which contributes to a homosexual outcome. Bieber and his colleagues found that in men with severe homosexuality there was a pattern of a detached hostile father and an overly close, seductive mother who dominated the husband.[5] He believes that the presence of a loving adequate father prevents homosexual development in the son.

There are, therefore, essential contributions by both parents if the family interactions are severely disturbed, and the homosexual son emerges as the focus of profound parental disturbance. The relationship with mother is close but ambivalent and the boy fails to let go of an early identification with her to form an adequate identification with father.[6] Socarides has suggested that the difficulty arises when parental needs override the child's needs for autonomy in the phases of separation–individuation.[7] This fits well with the formulation by Kolb and Johnson that overt homosexuality develops when it is supported and encouraged by the parents' conscious or unconscious processes.[8]

In the case which follows, the mother–son relationship is seductive and sexually stimulating, while the father is weak and passive and is later absent, a poor model for identification. The boy, who might attempt to flee the hovering presence of the mother, has no model of how to do so as a male in his own right. Instead, he works out a model of a receptive turning to men with a significant theme of castration and of guarding against it.

Richard, at age 26, longed to be heterosexual, but he had been attracted only to young boys (usually around the age of 12) since his own early adolescence. Although in many ways he was happiest while caring for them as a camp counselor, he felt guilty about his half-carried-out attempts to seduce them. On one occasion, he had persuaded a 12 year old boy to allow Richard to perform fellatio.

A year after beginning therapy, Richard met Maria. She was patient and understanding. She awakened in him a wish to be a father and husband which was in sharp contrast to his sexual love of boys. But when he attempted to make love with Maria, he was unable to sustain an erection long enough to achieve penetration.

Richard's past history included problem areas with both parents: his father was a weak, passive man who was most at home leading scouting trips for boys, but who had been unavailable to Richard. He had been rejected by Richard's mother when Richard was 12, and he had not seen him for the following year. Richard's mother was described as domineering and self-sufficient with little interest in men other than Richard. She had only one male friend after her husband's departure, an older man who appeared for dinner every few months over a period of years. There was no apparent sexual interest. Richard's most striking adolescent memory was of masturbating in his own bedroom with the constant preoccupation that his mother would burst in the room and catch him.

Richard's difficulty, as examined over three years of therapy, involved both parents. There was a feeling of a void in the center of his own relationship with his mother, yet an obsessional longing for and fear of her, signified by his masturbatory dread of and wish for her appearance. Yet her rejection of men, as in getting rid of his father, frightened him. It became clear that as a compromise to this ambivalence he had for years turned to his father for primary affection, something his father yearned to reciprocate. There he found a man with a shaky masculine identity which Richard could not rely on for defending himself against mother's 'attack' on his masculinity. His father's reciprocal longing for affection was not enough to enable him to remain available during the divorce, and his abandonment during the vulnerable phase of early adolescence contributed to Richard's unconscious identification with the young boys who were the continuing objects of his father's love. He identified his own yearning for love at age 12 with the 12- and 13-year-old boys whom he sought. With the advent of Maria to provide a non-threatening, supportive object, and a male therapist for identification, Richard began to feel he could risk change.

Richard's picture can be compared to that of Bob (chapter 7) who had issues of a similar sort, but presumably with different pre-dispositions and a different pre-oedipal object balance. Although Bob turned toward father receptively as a pre-oedipal object, his father seems to have been less passive than Richard's. He was able to identify with him actively against domination by mother. Bob's father pro-vided a better model for an identification and therefore a modified positive oedipal solution, while Richard's more passive father failed in this respect. While Richard could be read as showing a negative oedipal picture, a turning toward his father as a girl, the predominant mode of his affectionate life was actually that of identifying with his father taking care of and loving pre-adolescent and young adolescent boys. In this case a use of the term 'inverted oedipal constellation' (figure 7.2) is justified to describe Richard acting as a *boy* with father as the libidinal object. He then also reversed the situation and converted a passive wish into action (a projective identification) by taking the role he wished from father with boys chosen to reflect his own young self. This identification as a young boy represents a *defense* against mother's assault on his masculinity in what seemed to be a problem more at the oedipal level than the pre-oedipal. The fragility of masculine identification, which could be seen in Richard's fearful avoidance of women before treatment, was strengthened by an opportunity for a better paternal identification.

Richard's treatment transference involved the progressive identification with his male therapist, both as an effective man and as a non-intrusive mother. From the position of this new identification, he was able to withstand the threat of an attachment to a woman and to establish a prolonged heterosexual relationship. At the time of termination, which occurred because his therapist was leaving the city and which therefore occurred prematurely, Richard retained some hesitancy about his own competence and his attachment to Maria, as shown by an intermittent impotence which persisted.

Homosexual solutions in women share many major characteristics with those of men, previously discussed. However, they inherit the more complex history of the female's 'phallic–narcissistic' or 'first stage oedipal' development discussed in chapter 7. As in men, homosexual identification in women involves a mixture of pre-oedipal and oedipal issues, a failure in relation both to mother and to father.

Saghir and Robins note that a variety of patterns seem to exist from 'hostile, domineering mothers and detached, unassertive fathers,' to those lesbians who have had 'intense, seductive relationships with their fathers and had narcissistic, detached mothers.' In others, intense rivalry with a brother or even the absence of any notable family pattern occurs. They conclude that the common underlying factor is the presence of 'a strong antiheterosexual pattern in the home.'[9]

Socarides describes the female homosexual as being in flight from the man because of childhood guilt toward mother and because of fears of disappointment and rejection by father if she dared turn to him. She also may fear that father would either gratify (a masochistic danger) or refuse her (a narcissistic injury). Rather than face the horns of this dilemma, she turns to an earlier idealized mother. This may be accompanied by paranoid pre-oedipal fears as the persecuting object presses to destroy the idealized object.[10]

Most writers, then, have stressed both the deficiencies of early mothering and the unavailability of the father to compensate for this. The result is a powerful unconscious ambivalence toward both parents with either a direct search for a good mother to identify with, or an identification with father in seeking the mother. In the following case, the history makes sense of the patient's sexual orientation and object choice.

Yvonne is 31. Recently she gave up attempting to date men and told her family she was a lesbian. She lives with her girlfriend, Sammy, who is a tennis coach at a women's college.

Yvonne is the third child in a family with an older sister and a middle brother. The sister is flirtatious and extremely coy, while the brother is a successful hotel manager, very domineering and in control of everything. Father doted on the sister and idolized the brother. Mother was two-faced (by Yvonne's report) and denied Yvonne's feelings, giving distorted reflections. Yvonne felt that no matter how adverse her (Yvonne's) situation, mother would white-wash it. Mother idolized her relatives — even her father (Yvonne's grandfather) who exploited Yvonne sexually. When she was between 4 and 7, he had several times held her on his lap and used her body to masturbate to orgasm through his clothes.

As she grew older, Yvonne became the house's little 'errand boy,' fetching, carrying suitcases and mowing the lawn. When her aging parents need a jack-of-all-trades, they still call on her.

Yvonne is stuck at the early phallic–narcissistic or first stage oedipal level: the 'little boy' in the family. Her brother is the big boy and her sister is father's oedipal favorite. Her experience of mother's wish to keep her as the unthreatening phallic boy, father's refusal to approve of her as an oedipal girl, and rivalry with a brother and a sister all color her movement to feminine identification. Finally, she is content to appeal to both mother and father as a boy. She also does so in taking the masculine role with her lover. At work, however, she acts like the *mother* of boys, where she is a dietician in a boys' prep school, acting out the pre-oedipal mothering she wished she had received as a 'little boy' and thereby retaining a partial identification as a woman. Although the picture of a second stage negative oedipal constellation may describe Yvonne's attachment to her mother and to women, an explanation of her attachment to father as a boy only fits with a first stage, phallic-oedipal attachment to father (figure 7.2.) The components of Yvonne's attachments and the vicissitudes for her ego in attempting to maintain integral relationships to her objects are as complex as the mixed messages given to her by her parents during her development.

A patient who requested sex-change surgery

Patients who seek sex-reassignment surgery generally have a deficient ego organization on the borderline, narcissistic, or even psychotic level.[11] While Robert Stoller holds that there is such a person as a true transsexual who feels he or she has been truly a member of the opposite sex from very early childhood and who need not be significantly disturbed,[12] most writers have agreed that the early parent–child relationships, both of such 'true transsexuals' and of the larger group who seek sex-reassignment as a surgical solution to psychological upset, all have significantly disturbed mother–child and father–child relationships.[13] The gender identity disorders are more profound assaults on a central identity than most of the homosexual disorders, but share with them the collusion of both parents in undermining the early foundations of identity. The mother of a male transsexual, for instance, clearly recognizes him as a male at birth and proceeds to establish a close symbiosis in which he is feminized without acknowledging what she is doing.[14] The father is commonly absent and unable to correct this tendency, or if present is incompetent as an active father.[15]

The following patient proceeded from being a transvestite, aroused by women's clothes, to cross-dressing and desiring to become a woman.[16] The issues here can again shed light on our patients who have less overt difficulties with sexual identity.

> The patient, Oliver (or Olive) Winchester, is a 35-year-old super-masculine ex-Navy frogman, an 'aging transvestite,' and father of four children. He presented six months after celebrating his third marriage, this time to a dependent, ex-alcoholic wife who, as a beautician, helped Oliver cross-dress, appreciating him for his combined maternal yet masculine protective qualities. Although she offered to remain married to him if he had sex-change surgery, he felt trapped by her clinging behavior and grew suicidally depressed.
>
> He dissolved the marriage and increased the urgency of his demands for sex-change surgery. He then changed his name to Olive and began living and working as a woman in a new occupation. After much persistence, he found a surgeon to perform a sex-change operation and he is now living as a woman. He has since claimed to feel satisfied and fulfilled. It is worth noting that he has continued to function adequately as a parent throughout except during the few months surrounding the surgery itself.

During his first two years, Oliver's mother was depressed and generally unavailable. Father, a hearty and outspoken man, was absent, working overseas, and, as the patient later learned, chasing women. On return, father continued to be promiscuously involved in affairs with many women, and mother continued to be depressed. More recently, they have had an 'open marriage.'

There is a picture in the family album of Oliver dressed in feminine frills at 1½ years. From the age of 9, Oliver dressed in his mother's clothes occasionally, but he married at 19 and fathered four children, joined the Navy as a skindiver for several years, and then worked as a skindiver on bridge construction. He was a staunch father and loyal husband although his wife was unfaithful. Only when she died of leukemia when he was 28 did he begin to cross-dress. When a second and then the recent third marriage proved disastrous, he moved more and more urgently to demand sex alteration surgery, claiming that he felt nothing in his penis and that he could only find fulfillment as a woman.

This patient was able to achieve what passed for a positive oedipal adjustment until stressed by the progressive loss of the wife who stood for the early symbiotic mother. A bisexual identity then began the path of an accelerating reversal which eventually resulted in what *could* be understood as a negative oedipal constellation.

However, it is also clear that the underlying shift in this patient involved the reversion to a previously compensated alternate sexual identity as reaction to abandonment by the internalized symbiotic mother. She was appeased by the surrender of the hypermasculine activities at the same time that the patient turned *to* the pre-oedipal father for compensatory mothering; i.e., he then became the womanly object of the father's sexual caring.

Research on the etiology of transvestism is unclear. Often the first episode of cross-dressing occurs when a female imposes it on a boy to humiliate him; that is, a hostile woman attacks an established male identity and seeks to make him a phallic extension of her body. Later, cross-dressing is transformed into an exciting activity, becomes a fetish with all that is involved in the fetish as a representation of the mother's phallus. Still later, a woman's cooperation may be enlisted in the activity. Histories of adequate masculine — and often supermasculine development — are the rule.[17]

While these pictures of transvestism and homosexuality are far afield from the path of sexual symptomatology in many of the individual marriages which come to clinical attention, the ramifications of early issues of sexual identity, gender identity, and object choice are often present, reflecting the normal degree of human bisexuality. For instance, some marriages involving group sex may represent a covert way of accomplishing a link to a homosexual object in order to relieve anxiety felt in the heterosexual situation. Or patients like Bob (chapter 7) experience the inhibiting effects of covert sexual identity conflicts on sexual relationships. And in children such as Jackie and Tom (chapter 6) we can see *in statu nascendi* the development of skewed sexual identities as an attempt to solve a major conflict in the child-parent relationship.

Chapter 10
Adolescent precursors of sexual relationships:
The move from self to object

With the arrival of puberty, changes set in which are destined to give infantile sexual life its final, normal shape.

Sigmund Freud, 'Three essays on the theory of sexuality'*

In latency, the child relies on the capacity to split fantasy widely apart from bodily feelings, converting into neutralized games and researches the sexualized ideas and feelings of the oedipal struggles. But with the pubertal bodily pressures and accompanying ego-maturation, the separation can no longer be maintained for most children. Sexual expression and the relationship to the object world grow and change radically during adolescence. Puberty threatens the collapse of the repression of the connection between sexual fantasies and the family objects under the impact of the fueling of the sexual drive by hormonal and emotional development. Oedipal issues are re-energized at the same time that the young adolescent becomes newly narcissistic and ego-centric.[1]

Adolescent sex and play

In a sense, adolescence is the height of madcap play and playfulness at just that point at which life becomes deadly serious for the first time. *Romeo and Juliet* describes the interplay of life and death, childhood play, and seriousness in adolescence, as well as the intense interest of the adult world in it.

Adolescent development is partly ruled by the opportunity to 'play at being an adult,' although at a sophisticated level and with a new

93

and uncontrollable liability. In addition, the play now often involves the toy of the adolescent's whole body, but with a magical invincibility. The world revolves around the adolescent and he is magic! Nothing can really happen to him.

Early adolescence and masturbation

Masturbation (or the struggle to avoid it) is the phase-specific sexual expression of adolescence, especially early adolescence. The urgency of the hormonal and physiological shifts make the body a compelling, drive-motivated engine which puts a new urgency behind the previously relatively calm self and object struggles. The need emerges for the young adolescent to use masturbation as a vehicle for incorporating a view of his newly emergent body in his realigned narcissism and to compensate for his sudden loneliness in losing the family he begins to reject. In latency, without the pressures of sexuality and bodily change, he remains firmly attached to his family while developing new skills in which masturbatory equivalents are often subsumed, as in the jump rope games or games of skill. When he emerges from the latency cocoon, his wings are growing but he cannot yet fly. He has painful years of trial flight and modification ahead.

This struggle is almost always accompanied by fantasies, which coalesce with or without actual masturbation, into what Laufer has called the 'central masturbation fantasy.'[2] Masturbation may be suppressed by active, guilty, conscious obsessions, or unconscious repression, but a route must still be found for connecting the central masturbation fantasy to the body, or the impoverishment of expression and corresponding ego integration will be expressed along all lines of development.

The masturbation of girls is less universal than for boys, but the struggle is still crucial. Clower notes that masturbation is important in the development of a genital sense during a move from latency clitoral masturbation to the early pubertal wish–fear of vaginal penetration, and then further to the late adolescent use of clitoral masturbation as the trigger for spreading genital excitement which includes the internal genitalia in preparing for coitus.[3] At the same time, repeated experience of the body's self-gratification as belonging to the self supports autonomy and aids dissolution of symbiotic pre-genital ties, and then later is part of the fantasies which link the girl to progressively mature object choices.

There are important cultural and socio-economic variations. A noted exception to the use of masturbation among adolescents occurs in lower socio-economic groups of boys, for whom early intercourse is substituted for masturbation, and for whom premature closure on the elaboration of the central masturbation fantasy inhibits further cognitive and emotional development.[4]

The avoidance of masturbation in the deprived inner-city children seen by Meers was accompanied by the use of oral masturbatory equivalents such as drugs or voracious eating.[5] He viewed these habits as defenses against primitive and pervasive threats which were both environmental and personal. In this sense, even in the active shunning of overt masturbation, the derivatives were relevant to object-seeking behavior aimed at staying in touch with the pre-genital mothers.

For whatever reason, when intercourse is an early substitute for masturbation, reliance on the other person is often prematurely substituted for the individual adolescent's working out of his own narcissistic struggles. The adolescent uses the other person as a *projection* of the internal pre-oedipal mother or father to reflect approval, rather than relying on and strengthening his *internalized* parents in order to build a new equilibrium with his new body and goals. Deprived of the chance to develop internalized good sexual parents, this adolescent is much more dependent in the live other person, and may also feel himself thrown back toward the actual live parents who then may have to be rejected more violently. With these and other chances for failures of the maturational process, such authors as Hornick and Kestenbaum have argued for delay in intercourse until a time of readiness, even for adolescent celibacy.[6] So much sorting out is going on in ego-structure, identification, and object-relatedness, that the chances for premature fixation and closure are high indeed.

The work of understanding the role of masturbation in sexual development may focus on the following questions:

1   How did the patient react to the onset of masturbation in adolescence? Was the first ejaculation for the boy or menarche and the rediscovery of clitoral sensitivity for the girl traumatic, pleasurable, or guilt-ridden?
2   What was the kind of relationship to objects, including family of origin, peers, and future objects?
3   Were there competing fantasies which attacked or modified the central masturbation fantasy and how were they dealt with?

4   How long was the masturbation continued and how did it blend with later sexual experience?

The following example will illustrate some of these points.

Eric's first masturbation occurred at age 12, about a year after his parents' separation and divorce. While on a vacation trip to see San Francisco with his mother, he and a friend excitedly lit matches in their hotel bathroom. He also bought a pin-up calendar of Marilyn Monroe in a displaced enactment of his victorious oedipal possession of his mother. Soon after returning home, he accidently rubbed his penis against his leg and got an erection while doing so. Because he slept with his younger brother, he had to stay awake until after his brother was asleep to masturbate, but by 13 his mother cooperated in arranging his move into the guest bedroom. There he read by flashlight the books found in the family library which had sexy passages, preferring at first the manly, if sadistic, feats of Mickey Spillane's detective, Mike Hammer — an attempt to emulate and identify with his father. Pictures from photography magazines were remembered and discussed with male friends with an excited emphasis on breast development, size, and shape.

In the following year he had a dream which was used to form his principal masturbation fantasy. In the dream he was riding in the backseat of a convertible car with his two parents. This was his father's car, and since his parents were divorced, it represented the repair of their marriage. With him in the backseat, hair blowing, laughing at their having found each other, was a fantasized sister who had been adopted into the family and therefore was an available love object. The masturbation fantasies were variations and extensions of this situation into both intercourse and a more general acceptance physically than he felt he could get as a chubby teenager.

The dream and fantasy derived from it were used to form the 'central masturbation fantasy,' giving reassurance to Eric's concerns about bodily inferiority and connecting them to his object life and aspirations. As for most adolescents, the fantasy had an organizing function in his development and in beginning the move from narcissistic preoccupation to concern for others. The effect of Eric's central fantasy was to give him a new sexual object that related to his parents by helping to reunite them in his fantasy. This relieved his guilt about the oedipal victory while reclaiming a father with whom he could identify.

In this example, the sex is connected to both the original family and to another anticipated new one he would get by growing up. The finding of a new love object as a teenager is linked with the wishes and disappointments of the old ones — the parents. The fantasy expresses the hope that the destroyed parental relationship will be 'converted' (thus the convertible automobile) into a new life. This also represents finding a lost part of himself in the 'adopted twin sister' to make up for parents lost through divorce and through growing up. There are other aspects of masturbation to consider, however. The central masturbation fantasy had competition. As Laufer notes, these are conflicting elements which the adolescent has to juggle in his development.[7]

Another fantasy which excited and frightened him also derived from a dream. He lay on the grass with a boy classmate who was metamorphosed into a girl with large breasts and a comforting, reassuring body, face, and behavior. The homosexual element frightened him, but it stood for his own concerns both about his body and his struggle whether his breasts were too large for peer acceptance. This dream/fantasy solution was not acceptable to him, but the further displacement to the girl who was like him, and like his parental ideal, and who admired him as a boy-man, was a narcissistically acceptable solution.

The relationship to Eric's parents is partly spoken for by the dream origin of the central masturbation fantasy. The only time his father addressed the question of masturbation, he had told Eric 'Try not to masturbate too much. Wait (for sexual expression) until you are married.' A certain undefined amount of masturbation was acceptable. Once he had a fantasy that part of his brain had come out. He sometimes worried (though he knew better) whether his penis would become a stiff callus or would atrophy.

Eric and his mother never discussed masturbation. But once she wondered out loud if he couldn't do something about the mess on his sheets. He feigned ignorance of her meaning and she dropped the discussion. Sometimes he wondered if she would open his door, but she never did. He felt he wrung from her a silent, if grudging, caretaking of his body. The sheets became a transitional object against which he would rub while fantasizing, with the relationship to her gained through her washing them completely unacknowledged.

At 15 he told stimulating stories to a friend while both masturbated in the dark, but he was bothered by the homosexual elements
and thereafter he shunned sharing the masturbation with other boys.

From 16 on he had a series of girlfriends who filled in gradually
for the object in his masturbation fantasy. At 19 a serious steady
girl asked to be called 'Laura,' the nickname of the fantasy twin
girl in the dream. They began necking and petting for hours after
which he would masturbate alone. This pattern continued when the
first relationship loosened and he began in late adolescence to have
a wider range of girlfriends. The masturbation lessened in frequency
as mutual stimulation to orgasm became the practice, preceding by
two years his first intercourse at 23.

Eric's use of masturbation provides us with a relatively typical log
of the transitional use of masturbation in the journey from primary
object to the choice of sexual partner in late adolescence and young
adulthood. Compared to his experience, we can look at three examples
of masturbatory behavior which give very different pictures of the
development of the youngsters who have poor ego integration. For
these boys, the masturbatory activity reflected the difficulty in their
overall development at different stages of adolescence.

Wilson was a pre-pubertal 22-year-old who did poorly in school. He
was extremely accident-prone, and set several small fires while
playing with matches. He had been adopted at the age of 6 months.
He felt he was different from the rest of his family, unaccepted and
uncared for by them, saying that his sister, Dale, was like his parents
but he was different. Indeed he was more physically active and less
verbal than his parents or sister, but there was really no evidence
that they had preferentially rejected him consciously or unconsciously. His father did have episodes of screaming and spanking
Wilson, largely sparing Dale. More importantly, father had moved
out of the house eight months earlier. There had been a good deal
of bitterness between Wilson's parents over the year and despite
their later reconciliation, and their extensive participation in family
therapy, Wilson maintained that he hated his family, but especially
his father. In family therapy, he played an endless chain of
smuggling games in which the bad guys tried to steal the treasure,
fell off ladders or out of helicopters, shot the police or army, and
were shot themselves. Plate 3 is a drawing along these lines with

human figures shooting and being shot, falling out of windows. Violence abounds. In one family session he drew a picture of his family in which he pictured father as doing the same thing. Only the cat, who was incidentally called Mammy (short for 'Mean Momma') survived (plate 4).

This is a variation on the pre-adolescent regression in development. The fire-setting, accident-proneness, and excitement over the violence are all masturbatory equivalents in which aggression is fused with sexual excitement in a form of incestuous fantasy which is primarily aggressive. As the hormonal forces begin to have an impact, a regression to pregenital organization occurs in which the boy particularly fears the 'witch-mother.'[8] Here Wilson additionally identifies with the angry, murderous father against the whole family *and* with the sadistic, dominating mother who is the only survivor. He incorporates the parental fight with a viciousness added by his own developmental path and his version of the oedipal battle with father is more complete than mere castration.

A few months later, Wilson, now 12, began to bring explicit sexual material into his individual hours. Mainly he told how his 'girlfriend' would spurn him. He spent hours talking with other boys about whether to approach a girl, and then used the pretext of a glance from her to dash off in relieved exasperation, saying, 'I blew it. I know she hates me.' He refused to dance at his 7th grade school dances, but jumped around energetically committing practical jokes on boys and girls. He told me jokes about dirty girls, and finally broke his finger on the school bus, pretending that he was a mechanical talking doll which stiffly embraced boys, saying, 'Hi! I'm Susie! I'm a prostitute! Kiss me!'

Wilson's now early adolescent sexual development incorporated the earlier way his object world was dominated by violence. The accident-proneness pursued him into the new sexual fantasies in which women were alternately threatening and degraded. Wilson was actually able to give up most aggressive coloring of his bad objects and to achieve a considerable reconciliation with his family, so that these early adolescent 'jokes' and experiences were not particularly unusual. Nevertheless they continued the thread of his earlier development. Without intervention, Wilson might well have reached mid-adolescence looking like the next example.

A 16-year-old borderline boy had violent masturbation fantasies, images of his parents or sisters blowing up or his shooting them. When he developed a crush on a girl he barely knew, he became violently disillusioned because she failed to respond to his nodding greeting at school. He then went to her house at night and was filled with ideas of shooting her and of watching her house erupt in flames. When he recounted these fantasies in a therapy hour, he looked nearly orgastic.

Another mid-adolescent example gives a picture of the difficult struggle to expunge domineering, anti-libidinal objects in a budding narcissistic character.

Another 16-year-old boy, an only child, felt lonely and puny. He had no heterosexual experience but masturbated with images of women's bodies and thoughts of what he knew about intercourse. However, he was also feeling overwhelmed by his critical father and domineering, hovering mother. He began to exhibit himself, at first masturbating just inside their apartment door, hoping a woman would ring the bell. He later masturbated nude in the building basement. He fantasized that a beautiful woman would be impressed with the size of his penis.

Mid- and late-adolescence: Peering to pairing

Stressing that there is a great deal of overlap in the early, mid-, and late adolescent phases, we can still mark the trends which characterize them:[9]

1   Early: the narcissistic reflection of same-sex peers and the loosening of ties to family; same-sex pairing a background throughout adolescence.
2   Middle: tightening of ties to same-sex peers; the defensive distancing from family; loosening of resistance to sex with heterosexual movement in most mid-adolescents. (Same-sex pairing leads to heterosexual pairing.)
3   Late adolescence: the forming of heterosexual pairs, either exclusive ones or changeable ones, several of which now constitute the peer group.

Mid-adolescence is a time of shift from same-sex allegiances to heterosexual pairing, of testing oneself with others. But the back-and-forth quality leaves many vulnerabilities. The girl who jumps prematurely to use sex to get paired finds herself stranded when the boy hops back over the developmental fence to his friends and tells all about their relationship. When either boy or girl prematurely uses heterosexual links to avoid personal solidification, the break-up of the pairing may be followed by personal falling apart.

Sex has an important role in this series of events. A comparison of Kinsey's findings in 1948 and 1953 with those of Sorenson in 1973 and Zelnik and Kantner in 1979 shows that more adolescents are having intercourse earlier and, despite increased use of some contraceptive method, with an increased rate of pregnancy.[10] It is still true that slightly less than half the unmarried women and approximately one-third of the unmarried men do *not* have intercourse before 21.[11]

When intercourse comes at an appropriate time, it can begin to do for personal growth what adult sexuality can do. Bodily pleasure can be used in support of an intimate bond, reflecting personal confirmation and love from another to modify and develop the shaky self-images. An 'appropriate time' occurs when the individual feels sex is not going to undermine growth, a less risky venture for boys than girls, but still risky for many of both sexes.

When it is inappropriately early, intercourse can operate to do many things, making these adolescents the victims of the 'sexual revolution.'

1   It can increase a focused, imprisoned dependency.
2   It can widen the split between the ego ideal and the felt reality about the self, leaving the adolescent depressed.
3   It can increase the gap between adolescent and parent in the adolescent's mind as an imagined rejection by the parent, rather than by the adolescent leaving his parents behind when they can approve and support his growth.

The examples which follow illustrate the complexity of the situation.

Relationship of adolescent sexuality to parents

In an open-ended group which we called a 'sex rap group' at Children's

Hospital National Medical Center normal inner-city black adolescent girls, who were referred from the medical clinic, met weekly to discuss sexual topics and anything else.[12] The purpose was to increase use of birth control and to help with general life planning issues. A smaller group of boys came as well. The focus frequently was on teenagers' confrontation with their parents: what would parents do if they knew about sexual activity? For instance, role plays involved a pregnant girl and her boyfriend confronting their parents who were portrayed as harsh, unsympathetic, and punitive. Sometimes they were harmed (a threatened heart attack) by the news.

> One vocal member, Maryalice, age 17, decided at one point to get an IUD and made her friends swear to secrecy, saying her mother would kill her. At the end of the year, the group organized a parents' day meeting and managed role plays in which the parents were far more understanding than any of the teenagers had portrayed them. Presumably the less understanding ones stayed away, but two-thirds did attend. Those who came were flexible, several more liberal than their children.
>   Maryalice's mother was asked by another parent for her opinion on birth control and she readily said it was a good idea for a girl to have an IUD. Maryalice had projected her own guilt onto her mother and imagined a rejection which did not seem to be there.

What we often neglect is the part of the polarization over sexual issues caused by the maneuvers by the child to make the parent seem harsher and less sympathetic, a distortion created out of a splitting mechanism which leaves the child with the good internalized parent while projecting out the bad. (This can be understood as a normal regression to paranoid/schizoid splitting as a way of managing the surrendering of attachment to the parent by the adolescent.)

On the other side, the parent may treat the adolescent as a stereotypical sexualized object, the recipient of his own projected sexual feelings and frustrations, brought to life again by the adolescent's burgeoning sexuality.[13] The varieties of interplay between adolescent and parent are practically infinite, so that much adolescent sexual behavior can be understood as acting in accordance with the unspoken and often denied wishes of the parents, or in defense against their more inhibiting aspects.[14] Simultaneously the adolescent's sexual growth is a provocation to the vulnerable parent. (This topic is a principal subject of chapter 15.)

Sex as a tie to the pre-oedipal mother

A 15-year-old girl who had been a model of good behavior and academic performance and had never masturbated, became depressed and felt rejected by her parents, and clung to her boyfriend. A rapid sexual intimacy began with mutual petting and soon led to intercourse. She was desperate for intercourse, and her family actually believed openly in 'sexual expression' as a positive value. However, she always had to keep her brassière on in order to hide her small breasts. She was also not orgasmic.

At 16 she married her 19-year-old boyfriend to escape home. After marriage, she continued to avoid breast contact, but also began to find intercourse painfully unpleasant and progressively became aversive to intercourse altogether.

This girl was unable to confirm a healthy narcissistic feeling about her body. Not only did she carry this deficit into a prematurely intense sexual involvement even before she actually had intercourse, but the attempt to get her boyfriend to act like a pre-oedipal mother to mirror a validation of her body, take care of her, and make her feel good, did not work. Her sense of guilt and inferiority spread but so did her trapped dependency on him. The bad mother, originally bodily sequestered in her image of her own breasts, could then only be kept out by an enlarging avoidance of sex altogether while clinging to her young husband.

Earlier phase oedipal attraction lived out through pseudoheterosexuality

Irwin had not matured sexually until after 15. He lived at home until his junior year in college when he was 19. He had very little dating experience and had kissed only two girls. Soon after he moved into the college dorm, he met a girl in class and took her out for a drink that evening. When he walked her home and kissed her shyly good night, he was shocked to see that in her room was a boy waiting to sleep with her. He swore never to see her again, but she called Irwin the next day 'to ask his forgiveness.' He was unable to explain to himself his fascination for her given the situation and his outrage. He was drawn irresistibly to her and they soon began to go together and had intercourse regularly.

Psychoanalytic exploration of this situation years later led Irwin to the conclusion that the attraction had largely been to the hated rival, a libidinal transference figure for his father. The paradigm for the situation was both his witnessing of parental intercourse when he slept in his parents' room until the age of 2, and his father' barring him from watching his mother nurse his infant sister. On that occasion he felt not only excluded from his mother, but primarily rejected by father. A large part of the attraction to this triangulated relationship was the inverted oedipal attraction to the other man. After that he would stay involved with the man by an obsessional jealousy of him even though he had departed long ago.

An early ménage à trois

Jane was 19 when she consulted me. She was Catholic, living with a Jewish boyfriend, Joshua, age 23. Her parents were religious and so upset by the liaison they could hardly speak to her. She was determined that her parents should accept Joshua, however. She came because of her feeling he did not love her and wanted to break up. When Joshua came, as asked, he said that he had begun an affair with a second woman – a roommate of theirs. He wanted to keep the ménage à trois because he felt sorry for Jane and he loved her, but she was too childish. The other woman, aged 21, was more mature and he thought the two of them together could take care of Jane.

Jane at first denied the existence of the other sexual affair. Even when she found out, she couldn't bear to lose Joshua. She hoped against hope that she could win him back and was willing – and I thought even eager – to keep the threesome so as to recreate a loving, accepting parental couple to approve her independence and sexuality.

The last two late adolescents illustrate a wrinkle in pairing that can be set up by earlier deficiencies. Oedipal issues presumed to be about the parent of the opposite sex speak also for a disguised tie to the parent of the same sex. Jane's longing for mother's approval and love are expressed in the tie to 'the other woman' through Joshua. A carica-ture of a family is set up which allows a disguised incestuous tie while demanding constant sacrifice to the oedipal rival. This is a variation on a common earlier adolescent pattern of practicing intimacy by invoking a third person with whom to discuss the relationship.

In Irwin's case, the immediate replacement of his recently lost mother's love and care was also apparent alongside the tie to his father. In fact, he used his tie to women to defend against positive *and* negative feeling about father and about men in general. For Jane, the longing for her family and a considerable amount of anger at them for giving less than she wished over the years was expressed in the maintenance of a sexual and emotional object whom she knew her parents would actually reject. The hostile bond to both parents and to Joshua was evident in her clinging to this 'parental' adolescent couple.

Adolescent pregnancy

Adolescent pregnancy is, of course, essentially always a product of the issues we have been discussing, a combination of reactions to internal objects, actual current parents, and a hoped-for family which will repair past deficits.

> One such adolescent couple involved an 18-year-old boy who had been his family's black sheep and who wanted to compensate by taking care of a family of his own, and a 15-year-old girl who felt she had never done anything right and wanted to improve life for her unborn child. Her refusal to have an abortion made the point to her mother that she was independent and could win a control battle. At the same time, the couple was planning to live in a mobile trailer in her parents' driveway, perpetuating a kind of umbilical connection to her parents.

The role of sex in adolescence

Adolescent sex is about getting ready. In a way, it is not a thing in itself:

neither intended for reproduction nor being sufficiently practiced to play its part in making, in testing, and in cementing permanent bonds. This getting ready goes best if not pushed too far or too fast. There is the contrary opinion – that adolescents are increasingly mature and ready for full sexuality.[15] No doubt, adolescents in the United States, at least, are more experienced than they used to be before birth control and the 'sexual revolution' in that many have had intercourse by mid-adolescence and a majority by age 21 or 22.[16] But while some are mature enough for, or matured by, these experiences, others are not. Being more experienced at having intercourse does not mean that the intrapsychic work of sexual interrelatedness has been done. Adolescents who are fully active sexually still have to struggle with conflicts about sexuality, with integrating the sexual response with object choice and developing a capacity for intimacy, just as their parents did when they were adolescents who were experimenting with partial or symbolic expressions of sex. Although the sexual behavior is so different that parents may have trouble empathizing with these adolescents, the issues are very similar and parents who bear this in mind can still be helpful and understanding.

When full genital involvement comes more gradually, bodily testing can be graded in step with other aspects of the relationship. The danger in former days, when sex tended to come later in the development of a relationship, was that the bodily aspect might lag so far behind it would never catch up. The liability now is that too often it will race ahead, dragging the unprepared adolescents behind, floundering in a venture powered by their drives. Another way of saying this is to compare premature sexual activity to the premature invasion of the newborn's 'stimulus barrier.' When this occurs, the risk is increased to the infant, but the process of maturation is also accelerated. The outcome of such a crisis depends on complex factors: usually there are some losses and some gains. The same ambiguous potential awaits adolescents.

There is another pattern becoming a new norm in adolescent couples, and perhaps this is their way of negotiating this doubt: the sex is used occasionally in a low-key way corresponding to social mores, and meanwhile the adolescents get on with growing up in other areas.

One young couple like this consisted of a 19-year-old boy and a 15-year-old girl. He took care of her like a parent and she 'put a new light in his life.' They had intercourse infrequently because she was willing to do it for him, but she did not enjoy it much for itself, except for the concurrent opportunity to be held. When she felt the relationship was too smothering, she was unable to say so directly but arranged with her mother for a scholarship to an all-girls boarding school 500 miles away. The sex now occurred even less often but still at a frequency consistent with maintaining the relationship.

This chapter has considered the adolescent from the standpoint of his own development and the ways he looks forward to his own adulthood. The other aspect, the way he affects the internal life of his parents, is also important. They are often in mid-life and vulnerable to a renewal of adolescent issues insufficiently solved in their own adolescence. This reciprocal interaction will be taken up in chapter 15.

Adolescent sex in its most functional aspects is a synthesizing force, carrying and modifying relationships to past and current family objects, while anticipating hopes and fears with new objects and ways of relating. It stands mid-way developmentally between childhood and adulthood. Its Janus-like quality gives it poignance and helps us to see the way in which sexuality always has the potential for referring forward and back, to our families of origin and our families of procreation.

Implications for the therapy of sexual disorders of child and adolescent development

An understanding of childhood origins may be academic if a sexual dysfunction yields easily to behavioral or educational intervention, the first line of approach for many of the difficulties. But when these childhood experiences are more profound, sexual symptoms will not often yield so readily without psychotherapeutic or psychoanalytic work focused on the psychodynamics and object relations origins of the disjunctional aspects. Even in the more severe case, however, it may be helpful to focus initially on the more superficial aspects of the sexual difficulty in order to generate evidence from within the therapy which can help the patient see a need for exploration of more fundamental issues. It is important, therefore, to understand the early contributors to sexual dysfunctions, pursuing inquiry beyond the earliest specifically sexual experiences and into the quality of early family life.

Our estimation of a patient's capacity for forming a therapeutic alliance, whether around primarily medical (that is, body) care, or emotional issues, is determined largely by the earliest of these experiences. The extent to which the disorder is linked to underlying conflict will ultimately evolve in the course of treatment (whether analytic or behavioral), but may be estimated through an evaluation of internalized object life so that an appropriate recommendation may be made. If inner object relations are relatively sound, it is more likely that a sexual disorder will be easily treated by more purely behavioral, non-interpretive methods. If, however, because of unsatisfactory early object relations, not enough central ego (that part of ego involved autonomously in pleasurable aspects of bonding) is available, then an interpretive approach using transference will be required to strengthen the ego before addressing tasks of sexual intimacy behaviourally with the spouse.

Chapter 11
Breaking in: Bodily aspects of bonding in courtship and marriage

This chapter considers aspects of the role of sex during courtship, falling in love, the decision-making process, and the moment of actually getting married. Later chapters will look at the dissolution of these bonds in separation or death.

Those teenagers and young adults who wonder if they will ever be able to love are expressing a feeling they cannot allow someone in, or enter someone else's space, whether because they have not yet found the right match or because of more profound inability to fit with another due to fears of internal object life that are defended against by remaining unattached. These fears of one's own love or aggression may be so intense as to lead to a worry that the desired other person could be destroyed, or the fears may be projected onto the other person so that the inner threat is now felt to come from outside. In either case, the relationship is avoided to avert the danger.

It is easiest to examine aspects of bonding while the process of inter-penetration is either in a period of active formation or of breakdown. In the relatively stable time in between, there is a kind of homeostatic flow both between the two people and within each of them. The situation then can be compared to the difficulty an experienced worker may have describing what it is that constitutes the skill in his job.[1] Similarly, with the marital bond some aspects are much more visible when still forming, while other aspects may become visible only later. The negative or anti-libidinal aspects of the bond are often kept out of awareness early as the link is in formation, only to reach full expression some time after the commitment is formalized.

Often this change occurs at the point of marriage, but other events may signal it, including the birth of children, their growth or leaving, or the coming of old age. These are the subjects of later chapters. The general phenomenon of the return of the repressed or 'forgotten' anti-libidinal feeling is crucial to any theory of marital and sexual therapy.[2] In the beginning of a relationship, lovers can only see the ideal and the libidinal object in each other, while the anti-libidinal objects are projected forcefully onto others around them or are otherwise denied. They are a group of two against the world and anything hateful in the wider world often serves to heighten the power of their feeling for each other. In some cases, the world may be seen as a kind of frustrating 'environment mother'[3] while the lover is the solution to that frustration.

In the process of choosing and testing an object, two methods are traditionally mentioned, following Freud.

> Psycho-analysis informs us that there are two methods of finding an object. The first . . . is the 'anaclitic' or 'attachment' one, based on attachment to early infantile prototypes. The second is the narcissistic one, which seeks for the subject's own ego and finds it again in other people.[4]

It is possible to look at marital choice, however, as proceeding on a continuum in which some partners rely more heavily on the anaclitic, need-seeking aspects, while others rely more on narcissistic identifications, conscious and unconscious. If these elements are considered two factors in object choice, one can then discuss the degree to which each plays a role. For instance, a man may choose a wife because he sees her as weak and therefore in need of his *care*. He projects the anaclitic aspects of attachment onto her and substitutes 'taking care of her' for 'being taken care of himself.' In addition, he projects the part of himself seen as needy onto her, denying it in himself, and relates to his own needy part by this projective identification. In this case, and to varying degrees in all cases, the anaclitic aspect *and* the narcissistic element are both involved in object choice. Testing the degree to which this process provides for a fit between potential partners is the function of courtship which has to consider not only underlying wishes but vulnerabilities and defenses as well.[5]

Once a commitment is made, the pair become responsible for the total environment of life to each other. The 'bad mother' can no longer be split apart from life with the spouse who has implicitly promised too much in the way of repair for all loss and deprivation. Another way of saying this is to say that in the state of falling in love, the libidinal forces dominate the anti-libidinal ones, causing the person in love to project the anti-libidinal forces outside the loving dyad, to repress them within himself, and to deny their existence.[6] With the marriage or commitment, the spouse or lover is now held responsible for the more complete context of life in the way the early mother was. No longer is the spouse merely the *focus* for loving feelings. *Now* he is the context for a whole life and is responsible for its many and inevitable failings.

We see the same shift in a psychoanalytic treatment. Not until the analyst in the transference (after analysis has gone on for some time) becomes the focus of the wishes to be loved can he become the context for the patient's life. At times the patient is aware of making him the context first, holding him responsible for his own failures and frustrations without understanding that it is his own sense of unrequited love which is at the base of the personal complaint about the analyst's failure. Developmentally, we can see why this is so. The mother is responsible for loving the child and communicating that love so that his love of her reflected back along with her love of him becomes love of himself.[7]

The transference situation is similar in marriage. The cementing of commitment is like the crystallization of the transference into the structure of a transference neurosis. As the analysis becomes the analysand's 'illness,' so does the marriage become the setting for the ills of the spouses' internal world.[8] Some couples even know that they can hold this possibility at bay by not getting married and postpone the actual event for several years. The difficulty is also acknowledged in the joke about 'the couple who had to get divorced in order to be able to live together again.'

How sex influences this situation varies depending on the role of the *body* in the bond which is being formed. Emotional bonding may be facilitated by sex or by its lack. The discussion of this topic is continued later in this chapter and in the next.

Getting in

In young adults, especially in the last decade, sex is apt to be an integral part of courtship, accompanying the 'falling in love' rather than following it. Living together and a wide variety of other sexually active arrangements often precede marriage. What constitutes love itself is of course a complex philosophical question requiring the differentiation between the extremes of infatuation and mature love.[9] At the clinical level, the question requires differentiation of the sexual and emotional aspects of the formation of the bond. Therapists have always seen *individuals* clinically who were too blocked to get into a sexual relationship, but it is only relatively recently that they have begun to see representative numbers of pre-marital *couples* that already have difficulties or doubts. In what follows, the role of sex in moving toward and into marriage will be considered under the following headings:

1   sex as the reflection of the ability to relate;
2   paradoxical uses of sex;
3   sex and decision about marriage;
4   shifts in sex at the point of marriage.

In terms of mental representations, falling in love can be conceptualized as an ego state which happens when the ego invests with libidinal energy an external object which it can regard as an ideal object, and relates to it by projective identification. The self is felt to be impoverished except in relation to the idealized object which supplies what is missing, confirms worth, and insures against the potential loss. The world is a mirror and all of value is reflected in the lover's eyes. The vulnerability of love involves the narcissistic abdication to the object and the giving up ownership of the self to the other. There are endless personal variations to the solution of this vulnerable state. There have been historical periods when dedication to maintaining an unrequited yearning was cherished as an ideal, as in medieval courtly love. When this happens out of personal choice, however, the ability of such a person to live in a real relationship may be questioned. For most people, potential lovers must offer some opportunity to find fantasized satisfaction within the confines of reality. But for others, the fantasy may feel too threatening for them to even attempt to make it come alive. The role of physical sex will also vary. But it will have, throughout these variations, something to do with either letting someone in, binding together, or keeping them out.

Sex as a reflection of the ability to relate

Bob (chapter 7) illustrated the inability to get involved sexually being equivalent to the inability to relate. His immature and naive approach to women covered a deeper fear of them. The oedipal dynamics of his transference to potential partners were a part of this. However, it is of importance that when he *was* able to work on the underlying issues, the sexual disability became a barrier to testing the new ground. When he could then allow a beginning growth of intimacy the challenge of a sexual demand for performance by his partners still stood in his way. The usual dodges and refusals of invitations to a woman's apartment were used. He was eager to see if the relationship could develop, but he was equally terrified the woman would 'demand' sex. Nevertheless, his persistent interest in growth kept him at work with his therapist in developing new strategies and approaches. A more serious disability is illustrated in the next case.

Dick was 30 and fearful of sexual encounters when he came to see me. He had traveled extensively as a successful young banker but he had experienced impotence intermittently in his three previous attempts to have intercourse in temporary relationships. Shortly after beginning therapy, he found a sympathetic, non-demanding, but immature 26-year-old girlfriend who was sheltered by a close relationship to her parents. When he told her of his sexual difficulty, it seemed actually to be a relief for her. Still, he felt threatened by the idea of closeness. Early in treatment, he reported a dream:

He was a lone skater on an endless lake. He was enthralled with the skating. Then he heard a hum which came from the horizon. As he skated, he saw coming toward him a horde of skaters, arms hooked, humming and skating in unison. He felt paralyzed.

Despite the eerie threat of merger this dream portrayed, Dick was able to begin to have satisfactory sex with his girlfriend with her support and gentle understanding. But in the next two years, the extent to which his schizoid inability to relate had been part of the initial sexual inhibition became clear. One night before sleep he had 'an exciting fantasy that he was a criminal evading a famous detective.' He then dreamt:

I was witness to a plane crash. One plane came in at 180° and tried not to land because of another plane trying to take off from the same runway. It touched down, swerved and clipped the wings of a third plane which was deboarding. This plane then skidded to the water and tipped on its nose. People were getting out and swimming in the Potomac River. I was there to tell them not to jump, that there was no fire, but I was choking in my sleep and feeling 'I'm in no condition to help.' I turned and walked away because someone was coming after me. I couldn't get them to stay away.

An association to the 'Blue Plains Sewage Treatment Plant' and a connection between the 'planes' and human bodies let us know that the danger of two planes coming in contact referred to physical and emotional contact. Failing the escape, a crash was inevitable as was the danger of drowning in emotional and bodily pollution. He was paralyzed and unable to help. In this dream, the 'treatment plant' referred to the therapy and the dangers were those of staying in contact both with me and with his girlfriend (the second and third planes). Sexual contact was a threat he could bring himself to face, but he could not risk a more committed relationship. He eventually broke off both the relationship with his girlfriend and the treatment.

The paradoxical use of sex to foreclose the need for a relationship

There are other patterns also designed to short-cut or avoid the difficulties of relating.

Ingrid, who was Swedish, was not in conflict about bodily sex, but she was confused as to who was suitable for marriage. No man measured up to her beloved father. She lived for a while in a ménage à trois as a mistress to an Italian professor of archeology, working devotedly as his assistant. Shortly after her own father died, she returned to Sweden and found a man by whom she became pregnant. This man was a dependent person, disorganized in his work life, who would have liked Ingrid to support him. With him, she could play father to his being the dependent child. Ingrid was very clear that she would not marry him, and she left him. After the birth of her son, sex took on two patterns with a variety of men: getting held and cared for by older, fatherly men who were married or otherwise unavailable; and taking in younger, dependent men whom she could parent, support, and protect while they often exploited her. Both gave her company and a bodily satisfaction. The sex was used in recapitulating her identification and oedipal romance with her father. Her son inherited the role of her father and she sought a life alone for the two of them. Only after a period of this shared isolation, was she finally able to meet and marry an eligible and reasonably self-sufficient man.

Sex and the decision to marry

Only a few variants of the role of sex around this most complex passage can be discussed here. Many of the case illustrations elsewhere also bear on this moment in the life of a couple. The ex nples are listed under headings according to the predominant shared or complementary anxieties presented, consciously and unconsciously, by the couple. The sex then expresses and/or disguises these anxieties as the attachment deepens.

Sex representing anxious attachment and fear of entrapment

Often sex feeds dependency wishes in which a woman fantasizes she will be taken care of like an infant. The sex is used to establish a relationship but unconsciously it is connected to an unacknowledged wish for pregnancy. The fantasy is that the pregnant girl will get mothering from several sources: from her real mother, from her boy-friend, and from herself in giving to the baby what she either never had or had but lost in growing up.

Tanya (chapter 6) and Judy Green (chapter 7) represent examples of this dynamic in adolescents who wished for a baby. There, marriage was not part of the fantasy. However, marriage is often more sought than the pregnancy. For instance, the dependent relationship for both a boy and a girl may offer a way of avoiding the anxiety of leaving home and becoming independent. Sex is then employed to build a substitute attachment and pregnancy is only the stamp which seals such a bond.

Mr and Mrs M were from very different backgrounds when they met in college. Mr M was wary of marriage, citing his own parents' poor relationship and hard-working life. Mrs M's father was a successful military man and an alcoholic. He beat her and her brother occasionally, but he was frequently verbally abusive of them and of Mrs M's mother. Mrs M felt her mother was well disposed to her, but completely unable to protect her. The late adolescent sexual

relationship to Mr M was an integral part of finding him a safe
haven, but this restlessness about commitment made him a challenge
for her which had echoes of the lack of safety with her own parents.
When she became pregnant, Mrs M was consciously 'almost relieved'
and unconsciously even more relieved of the fear of being abandoned
for the time being. She even agreed to have an abortion if Mr M
would marry her. Although he did, the marriage carried forward for
many years the complementary patterns of her desperately anxious
attachment and his sense of being trapped into an ambivalent union.

Sex as link into and out of marriage: Hidden aspects of an oedipal bond

As far as he knew, Irwin (chapter 10) was attracted to his first serious
girlfriend at 19, despite her casual sexual involvement with a cavalier
youth who was already in her room waiting to have sex with her as
Irwin brought her home from their first date. Several years later in
analysis he discovered that a large part of the attraction for her was
the 'homosexual' aspect of the jealousy of the man.[10] Irwin was jealous
of his own father, enjoying his competence and power, and wished to
get that competence from him for himself as well as the affection from
him for which he longed. This dynamic was stirred up at the moment
of this adolescent encounter which occurred when he felt lonely and
insecure, having just moved out of his parents' house when he transferred to a new college for his junior year. Thus the attachment to the
girlfriend who would satisfy his passive, dependent yearnings was
considerably augmented by the symbolic connection to the man through
her body. He thereby was symbolically supported by both parents
through the anxieties of leaving home. These factors remained in
operation until the day, as he put it, that 'he popped the answer' and
they agreed to marry so that she would support him through graduate
school. Upon marriage, he retreated from sex, began to substitute
masturbation with fantasies of other women, and quickly began an
affair. Sex, which had been a temptation into a relationship, was now
used as a way out of it.

A paradoxical role for sex: The absence of sex as an attraction

Ellen P had been active sexually since her mid-adolescence, enjoying

many partners without any conscious sense of conflict. Although at
times she wondered if she might be a bit promiscuous, in the main
she felt comfortable with her sexual activities. But when she met
Sam, she felt challenged. He was 14 years older and had never had
intercourse. He was so shy and reticent that she had to seduce him
the first time. Because he was so inexperienced and reluctant, Ellen
was unable to enjoy sex as she formerly had, but she readily assented
when Sam proposed. As far as she knew, she did so *despite* the poor
sex, but in therapy she discovered that it was largely *because of* the
lack of sexual interest and ability that she married Sam.

Ellen's mother had been a negligent and narcissistic woman, so
wrapped up in herself that she thought nothing of exposing Ellen
to her many flagrant affairs. When Ellen was young, her mother
forced her and her sister to aid her in her shoplifting by wearing
clothes out of stores, and later she insisted on making Ellen her
confidante about sexual matters. Father left his wife alone, turning
a blind eye on the family, and living apparently without sex himself.
Ellen reacted by distancing herself from both parents. She thought
of herself as needing no one and she concentrated on academic
achievements and on 'making herself completely independent.'
Her only real attachment was to a much older high school teacher
whom she idealized. She split off the sex and at 16 began to enjoy
it with a variety of boys and men without conscious remorse, and
without the threat of meaningful attachments that might then be
lost.

When she met Sam after several years, he seemed to offer Ellen
a perfect compromise. Her wariness of mother's rampant sexuality
and her own unconscious guilt could be relieved. An attachment
to him offered her a caring figure who would indeed return her care
while offering safety. And his relative sexlessness was a reminder
of her apparently sexless father. While making a conscious decision
to marry Sam because he was sweet, innocent, and teachable, Ellen
was unconsciously choosing him because he was dependent, naive,
like the 'father who could be fooled,' but especially because he
was asexual.

Sex and the decision not to marry: A normal variant

Foster Lomas is a 36-year-old twin, a botanist, who asked for a consultation. He was engaged to marry a girl whom he had known for six months. Although he was very fond of her, he didn't want to marry her. *She* maintained that he was neurotically frightened of commitment. *He* said he was not so much frightened; it was just not his preference.

'I like sex and I like people, but I just never want to marry. I'm very close to my family. My twin brother is married – I love him, his wife, my parents, and my sister. Maybe it's because I have enough closeness and trust. And I'm very fond of Shirley – as fond as I ever have been of anyone. I feel I got fooled into thinking I *should* want to get married. She and her mother sure want me to. I agreed to see you because I'm not sure if they're right – that I'm abnormal. I love my work and I like people. I like sex even better when I really like the woman, but I like the personal freedom. I have good relationships. I just don't want to get married or have children. I never have. I hate to let Shirley down, but it's no good marrying feeling like this.'

In the evaluation, it was not possible to uncover anything which could be called neurotic in Foster's presentation or development. He was aware of the limitations on commitment, but he preferred things left that way. Perhaps he was right that his family did provide enough long-term intimacy, or even too much, and that being a twin left him wanting less intimacy instead of more. The sex and intimacy were fine until they reached his personal limit which stopped short of marriage. Foster seemed normal; his choice seemed to be one of normal preference even if it would not have been the choice for many people.

The prolonged delay in marriage: Sexual disjunction before marriage as insurance against commitment

For some pre-marital couples, the sex can express the reluctance to commit, despite their caring for each other. It can be a shared or unilateral reluctance, but often two such people find each other.

Dolph and Frances were in their mid-twenties and living together when they came for sex therapy. Frances reported that she was inexperienced and moderately aversive to sex. Dolph felt deprived by her aversion and disinterest, but upon inquiry we discovered that he had a lifelong history of premature ejaculation. Behavioral sex therapy 'cured' things technically. Dolph's premature ejaculation could be controlled and Frances enjoyed sex more than before. But when physical functioning was improved, a more profound issue was unearthed. Dolph and Frances now began actively to avoid each other physically and their ambivalence about getting married became a focus. Both had unconsciously regarded the previous sexual stalemate as insurance against a threatened demand by the other to get married. All the dynamics of their relationships to feared and envied internalized parents were now exposed with each other. They longed for connectedness, but in their fear, made it a point to stay disconnected! The dysfunctions were unmasked as really representing a shared disjunction. The sexual representation of the need to stay unconnected stemmed from a shared fear of being swamped and overwhelmed. They now had difficulty attuning to desire at the same time. This pattern remained through two years in which each had individual psychotherapy with the same woman therapist.[11] In this format, oedipal and pre-oedipal issues tended to focus in a triangular transference. The transference was to a shared anti-libidinal parent who was seen by Frances as the dreaded engulfing and critical mother, and by Dolph as the controlling father. Ultimately these feelings toward the therapist and toward each other were worked through. The therapist could then be experienced as a cooperative helper. They felt increasingly free to be committed to each other and the sexual relationship followed suit. They sent their therapist a wedding announcement from their honeymoon. On the back was scribbled:

> No need wishing – you are here!
> We couldn't have done it without you.

Broadly speaking, the five examples given above demonstrate that (a) the sexual bond may operate partly in concert with the general direction of the relationship; (b) partly it may run directly counter to it; or (c) it may serve to encapsulate split-off aspects in a way which allows the decision to marry to proceed despite unconscious reservations. In practice, the sex often expresses both the conscious aspects of a bond *and* the unconscious countervailing (denied and split-off) aspects. No matter what the shared or complementary anxieties of the couple, when the sex is sufficiently cut off from an awareness of the unconscious fears, there is a significant potential for later difficulty.

Shifts at the point of marriage

The period immediately following marriage has proven a difficult passage for many. Patients who are fond of each other, experience physical comfort or even sexual fulfillment with each other pre-maritally and who share each other's personal and cultural values, find that from the point of marriage feelings cool and sexual interest flags. There is more than one cause for this, and more than one temporal pattern. It may happen in a day, or slowly over the years. But something about the fact of being married has an ineffable role in the switch.

In his book, *Marital Tensions*, Henry Dicks divided marital bonds into three subsystems: [12]

Subsystem I: The socio-cultural values and norms – the public reality. Agreement at this level is necessary for a first attraction in many marriages.

Subsystem II: Personal norms – the conscious personal reality. At this level 'the ongoing pulls and pushes' for role performance go on, the *conscious* contracts, agreements and wishes are negotiated by the central egos in their characteristic styles derived from the developmental background of object relations and pre-marital social learning.

Subsystem III: Individual unconscious reality. This system includes bonds of both positive and negative kinds. The unconscious reality is the locus of drives toward satisfaction of object-relational needs and consists of repressed and split-off ego elements and object relations.

Dicks feels it is in subsystem III that the longer-term quality of marriage is determined. If all three subsystems are congruent, courtship and marriage proceed apace. But if the needs in subsystem III do not fit the other two, conflict is all about, especially if I and II are a public interpersonal façade for a deep lack of fit in the unconscious realms.

What we see at the point of marriage, in these couples who experience a shift in feeling from positive yearning to fright, to a detached apathy about each other, may be conceptualized as a shift in subsystem III. The unconscious denial of an identification of the spouse with an anti-libidinal object, a hated or feared parent, a critical superego, a controlling object, can not now be maintained. Before the marriage the partners relate mainly to each other as ideal objects with the libidinally invested, relatively conflict-free central egos. At the unconscious level, ambivalence toward the object is inevitable. While the repressed libidinal ego pulls toward the object that is exciting its needs, the anti-libidinal ego pulls away from the object that might be rejecting. The central ego's union is threatened by the unconscious ambivalence and it strenuously maintains repression of the threat that the neediness and loving of the libidinal system will overwhelm the object or that the aggression of the anti-libidinal system toward the frustrating aspects of the object might destroy the object. In either case, what is longed for would be lost.

After marriage, when fear of loss of the relationship is at least temporarily assuaged, these repressed object relationships can gain expression in a number of ways. An unwanted part of the self may be projected onto the other and the other valued for accepting the un-wanted projection, a dynamic founded in the wish to cure a defective part of the self projected onto the other or found and identified with in the other. Or perhaps an idealization of some parts of the other will be formed to allow the central ego to blind itself to faults. Once these repressed relationships have surfaced, they can be relived, reworked, and repaired in the normal context of the reasonably healthy marriage.

In earlier examples defects in sexuality were actually a positive reason for choice of a partner, a choice made for instance in order to make reparation by cure - a frequent adolescent and young adult Pygmalion fantasy. Sexual symptomatology has no unique role in these patterns, but its operation has a special poignancy because if it works it can catalyze growth of positive forces and if it fails, it tends to catalyze the negative ones.

Just as sexual sharing speaks for coming together while its frus-tration, failure, or absence speaks for forces of separation, so once the one side of ambivalence which seeks approach and fears coming apart is satisfied, the other side of preferring to stay separate springs to life. Now the person fears attachment (for his own personal historical reasons) and he seeks separateness. The sex which accompanies fear of attachment is fearful, aggressive, or controlling. It fails or is withheld. Apathy, loss of desire, or 'non-sex' is its ultimate form.

So the shift which takes place, probably almost always to *some* degree on or soon after the wedding day when the relationship is secured, is the resurgence of the avoidance side of ambivalence.

Many couples have come to therapists with this picture, with either husband or wife showing a secondary sexual disorder sometime after the wedding. Emma Smith and Enid (chapter 7), and Penelope S (chapter 4) were all women who enjoyed the physical closeness of sex without orgasm before marriage, but lost interest afterwards. But the same can happen to sexually fully functional people, as in the case of Tamara (chapter 7) and in the following example.

Ron, aged 31, came to see me after a year of marriage. Before marriage his sexual life had been fun and apparently had felt complete to both him and his wife. Intercourse had not been frequent, at most once or twice a week, but then they had never lived together and Ron's job as district representative for an agricultural supplier required frequent travel. His wife was reported to be easily orgasmic, and Ron said she appreciated his witty empathy for her. He was proud that he was also well liked by their large circle of friends who frequently sought his advice. His wife was the object of friendly jealousy socially for her good 'catch.'

But in the months following their marriage, Ron lost interest in sex completely. He also began to badger his wife about previously unnoticed petty things. He was responsive and social with friends, but unable to exhibit any interest in sex. They had been to his wife's gynecologist who told them about 'sensate focus' which they tried. Ron only felt colder and withdrew more, turning frequently to escapes from home by stopping at a bar on the way home. The origins of his withdrawal became clearer when his 55-year-old mother became seriously ill. She was diagnosed as having rapidly spreading cancer. An identification with her is evident in the following dream which also allows a view of his fear of women.

'The dream was about my crucifixion. I was crucified on the wall opposite the elevators. It wasn't a particularly painful experience although I was frightened. I knew I was dreaming. My feet were nailed and I had my clothes on. It was not a Christ-like crucifixion. Next I remember being crucified on another wall by Sandra, a woman I work closely with. She hammered nails into my hands very slowly. I thought to myself, "I am going to die by bleeding to death," but I don't recall being particularly scared by that thought. I saw myself as a white body with all the blood gone and thought how the undertaker would handle the viewing. I woke up hearing church chimes. As I woke, I thought of Sandra as Judas and the phrase "You will betray me before the cock crows." '

In this dream his affective detachment, his fear of women, and a narcissistic identification ('It was not Christ-like') are evident. He gives a full description of the withdrawal from sex as an essentially life-saving retreat in the phrase 'You (a woman he works closely with) will betray me before the cock crows.' The inhibition of sexual interest in his wife protects him against the projection of his own sadistic inner world onto her.

In a dream the night before his mother died, the sexualized longing for a libidinal mother is acknowledged.

> 'I was in a small, sparsely furnished hotel room. The bed was elevated like a hospital bed. My landlady, who is in her mid-fifties, was there. She was hard like a whore, rough and tough. She asked me if I wanted a blow job. "Do you want me to help you out, to make you feel good? I did it to your father recently. He really liked it." I got on the bed. She was wearing green knit slacks like my wife's. She went down on me. I wondered what I was supposed to do . . . I tried to make love to her and grabbed for her breasts, trying to kiss her. Then I woke up. My wife said she thought I was making love to my mother, trying to get my mother to love me. The landlady looks like my mother, and she had an affair with a neighbor of ours.'

Despite the clarity in this dream about the longing for his mother, Ron was unable to mourn her or to feel sad at her death. He felt he had never really known her or been loved by her. His father's detachment from her was clear to him, and he began to see that the inability to mourn his mother was related to his sexual withdrawal from his wife. We agreed that intensive therapy was required and he agreed to begin psychoanalysis.

Ron's shift from a loving, affable, and supportive 'Henry Higgins' to a retreating, scared rabbit illustrates the shift at the point of marriage from operation on subsystem levels I and II to the domination of the anti-libidinal ego of level III. He was at ease with socially intimate relationships which did not penetrate to the unconscious level, but could manage more intimate primary relationships only when he could dominate and control his object as in the pre-marital solicitousness of his wife and the post-marital bullying of her. His internalized model of women alternated between the sadistically internalized, frustrating anti-libidinal mother and the exciting incestuous object. His loss of sexual interest and his difficulty getting an erection spoke for an urgent need to withdraw.

Sex as bondage

Before birth control and abortion, pregnancy used to enslave women to the bondage of their sexual impulse and to unconscious choice. Other events can still bring the same. For some men and women, once their body is involved sexually, a bond is sealed. When this has been done in a risky situation, the bond may quickly change to bondage.

> Nina was a virgin at 20 when she slept with Seth. Although they were to be married, she felt unsure of his love. After a few months of sleeping together, her tolerance of sex was just beginning to turn to pleasure when Seth got cold feet. He suggested they date other people even though they should remain engaged. She was shocked and numbed. Even though he came back only three days later, saying he had changed his mind and still wanted to marry her, Nina could not fully recover her trust. She never discussed her hurt with him, hiding her now-permanent distrust because she felt she was a ruined woman who was completely at his mercy. She was able to feign enthusiasm sexually until shortly after their marriage, but as the years wore on, she found she continued to resent being Seth's hostage and she was less and less able to respond.

In this case, the shift did not develop at the point of marriage. The mistrust was planted but did not put shoots above ground until the marriage was secure. Then all the fears and resentment blossomed. Not surprisingly, Seth was subsequently 'driven' into having an affair before the situation began to change. When Nina began to investigate why she had become a hostage to her own dependency, she discovered that her relationship to her mother was an ambivalent and anxious one in which without knowing it, she had constantly feared disapproval and disfavor. The bond to Seth had recreated many of these elements.

Married chastity

A final pattern is the change at the point of marriage when there has been no intercourse before marriage, usually because of moral or religious beliefs, often coupled with some degree of sexual naivety. Once married, the couple is huddled together, unable to get going unless they can find a benign authoritative figure to help them begin. Experience with a few such couples has demonstrated more naivety than other groups. This again recalls the internalization of parental over-protection.

Heidi and Peter Z were naive, but enthusiastically in love. Both were from strict fundamentalist religious backgrounds but had shed most of their faith. They kissed and held each other before marriage, but did not advance to petting. On the wedding night penetration was not possible. Attempts during the honeymoon were painful. They battered each other for two weeks sexually without success, and finally consulted a gynecologist who did a hymenectomy. Even so, it was a few weeks before intercourse was possible. From this point on, Heidi submitted to Peter three times a week for eleven years with no enjoyment. From time to time she would grow bitter about the sex, but would relent when he insisted. As her interest failed to improve over a decade, Peter's patience and hope that he could heal her gradually wore thin. Finally he felt the marriage would not long survive without a change. At that point, he was able to convince Heidi to come reluctantly for help.

In this case although intercourse began several weeks after the marriage, there was never any effective physical bond. Even the pleasurable holding they enjoyed before marriage now failed to give comfort. By its failure sex began to operate as an anti-libidinal disruptive force which slowly grew to rival the holding power of the libidinal bond in an otherwise healthy marriage.

For all its potential to connect libidinal currents and undercurrents constructively, sex also has the potential either to produce disruption or to express it. When the point of marriage calls for new closeness and bodies fail, whether because of inexperience, anxiety, or disability, the wish for intimacy is frustrated calling up reverberations of painfully frustrating inner objects. On the other hand, when the anti-libidinal ego has been barely kept at bay, split off but active in the unconscious, the moment of marriage often opens the way for its dominance in the relationship. Sexual life may then be one of many voices speaking for a distancing in a relationship which is thorny throughout. Or sex may be the lone voice speaking centrally, and *seemingly uncharacteristically*, for the wish to be apart, which later turns out to be a dominant wish of one or both partners.

The examples in this chapter have focused on the difficulties which may set in at the point of marriage. For most couples, despite some of these difficulties, sex becomes a source of healing and repair in marriage, a mutual expression and maintenance of the ideal object relationship above all others, but *not* to their exclusion. The balance of these constructive and disruptive forces is the focus of the next chapter.

Chapter 12
The power of sex to sustain or disrupt marriage

This chapter examines the myth of the couple that stays together principally on account of their sexual life. While investigating the role of the sexual bond within marriage, therapists often see such people, whose tolerance of each other as marital partners is surprising, beset as these couples are by bickering, mutual criticism, emotional distance, and hostility. Such a marriage raises the question as to whether mutual sexual interest alone is enough to sustain it, or whether other factors are operating. In the past, behavioral sex therapy has tended to treat such a couple's sexual dysfunction as though it were an encapsulated illness without reference to such other factors. For instance, one couple was referred for treatment of the husband's secondary sexual dysfunction that came to the foreground after previously successful behavioral sex therapy for the wife's dysfunction. In the first treatment the decaying core of their marriage and his lifelong pattern of affairs had been overlooked (see chapter 17).

Some couples support the notion of an independence of sexual life. They believe that mutual sexual interest is enough in itself to maintain their marriages, stating that it is the chief thing they share, and acting as though it is all that holds them together. But beneath the surface, one of two situations will pertain.

Either the mutual sexual satisfaction *symbolizes* and *speaks* for what is really 'good enough' in a fuller sense, drawing on diverse emotional elements and providing the integration of them. (A couple for whom this is the case will be most aware of a sense of well-being during their sexual life but they will do well in other ways too.)

Or, alternatively, the sex hides and helps to deny an otherwise barren emotional climate, helping the couple tolerate a loveless marriage which survives despite the emptiness of the apparent physical victory of love over hate.

Questions of historical and cultural relativism arise here as to what constitutes a 'good-enough marriage.' Here, as in the later consideration of extra-marital sex and infidelity, philosophical debates and value judgments can be avoided by adherence to a clinical point of reference. In assessing a marriage the question will be limited to: 'What does this patient or couple want from the marriage and what is the barrier to their getting it?' By virtue of the fact that a couple seeks help, the couple can usually be said to be defining themselves as having difficulty with their relationship and as giving it priority.

In asking whether sex sustains or undermines a given marriage, further clinical questions arise. How does the sex support, attack, or fail to uphold the marital bond? What is the nature of the bond; i.e., is it loving, over-excited, aggressive or sado-masochistic, complementary, supplementary, or symbiotic, fused or differentiated? And what is the patients' best interest individually and jointly, consciously and unconsciously? The clinical judgments refer, then, to the best interest of each patient individually, the couple considered jointly, and the larger family – not to the therapist's preference. Of course, personal values do influence perspective, but professional judgment should be based on considered opinion that is defensible by evidence, reason, and experience, rather than on a therapist's beliefs internalized in childhood.

An example of two quite different kinds of sexual relationship formed by the same patient in consecutive marriages illustrates the role of sex in sustaining or disrupting the marriage.

At age 30, Michael felt his marriage could no longer endure. He had enjoyed many aspects of living together with his wife and son, and this enabled him to tolerate his sadness that for many years he and his wife Ethel never had pleasurable sex as she had always found sex uncomfortable, had no orgasm, and generally preferred he make no sexual demands. While he kept hoping for change, he could put up with this deprivation himself, but became more upset to notice that Ethel was not able to express affection for their 4-year-old son either. While previously he had been able to ignore the sexual difficulty, hoping for future improvement, the two aspects of disappointment now added to each other, and were felt by Michael as a rising anger in response to his increasing awareness of the sexual difficulty and its expression of larger issues. When he finally decided that the limitation in sex and in affection in the marriage was more than he could tolerate, he left. He made an effort in testing out future relationships to find one that would offer him the longed-for intimacy. In a second satisfying relationship at age 36, the sexual expression took on a central, symbolic, and communicative role. With Lucy, who became his second wife, sex provided a mutual sense of caring, soothing, and satisfaction, although it was not always exciting.

The difference in sex in the two marriages paralleled the degree of intimacy and mutuality in each. It was not the single cause of the intimacy, but it did serve to confirm a better fit in the second relationship.

This case briefly illustrates the potential of sexuality for the communication of wider needs in the context of marital commitment. As a largely non-verbal route of communication, it has crucial links to the earliest forms of physical nurture and reassurance in infancy and childhood which have been discussed earlier. That is why it hurt Michael to see his son not cared for either in his first marriage, for it was a reminder of himself as a child. The sex, paralleling other aspects of Michael's first marriage, failed to provide an avenue of communication in a relationship in which intimacy was blocked in general. In the second marriage, it was one form of proof of the viability of the intimacy.

The first part of this case illustrates the formidable power of sex for disruption. In many ways, the marriage was not bad. But many of the destructive aspects were embodied in the missing sex. Men without dysfunctions themselves are more often distressed by a wife's dysfunction than are women in the situation of having a dysfunctional husband.[1] They bring their wives or partners for therapy because they feel the marriage will dissolve without sexual improvement and the wives often acknowledge the risk to the marriage caused by their dysfunction. There are, however, definitely cases in which the potential for sexual disruption has been demonstrated when the husband has the dysfunction. In practice, although more wives may agree to live with an on-going dysfunction, the ones who will not account for the couples who present *their* distress, stating much like their non-dysfunctional male counterparts, that the marriage itself it at stake.

'We only stay together because of the sex!'

When a couple *says* that the sex is what principally binds them, theirs is often a tenuous marriage, as in the following example.

> The Parsons claimed that sex was not only the best part of their relationship, but that it was the sex which played a large role in keeping them together. It had also been a large part of their initial mutual attraction to each other. While the sex continued to be good, varied, and frequent, other problems had set in. Mrs Parsons no longer respected her husband who was not ambitious, took frequent sick leave from work, and preferred letting her take care of him. Mr Parsons complained that his wife was too aggressive for him. She dominated their decision-making and their children. Despite a considerable waning of affection, each saw their sex as a source of pleasure and valued the spouse for enjoying and giving through sex. The social worker who interviewed this couple described her feeling that the sex had been disconnected from the emotional life of the couple, and that the underlying hostility between them was only beginning to emerge. The sex was isolated from the major bond, a hostile, dependent one which relied on anger more than loving feeling. A short time later, the couple became more openly quarrelsome and broke off counseling, indicating that they thought it was stirring up trouble. Their fragile defense against the split between body and feeling was obviously in danger.

For a couple to say, 'It is *only* the sex which keeps us together,' implies that positive feelings are otherwise lacking. Clinically one sees many couples who cling together despite their mutual dislike or even hate. Their masochistic bond underscores a desperate dependency. Sex is then burdened with the need to maintain a bond despite widespread disaffection, providing a slender excuse to stay together. It helps disguise and isolate the sources of hate and discontent, but this maneuver often leaves one or both partners clinically depressed. This can be understood by pointing out that it is only when the anti-libidinal elements have overshadowed the relationship between central ego and ideal object that a split-off libidinal system becomes the primary conscious bond for a couple, isolating the sex as the sole conscious answer to a sense of mutual dislike.

When one speaks of a marriage *really* being held together by the physical sex alone one must conclude that there is a great deal of hostility between the partners. Whether it is acknowledged by them or not, they are usually living in a desperate situation. This can be contrasted to the situation of the couple who maintains that the sex is perhaps the best thing about their marriage, but in whom it can be seen to parallel other positive aspects of their bond even if they are non-verbal or if the couple is not able to articulate them. In these cases, the sex may symbolize good aspects of the marriage, but it is far from its sole support.

What does sex do within a marriage?

The evidence that sex does indeed have some power to help sustain marriage comes from diverse sources. Many couples report that sex is an important and pleasurable support in times of difficulty. But in the clinical setting one more frequently sees couples who are missing something in their sexual life, and under the impact of what is missing, their marriage is in danger despite an overall sense that this is a loving and committed marriage. From the standpoint of a 'physiology of marriage', these can be conceptualized as unintended 'ablation experiments', on the model of physiologists who remove an organ to see how an animal functions. In those cases in which the sex can be restored by a relatively simple form of sex therapy, something can be learned about the emotional physiology of sex in its role of sustaining marriages.

Restoration of normality in marriage

Sol and Nancy were in their mid-twenties and had been married for four years. They were fond of each other and supportive in most ways except sexually. Sol felt more and more depressed because Nancy never enjoyed sex. Nancy felt more and more pressured whenever Sol came to bed or tried to hug her. In sex therapy, they discovered that Sol shared in the dysfunction. His premature ejaculation meant that Nancy had never had enough of an experience with intercourse to enjoy genital stimulation even if she had known how. For Sol, the sexual experience precipitated the kinds of feelings he had about his intrusive, possessive mother who critically denied him the right to have pleasure. When he was 19, for instance, she had walked suddenly into the living room where he was timidly holding hands with his first girlfriend. 'I know what you're doing,' she announced, 'and you had better not!'

For Nancy, the prospect of allowing herself to experience womanly sexual feeling threatened to keep her from continuing to play her habitual role of a child, a role which had allowed her to retain a longing for her father without overwhelming guilt about replacing her mother. This sharing by both Sol and Nancy of a fear of mothers contributed to their joining in keeping Nancy from acting and responding like an adult woman.

In sex therapy, it was Nancy who expressed a heightening of anxiety about trusting, a sense of being potentially overrun, a fear of invasion. Although Sol was quite gentle, he had to struggle to learn patience and restraint. He had difficulty responding to Nancy's fears with more sympathy than anger. With these new efforts, they grew more trusting, giving, and tolerant of each other's difficulties. The new pleasure of their successful sexual life reinforced these improvements which, at first, were tenuous.

A year later the restored sex had a new function in their lives, but was no longer the prominent feature of their relationship that it had been when it was missing. It was now available to them for pleasure and repair during times of strain. Although sex was occasionally exciting, more often it pleasantly reinforced their mutual caring. Anger, from whatever source, tended to keep sex from working well until they were able to begin pulling together, at which point it usually became an instrument of the reunion. Like many couples, once sex began to work for them, it became an integral, and occasionally exceptional, part of their life together.

Functions of good-enough sex in the marriage

The first chapter reviewed the functions of 'good-enough sex,' a term modelled on Winnicott's 'good-enough mothering,' from the point of object relations repair and integration.[2] Good-enough sex with the partner allows him to be experienced as a whole object – frustrating and ideal – just as good-enough mothering allowed the infant to get to the stage of concern for the whole mother and to be able to hold her in the mind as a whole object that need not be split into good and bad. The particular functions include:

1 repair of the internal and external object damaged by ordinary wear and tear, damage felt partly to have been done by the self;

2   reparation, making up to the object and earning forgiveness;
3   renewing of the overall bond and preparation for the separation which will inevitably follow;
4   integration of bodily drives with the overall current of the marriage.

On the other hand, there is also the need to meet demands from both the internal objects that are ambivalently held and those composing the superego.[3] So another function of good-enough sex is:

5   striving to satisfy the critical and standard-setting aspects of internal objects (under pressure from the anti-libidinal system);
6   making up for the deficiencies which are felt in the internal objects and in the corresponding aspects of the self, so as to reflect a more positive self-image, particularly in comparison to the ego-ideal.

Nancy and Sol both longed for less intrusive and more empathetic mothers. While struggling as young adults they were both struggling with the feeling of not living up to the unrealistic (but now self-imposed) demands. Before sex therapy, these self-criticisms were constantly aggravated and the old frustrations rekindled. Afterwards, the gaps could be filled periodically and the expectations met by a satisfying experience in the 'transitional space' between them which then 'contained' the depressive anxieties. Experiences such as the one recounted here demonstrate that *when sex is missing in a couple's relationship, their perspective often alters so that it seems to become the major issue between them. When it is restored to normal functioning, it becomes only one aspect of their relationship, usually with no special overall prominence. This approximates the usual situation in most normal marriages.*

Sex and personal boundaries

Sex also has a role in maintaining distance and setting boundaries between two people. In the confines of marriage, partners struggle with too much closeness as often as with too little. For many, the question is not how to get closer but how to guard his or her territory. For women, the fear is most often of the threat of being taken over by the husband; for men there is the reciprocal fear of being trapped, taken in, or swallowed up. In all cases, a profound unconscious fear of becoming a hostage to the spouse through sexual intimacy dictates that keeping one's distance is the safer course. A number of examples in several chapters have given the details of this aspect of intimacy.

This issue may explain a paradoxical kind of failure in sex therapy: as sex improves the marriage does not. For these patients, an improvement in sexual functioning does not restore trust in the marriage or intimacy. Instead, the improved sex represents a force of invasion beyond the limits of trust. In this case, restoration of physical sexual functioning reveals that its absence was part of a defensive shield designed to keep the partners at a safe distance. For some, this was felt to be an almost life-protecting function.

Mrs R was an angry and brittle 36-year-old woman. Initially in sex therapy she was able to become considerably more sexually responsive. At the same time her husband seemed well on the way to overcoming the difficulties with secondary impotence and premature ejaculation which had set in as she lost interest in sex five years previously. The couple made satisfactory progress in the 'sensate focus' and 'genital massage' phases of therapy.

But because of her rigid character defenses, the therapists did not feel they were able to make any headway in encouraging her to be more emphathetic with her husband. Still, she stayed hard at work in the sex therapy despite the paranoid anger which was frequently focused on people in the periphery of her life. The struggle was, and had been for five years of improvement in psychotherapy, to maintain a split in objects which allowed her central objects and her therapists to be felt as supportive and trustworthy.

However, as the sex began to return to function and her husband became more hopeful, her anger could not be suppressed. With an exercise which prescribes penile 'containment' in the vagina without movement, the anger began to be openly expressed.[4] In the next phase as they were both supposed to begin slow movement, Mrs R could not tolerate the loss of control of her own sexual arousal. Feeling at her husband's and the therapists' mercy, she became unremittingly angry at the same time as she was becoming sexually responsive. Progressively she felt no one understood her. The female co-therapist scheduled extra individual sessions but was nevertheless defeated in her attempts to work this through. Reluctantly the therapists terminated with them. The Rs settled back into something of the same kind of hostile truce as before the sex therapy, even though sex was now available to them.

One of the uses Mrs R had made of the sex therapy was to use it to separate from therapy altogether. She had been working profitably for years with one female therapist, and transferred to the co-therapists for sex therapy. She seemed to be using the acquisition of sex as a transitional phenomenon not to get closer to the transferential mother, but as an area in which to seek control of her own sense of separateness. The cry to be 'understood' seemed to be the need for a maternal understanding of the need for separation despite denied but desperately felt symbiotic yearnings. The new attachment figure, from whom she also feared damage in union, was her resexualized husband. The acquisition of sexual functioning was used to terminate treatment, although the person she talked about shutting out was her husband. Once over the angry 'weaning,' she seemed to settle down with a small advance on maturation and an overall sense of relief.

Virginal marriages

The group of marriages that seek help because of non-consummation has been described by Leonard Friedman in *Virgin Wives*.[5] The small number of such marriages the author and his colleagues have seen directly have been between naive partners, both of whom came from restrictive, religious backgrounds. The comments in chapter 7 concerning the way in which individual experience with their particular parents transmits the religious orthodoxy apply here. The partners have had a child-like quality and have lived sheltered lives in which they were unusually dependent on and close to their parents. Clearly, it was not the religious orthodoxy *per se*, but its transmission through parents who were overly close and protective. Some of these couples have been united in wishing the sex to function. In other marriages, one spouse was essentially content without it. The following case fell into this group until the wife began to want children.

Louis and Rachel were an orthodox Jewish couple who had been married for four years. It was Rachel who initially had sought help for their unconsummated marriage because she wanted children. Louis was 41 and had had very few dates before they met. He had lived at home, dominated by his widowed mother. Rachel, now 33, had also lived with her parents while teaching nursery school. She had dated but physically had never progressed beyond kissing. Her parents found Louis a suitable mate, but his mother was less friendly to Rachel. She would have preferred to keep Louis to herself.

The sexual dysfunction which prevented conception consisted of a combination of Rachel's vaginismus and Louis's 'primary impotence.'[6] He lost his erection on each attempt at penetration. In the therapy, we were most struck by their shared naivety which appeared to be aggressively maintained by each individually as a protection from close contact. Rachel was quite bossy, presumably much like Louis's mother. Although she was usually sure she was right, she was frightened, anxious, and dependent. It scarcely occurred to her that conceiving children could be pleasurable. Throughout the therapy she remained critical of Louis's boyish enthusiasm, which, for instance, surfaced the first time his experience went beyond occasional guilty masturbation. Rachel maintained single-minded dedication to the process of having children. She was interested only in getting his penis far enough inside to accomplish what was necessary and even at an advanced stage of therapy inquired about artificial insemination. She remained the controlling mother to the end, when she did in fact become pregnant. Louis did not mind. She was taking care of him in the style to which he was accustomed and he was delighted with his new-found modicum of sexual enjoyment, exhibiting a kind of delight Rachel could tolerate without sharing.

The lack of sex in this couple facilitated the shared early symbiosis which functioned as the basis for marriage. Their immaturity was reminiscent of a bond unaltered since the first year of life. Louis and Rachel had each maintained an overly-close, poorly-differentiated relationship with mother. Now each was an undifferentiated and non-sexual surrogate for her to the other. To sustain this union, they had to eliminate the aggression that would have threatened to separate them, that is to propel them toward the separation phase of development. This was cooperatively accomplished when Louis abdicated any aggressive role, allowing Rachel to carry it for both of them. She was in a way a doubly aggressive woman, controlling of Louis and of others, and frustrated at the lack of support and confrontation. Sex would have threatened them because it was seen as aggression aimed at Rachel *unless* she was fully in control of it. Vigorous naivety was a shared defensive style which protected Louis and Rachel against the return of this repressed and projected aggression. This naivety can be understood as a defense against the cognitive growth which accompanies separation from mother. The style of character defense remained solidly intact long after the sexual dysfunction, which had been a prominent component of it, had been largely treated.

Homosexual 'marriages'

Many of the same principles previously discussed apply to these homosexual unions in which both partners have a sustained commitment to each other. Here the sexual life represents the continuing bond between partners in the same way it does for heterosexual couples. As noted in chapter 9, the choice of a same-sex partner represents a compromise of object choice with roots in developmental lines. The male homosexual usually has a fear of women and a sense of inadequacy as a man, but it is also true that most heterosexual couples have to live with various compromises of different sorts in securing their marriages, and that the pathology they must live with may be as severe as that indicated by the choice of a homosexual partner. Having noted this developmental deviation, we can proceed to consider a homosexual partnership in terms of the principles elaborated for heterosexual couples.

Jack came to see me because he felt his 'marriage' was in danger. He assured me that he had no interest in giving up homosexuality, but was in distress because his lover and partner of five years had been uninterested in sex for almost a year. In the last few months, Jack had found himself looking at other men and had even sought out a promiscuous relationship with a man with whom he became impulsively infatuated. He described this man as 'a mindless young fellow with a good body.' The sex had been exciting and in itself satisfactory, but Jack had felt cheap and disloyal. He said, 'I only want the relationship with Rick, and I don't know how to interest him in it. He says he is committed to me, but acts depressed, angry, and uninterested. He never wants to go out anymore or get involved in sex. He seems to feel I'm no good. He acts like an old maid who puts me down for everything.'

Since Rick was not willing to come for a consultation, I urged Jack to tell him of the outside sexual involvement and of his concerns. Things seemed so bad that, like it or not, Jack thought he would have to leave the relationship. I thought that Rick might as well have a conscious choice about whether this was what he wanted, whether the message of dissatisfaction he was sending was the one he meant to send. When Jack told him of the outside sexual activities, Rick responded immediately. It was as if a sheet of ice had been cracked. His depression melted, he became interested in sexual activity and responsive to Jack again. In fact, they had a kind of honeymoon of sex and intense feeling over a two-week period. Later it took on a lower profile as they were able to renew their commitment to each other. Jack's interest in other men disappeared promptly, to his relief.[7]

The power of sex to support intimacy, to renew a sense of well-being, and to calm childhood fears of abandonment were revived for this couple in the same way as for many heterosexual couples.

The functions of sex in marriage

When sex is available as a resource in a marriage, it operates at conscious and unconscious levels to give pleasure, to promote and renew the bond between a couple, to offer reassurance in times of stress, and to act as a healing and integrating force. In doing so, it has the power to overcome the fears within each partner which represent the irrational remnants of infancy and childhood, fears which often threaten to divide couples who wish to stay together. In sum, it aids in the maintenance of the integrative forces of the depressive position against the developmentally earlier forces of paranoid/schizoid life.[8]

But because sex is so important in these constructive and integrative ways, when it goes wrong it has enormous disruptive potential. It can be the sign of a failure in interdependency, of a failure to fill the needs which are left from earlier years, or the inability to respond to the assault of developmental changes. A husband's looking for an affair or a wife's loss of sexual interest are signs of important failures of intimacy. Lack of a sexual life exerts an additional powerful force for the dissolution of the marriage by setting new forces for disruption into action. The couple who have a basically sound relationship which is upset by a sexual problem which does not seem to stem from a problem in their shared intimacy suffers mainly from this disruptive factor. In these relatively unusual cases the therapy generally goes easily and the couple embraces the new sexual life without significant reluctance.

But for most couples, the power of sex for repair or disruption is more complex. Even after exploring the origins of their sexual failure, they will need to recommit themselves to each other for the sex to begin to help them reconnect. They will have to suspend, at least temporarily, the sense of injury and frustration previously felt at each other's hands. To the extent they are able to do so, sex can offer a tool for reconstruction. To the extent they cannot, sex will remain powerless to help.

Chapter 13
Facing the brink: Sex and separation

> . . . not only young children, it is now clear, but human beings of all ages are found to be at their happiest and to be able to deploy their talents to best advantage when they are confident that, standing behind them, there are one or more trusted persons who will come to their aid should difficulties arise. The person trusted provides a secure base from which his (or her) companion can operate. And the more trustworthy the base the more it is taken for granted; and the more it is taken for granted, unfortunately, the more likely is its importance to be overlooked and forgotten.
>
> John Bowlby, *Separation, Anxiety and Anger**

Emotional attachment to another human being is the condition in which everyone feels most secure. Falling in love is the condition of making such an attachment and the attachment itself is buoyed by the multiple experiences of refinding the loved one after short separations or of overcoming the distances which are inevitably created in the life of a couple. Loss of the loved object is the most painful of human experiences. Even to observe the ending of a relationship which has been sustained and loving is painful. The process of mourning which facilitates the healing of the wound is so distressing that it often seems as if the grieving will never end.

Mourning, as previously discussed, proceeds through a series of four overlapping phases: numbing; yearning and searching; disorganization and despair; and reorganization.[1] A person may be held up in any one of them in a pathological or incomplete grief reaction.

Loss of a spouse through death is an expectable event of old age. While it does occur in younger marriages, it is not expected. However,

140

marital separation has now become an extremely common event of young and middle-aged marriages, so common that almost half the marriages now being formed in the United States can be expected to end in divorce.[2] It is this aspect of marital loss to which we now turn.

Separation: A syndrome of catastrophic reaction

'I always thought,' a lawyer and widower told me, 'that losing my wife was the most painful experience anyone could possibly have. But since then, as a lawyer, I've seen people going through divorces. It has to be much worse. Not only do they lose each other, but the love turns to a hate which keeps on hating.'

The experience of marital separation rings unique changes on the painful but relatively straightforward pattern of loss of a spouse. When a spouse is unexpectedly confronted with the news that his husband or wife is leaving, the result is often the kind of physical and psychological panic reaction to be expected in cases of disaster and abandonment. A wife whose husband tells her he is leaving often becomes tremulous, expresses disbelief, cannot sleep or eat, and may become nauseated. Over a few days and weeks she may lose weight, sob uncontrollably, and sink quickly into a clinical depression. Although she might well feel angry, often the anger is held in abeyance or turned against herself. Suicidal thoughts are common. In the beginning, there may be an embarrassingly obsequious clinging in place of anger toward the departing spouse. There is often an inexplicable wish to be helpful, perhaps in helping the husband pack as though he were going on a business trip. A number of women who have been distant or unavailable sexually may suddenly feel desperate yearning and offer themselves sexually to their husbands almost as they go out the door, degrading themselves in an attempt to keep the husband from leaving. A part of themselves has not simply been lost, but has been violated in such a way as to question the validity of all internal security.

In the immediate situation, a person treated in this way seems to have a limited number of options. One is to denigrate himself or herself in order to try to preserve the object as ideal. The other is to denigrate the object to preserve some self-respect. Often the self-belittlement comes first, presenting the picture of aggression turned against the self which paradoxically is designed to save the self from feeling abandoned by the good internal object. Only later when the self feels it can survive alone can the previously internalized object be externalized, attacked, and hated, facilitating a detachment from it as a former part of the self. This detachment comes with great difficulty because the object was interconnected with other vital parts of the self, and because the connection had a bodily expression. Hate and active efforts to separate from the object may become an almost permanent part of the continuing psychological picture. In this case, they are a constant vigil against the traitorous object, lately so beloved. Saul Bellow's novels, *Herzog* and *Humboldt's Gift* explore the anger at the ex-wives of the protagonists and the difficulty of making significant reattachments. This hating may become so prominent that one gets the impression that a divorced patient 'loves to hate' his or her ex-spouse.

Sexuality and the fear of separation

Some patterns of deviant sexuality are designed to avoid psychological separation. They defend against a feared marital breakdown by paradoxically substituting a psychosomatic detachment. For instance, a number of patients who have been previously described (Emma Smith and Enid, chapter 7; Ron, chapter 9) withheld sex because of an encapsulated conviction of ultimate betrayal. This conviction is based on the childhood experience of either actual or threatened loss of a parent. The predicted and feared loss is prepared for by withholding the sex so the loss will be minimized. The loss is thus anticipated by sexual enactment of detachment from the object. At the same time, efforts are directed toward preventing the loss by the apparently illogical withholding of sex, in the name of protection of the spouse against the harm sex is unconsciously thought to threaten. In this last aspect, the patient treats the sex as aggressive. The harm he or she would do to the spouse by being a harmful person who would castrate her husband or by hurting the wife with an aggressive penetration is being avoided to protect the loved part of the spouse. The multi-purpose function of the defensive withholding of sex becomes so compelling for many patients that there is no undoing of this response without a painstaking reworking of each early object-related experience. These patients generally had a profoundly anxious attachment in early life with multiple threats of withdrawn approval or abandonment.

The use of sex to continue a threatened relationship

Another variant of this situation develops when someone offers sex in order to hang onto a relationship in which they are otherwise holding out. This pattern is more frequent in women and represents another wrinkle in the pattern of being hostage to one's own dependency. While the sex usually becomes lackluster and burdensome, the women continue to use their bodies to avoid being alone and frequently feel they are prostitutes. The woman's view of both her husband and herself suffers in the process. Frequently, the method of dealing with objects and of object choice which led to the compromised relationship can be seen in the therapeutic transference.

Faye, aged 35 years and in her second marriage, made a suicidal gesture and was briefly hospitalized when I was a psychiatric resident. Her first husband had been unreliable and impulsive. After he left, she impulsively married a minor business tycoon twenty years her senior with whom she formed a folie à deux. She felt denigrated but protected. She dreaded sex, but she held on and 'delivered' her body, fearing the threat of being left alone with her two small children.

Shortly after disclosing to me that she felt like a 'high class prostitute,' Faye brought me a gift of two bottles of Scotch whisky. When I inquired about her motivation, she said that her husband had bought her two cases of the Scotch despite knowing her dislike for it. She thought perhaps I could use it because I was, as she put it, 'just a student.'

When I recovered from feeling narcissistically belittled, I was able to recognize that her denigration of me represented her own internal self-denigration and struggle to feel less envious and less belittled by pulling me down with her. It recreated the oscillating interaction of her marriage in the transference. By not accepting the gift, I was able to help her understand how her own feeling of denigration impelled her to offer it to me.

Sex in a loveless marriage

A third effect on sex occurs when a spouse hangs on in a marriage despite disaffection which may even be conscious. The following example illustrates one of many possibilities.

> Mrs A was a 31-year-old childless woman who came for a consultation because she wished to leave her 42-year-old husband, although her religious and moral values forbade her. As a freshman in college she had developed a crush on him when he was her literature professor. When she became pregnant, they married although he insisted she have an abortion. He wanted no children, feeling it would interfere with his writing. As the years wore on, Mrs A felt less and less in love with him, but kept on having regular sex which she enjoyed. Recently, however, she had lost interest in sex, and then began to find it repugnant. In the consultation she asked that I offer her a way to tolerate sex and her life with her husband. Her conscience would not allow her to leave. She was unable to voice anger at his self-centeredness, although I felt it was apparent. She had long ago decided that she would never have children with him because he 'would be a bad father.' Although she could 'rationally' decide to stay with her husband and forgo parenthood, the deterioration of interest in sex and the progressive inability to become aroused indicated the shift in her emotional current. A more thoroughgoing depression followed some months later.

The threat of separation

At times, however, an acute threat of separation may have the effect of penetrating the kind of defenses discussed above. A man or woman who is about to be left may be able for the first time to feel sexually aroused. While this is part of the pattern described earlier of clinging to the object that is threatening abandonment, it may have beneficial effects. With the ultimate failure of the multi-purpose 'protective' defense, the wish for a loving attachment may find adequate expression through sexual feelings only now freed from the binding defensive habit. When a good deal of work has preceded this threat, the movement to sexual feeling may be quite solid. However, more usually the freeing up is temporary, resulting in a brief hyperfunctioning of sexuality. It represents a kind of flight into health which is like the previous denial of sex in that it is also designed to avoid abandonment. When the threat subsequently recedes, the sexual feelings also recede.

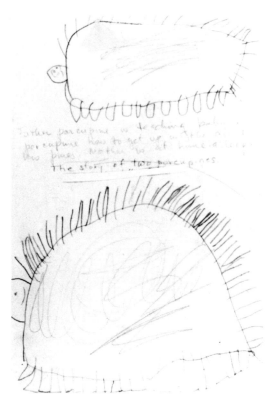

The story of two porcupines

1 The story of two porcupines. 'Father porcupine is teaching baby porcupine how to get up in the air and shoot his pines. Mother is at home asleep.' Note that the baby has some male elements (shooting *his* 'pines') typical of a first stage oedipal situation. See chapter 7 for a discussion of this aspect of oedipal development

2 below The story of two turtles. 'Father and baby turtle are going to swim together in a pond. Mother turtle is at home over the hill'

3 Wilson's picture of violence

4 Wilson's family picture

5 A 6-year-old girl's oedipal picture drawn with her father

6 The heart with hat removed shows the sexualized intent of the completed picture

7 A 10-year-old boy's picture of his divorcing parents' relationship

8 A 7-year-old boy's picture of an oedipal victory which nevertheless frightened him

SALLY

DADDY

GRANDAD

MOM

GRANDMA

AUNT JOAN

ME

9 A house is 'barning'

10 'King Kong kills some little animals because he tries to be friends
with them and they are mean to him'

11 above Gordon's
family picture

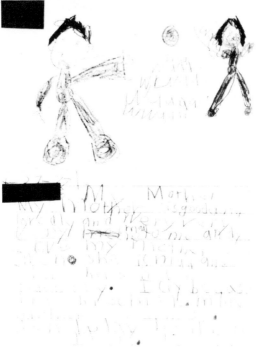

12 Gordon's
Mother's Day picture
for his mother

13 The other side of Gordon's picture

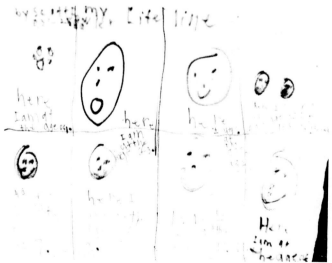

14 Gordon's life-line

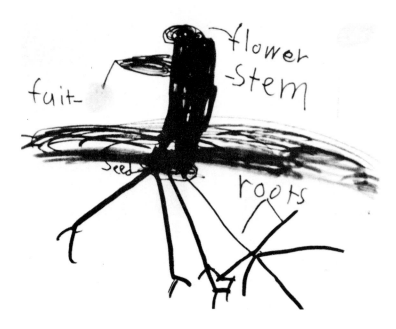

15 above A flower

16 'Popis Bay' – a picture representing both parents and the treatment transference

After separation

So far no mention has been made of the departing or threatening mate. When one partner decides to leave, he begins the separation in a more protected position, usually keeping more of his self-esteem intact. For many, the separation will have been in response to marital failures which included sexual dysfunctions and disjunctions, and sex will work more readily with new partners. For others, despite having initiated the separation, the feelings of being left alone and grieving will predominate. In the process of mourning, sexual feelings may also wither. The ability to make a new significant attachment is often impaired during mourning. Nevertheless, one defense against the pain of loss is a precipitous indiscriminate reaching out to anyone. Promiscuous sexuality, one common picture in the post-separation period, is a form of the denial of loss, a manic defense against the pain of mourning.

For the person who is left, the pain, shock and diminished self-regard are often prominent early reactions. The other side of the ambivalence may then gradually emerge with a sense of relief. For this abandoned spouse too there are varying pictures of sexual life. A previous desperate inhibition of sexual life may be released. Or an adequate sexual functioning may wither in the disappointment and grief. Or a sexualized bodily reaching out may present a manic defense to loss and hurt, perhaps leading to a later feeling of self-disgust and secondary sexual withdrawal. For some, the blow to self-esteem is so severe that bodily care and presentation of the body decline and the person treats himself or herself the way he felt treated by the spouse.

Sex after marriage: the reconnection

For many of those who are permanently separated, new attachments develop which lead toward permanent commitment. At this point anxiety sets in about whether 'this time' will be better. An increasing number of such pre-marital or recently remarried couples, feeling buffeted by one or more previous marital failures, request consultation hoping to insure that things will go differently the second time. For most of them, the 'fit' in the second marriage is better and the sex will accordingly go better. They will also have learned from the experience of defeat and loss. Even the act of asking for consultation to seek help and reassurance represents a willingness to investigate the relationship and to make reparation. Some couples, however, are compelled to repeat a neurotic interaction.

> Peter, aged 49, presented for help after the failure of three marriages. Although he had experienced intermittent premature ejaculation and impotence in all three of the previous relationships, it had only recently become crippling. In a new relationship with a woman named Gloria, he had experienced such frequent difficulty with erections and ejaculatory control that he now became aware of a massive anxiety about sex. Even in the initial consultation he was able to acknowledge that the sexual difficulty represented a growing doubt about his ability to sustain any loving relationship. A newly acute concern about harming the object of his love led to an active worry that Gloria would leave him and that he would again feel abandoned and degraded.

Children and divorce

It is not the task of this book to deal extensively with the specific effects of parental separation on children, although it must be acknowledged that an understanding of the child's reaction to any sexual matters in either his or his parents' life will be understood primarily in the context of his overall reaction to the divorce. The reader is referred to the book *Surviving the Breakup* which clarifies the specificity of the response to parental separation to the developmental stage of the child.[3] The brief comments which follow are confined to the direct effects of the parents' relationship and sexual life on the sexual development of the children.

Children will have been influenced by the parents' pattern of interaction, including sexual interaction, in the years before separation. This topic will be explored more fully in the next chapter, so here one drawing by a 10-year-old boy of his parents' relationship will suffice to make the point that his experience of his parents as a couple had been terrifying (plate 7).

Secondly, there is the child's experience of the separation itself and his interpretation of the loss of one parent in the light of his own stage of psychosexual development. This is illustrated by several examples with drawings by the children.

In the first example, an 11-year-old boy drew (plate 4) a picture of his family representing the father murdering everyone except the cat. At the time the picture was drawn, the father was living separately but was soon to return. This boy identified with his mother's sense of being abused by the father. He consequently had difficulty forming a relationship with his father even when the mother welcomed father's return, because the parents' aggressive relationship reinforced the pre-pubertal reactivation of aggression in the child. Sex and aggression became easily confused in this boy and the separation reinforced a 'murderous' meaning for sex for him.

In the second example, a 6-year-old girl whose parents had been divorced a year earlier, was seen in alternate sessions, first with her mother and then with father. She played themes of having a family whose members were too numerous to count, but some of them were allowed to leave the 'family compound.' In one session with her father she drew a picture (plate 5). In plate 6 this picture has the 'hat-penis' removed showing not only the conscious love for her father, but the seductive oedipal sexual element as well. The 'V' of the heart forms an invagination for the phallic paternal hat. The oedipal pull to father, specific in her stage of development normally, was reinforced in the repeated physical separations and reunions of the visitation pattern, impeding this girl's movement into latency.

A final example is provided by a 7-year-old boy who drew a picture (plate 8) of his family six months after the parental separation. Although he felt desperate without father and in danger of engulfment by mother, the picture pairs his sister with father whose space suit otherwise completely isolates him from life on this earth. The boy is the most adult man on the scene, paired securely with his mother. What concerned me was not that this oedipal configuration was abnormal, but that while hanging on to it, he was so desperately fearful of loss and harm because of the loss of his father in his empty oedipal victory.

Once again in this situation, the reciprocity of issues between child and parent is critical. The children are directly affected by the new sexual life of their separated parents *and* the presence of the child in turn affects the separated parents' sexual life. A single parent who is dating has a young 'chaperone' or companion who may reincarnate a parental object in being an obstacle to a new sexual life. Some single parents flaunt their renewed sexuality, as if before an impotent anti-sexual parent, while others suffer the inconvenience with varying degrees of resentment or compliance.

In turn, children live with their parent's new sexual adjustment in different ways, depending not only on the child's age and psychosexual development, but upon many other factors such as the progress of the child's mourning, the discretion the parent exercises about his sexuality, the overall nature of the new parental sexual relationships, and the security of the child's bond to each of his parents. Although the patterns vary endlessly, children may adjust relatively easily to the now relatively common situations which were unheard of a few years ago. More will be known about the vicissitudes of these adjustments as time gives more experience with them.

Although the pattern of sex leading up to and resulting from marital separation varies widely, the anxieties involved center around the reaction to lost attachments and their effects on the self. The children are affected more by the general loss than by the parent's sexual life, but if the parent resorts to a defensive isolation or promiscuity, it will have an additional effect on them. In turn, the child's own development, including the sexual component of it, will affect both his parents' relationship and their feelings during separation and reattachment.

Chapter 14
Children of parents with sexual dysfunction

> If there are quarrels between the parents or if their marriage is
> unhappy, the ground will be prepared in their children for the
> severest predisposition to a disturbance of sexual development
> or to a neurotic illness.
>
> Sigmund Freud, 'Three essays on the
theory of sexuality'*

The relationship between the sexual issues of parents and symptomatology in the rest of the family has been observed by family therapists
for the last 25 years, and referred to in the psychoanalytic and child
psychiatry literature for much longer. Freud's report of the Dora case
in 1905 is probably the first example, remarkable among many things
for the specificity of interaction between the parents' sexual blockage
and the personality development of their adolescent daughter at a
time when Dora's adolescent sexual development was prominent.[1] In
that case, flagrant sexual acting out by Dora's father, withholding by
her mother, and a series of incestuously-tinged seductions of Dora by
the husband of her father's mistress (a woman with whom she heavily
identified), resulted in sexualized symptomatology and in permanent
hysterical character disorder. Felix Deutsch's chance follow-up visits
confirm the lifelong effects of these events,[2] and his and Erik Erikson's
comments contribute much to our understanding of the transmission
of sexual symptomatology as a component of personality formation.[3]
For the rest of her life, Dora remained a shrew. Her personality – and
presumably her sexual behavior – represented a permanent record of
her rejection of her family's version of sexuality, namely disappointment
and the often futile attempts to assuage it. (Further comments on
Dora and especially her early development will be made at the end of

the chapter.)

In modern family therapy, cases present which are similar to that of Dora in that the family requests help for a child's difficulty. Frequently these reach an impasse which is only resolved when the parents are able to begin discussing a sexual problem of their own, even if this discussion goes on out of the child's hearing (as it almost always should). The sexual problems of the parents, then, are a frequent contributor or cause of family-wide dysfunction.[4]

For the child, these parents who struggle with their own difficulty are not only his current real objects, but also provide the basis for his internal objects. The central issues lived out in the sex between them are also lived out inside him. In his development, he must often solve certain problems presented to him by the parental relationship in order to get on with growing. In the process, these conflicts become internalized landmarks in his growth.

It is worth noting that the child is not a passive participant in family processes. The very issues of his development discussed in earlier chapters spur him on to involve his parents in the issues of his internal life, too. One may *balance* the picture by assigning a greater role to the parents' influence on the child than to the child's influence on the parents. In keeping with this, the role of the parents' effect on the child will be presented first in this chapter, followed by the child's effect on the life of the parents in the next chapter. However one may assign the balance of *relative* influence of the child's effect or the parents' contribution in any single case, the viewpoint of this book is not only that each is important, but that what is critical is the reciprocal interaction between them.

I would like now to describe three children of patients whose sexual dysfunctions I treated. A study of the interaction between the parents' sexual symptomatology and the children's issues as they surface during development affords an opportunity to compare the *psychosomatic link between the parents* with the one *between parent and child*. The opportunity of doing these evaluations exposed me to the impressive correlations between the issues expressed in the parents' sexual lives and those embodied in the development of their children who have ranged in age from infancy to adolescence. (Other children will be presented in a later volume.)

The first child, the youngest, is the only one of the group of such children who has been diagnosed as having a significant inborn developmental impairment.

Jack and Emma Smith (see chapter 7) came for the treatment of
Emma's aversion to intercourse and absence of orgasm by any
method.[5] Treatment was slow and difficult for her, and went
through several phases, including conjoint sex therapy, marital
therapy, and a pre-orgasmic women's group in which she did finally
achieve orgasm by masturbation. Intermittently, the Smiths used
conjoint psychotherapy to consider their relationships with their
children and their original families. In all, I worked with them for
almost four years. Emma's aversion to sex represented the
crystallization of complex issues from many sources – early religious
inhibition, hostility between her parents, and primarily problems in
her own relation to each of her own parents. To recapitulate some
of the relevant information, I will remind you that Emma's mother
was distant from her. Emma had been sent to a religious boarding
school at the age of 5. The relationship with her mother remained
one in which Emma sought attention and could never get it. In
addition, her father drank and the parents fought, and while
growing up Emma found herself each evening a willing participant in
exciting family quarrels, baiting her father and defending her
mother before her father finally staggered off to bed. There was
violence and occasional knife-brandishing. Her father sometimes
wandered through the house drunk and nude at night.

Jack's experience with his parents was similar, although less
dramatic. His parents were both children of large, poor, immigrant
families. In marriage, they had become isolated from their own
families and focused on Jack. Both had drunk heavily and became
increasingly bitter toward each other. As time passed, they had only
their religion and Jack as reasons for living. Jack's mother had a
hysterectomy after a stillbirth of a child who was delivered several
days after her amniotic sack ruptured. As far as Jack knew,
ignorance, religious tradition, and social isolation had interfered
with any sexual enjoyment his parents might have had, as these
things had in most facets of their life. At 16, he had renounced
religion and in consequence his relationship with them had withered.
He had not been able to escape home until after college, however.
Since then he had a distant and cool relationship to them. He felt
that his parents were each other's enemy, locked by circumstances in
the same house.

Although sex had been a pleasant and exciting link for Jack and
Emma before marriage, and for a year afterwards, it soon became

frightening. Emma began to have fantasies of being stabbed and thoughts of wanting to stab Jack when he penetrated her. This shift in her feelings about sex occurred just after she became pregnant with Tommy, their first child, recalling for her and Jack that they had both been only children in warring households while growing up, and had held themselves responsible for their parents' disaffection.

The pregnancy with Tommy and his birth proved to be a stress in their relationship. He was full-term, but weighed only 4½ pounds, a finicky and colicky baby who gained slowly and was a cause of anxiety. He had a milk allergy, and from the first was felt to be negativistic. During the sex therapy he came to our attention because at 18 months of age he demanded to be let into their bedroom and invaded their privacy by putting his fingers under the door when they wanted to be alone. By permitting this disruption, the parents used him to express Emma's sexual reluctance and he became an instrument to protect her from intercourse. When he was 3 years, 4 months I was asked to evaluate him for stubborn behavior, 'hyperactivity,' slow speech development and clinging.

I found Tommy to be a small, wiry, clinging, and negativistic child, one who would be difficult for any parent. In the playroom he was extremely active, darting from one activity to another, getting into everything. Walking and crawling around the room he gave an impression that he might be hanging from the tallest limb on a tree, confidently accident prone. He was below the third percentile in height and weight for his age, and was the kind of child who adjusted to new circumstances by withdrawing and becoming stubborn, and even angry. Yet he clung to his mother (who stayed with him) and told her he loved her frequently. He played immaturely and destructively with toys, using them as aggressive objects. He enjoyed knocking them down and throwing them more than playing thematically or constructively. He was almost sadistic to stuffed animals in my office. His speech was immature, and he would often refuse to use even what words he did have and turned to manipulating his mother instead. Emma reported that ordinarily at home he was frequently extremely independent at times. He would take off and go blocks away from his house. Yet he refused to stay at playmates' homes without his mother and he cried anxiously when she tried to leave him.

When Tommy was 2½ a brother had been born (conceived during

the partly successful sex therapy). Jack and Emma found this birth liberating for their sexual adjustment. They no longer felt bound by having a single and destructive child and felt released from repeating their own pattern of being only children. Tommy, however, had become more clinging and angry, alternately hitting his mother and telling her he loved her. He had been in day-care five days a week until age 3½, but on my advice he now began to attend nursery school only two mornings a week. This allowed some consolidation of his anxious attachment to Emma. He responded by becoming easier – more clinging but less negativistic with Emma, a shift I regarded as a healthy move away from his previous angry ambivalence.

Tommy has also been found to have difficulty in the acquisition of language, a fairly common problem in underweight full-term babies. This developmental aphasia cannot be attributed to parental behavior and is itself a major factor in his turning to negativistic behavior when words fail him. He is still a child who has frequent recourse to saying 'no,' to being provocative and striking out unpredictably. He prefers his father to his mother and causes disagreement between them. Yet he can be a source of loving pleasure when he is happy and relaxed. Since the evaluation, special schooling has offered remediation for the aphasic difficulty and its sequelae as well as some of the more general emotional issues in his growth.

I would now like to turn to those issues of Tommy's growth which represent the emotional inheritance from his parents. The ambivalence around closeness which stems from both Jack's and Emma's own childhood echoing the discord of both sets of parents came to a pitch during intercourse when Emma felt under attack, longed for caring, but fantasized retaliation. At the moment of hoped-for closeness, she was most frightened and was flooded with murderous fantasies. Abandonment and separation were an integral part of the conscious and unconscious preoccupation of both Jack and Emma.

Tommy has echoed these issues in his own growth. Sent out each day in his early life, he became prematurely independent or 'detached', in Bowlby's terminology. But when Emma was able to give more to him, the clinging betrayed the hunger for a more mothering relationship. They shared the fears of separation (psychologically recreating separation fears from the time Emma was sent to boarding school at age

5), a misplaced compensatory pseudo-independence, and a longing for love. His negativism and destructiveness which accompanied the emotional detachment echoed her own struggle with sadism. This aggressiveness, directly expressed by Tommy, was often out of his control. It was not so obviously out of Emma's control, and yet its indirect expression through the projection of angry impulses onto her husband felt so threatening to her own control that she had to inhibit her sexual response. In Tommy's case her inability to set limits provoked and exacerbated his aggression. In a parallel but reinforcing way, her fearful sexual withholding tended to incite Jack's anger and aggression, just the response she feared. As Emma became more open and available to Jack, and more available and limit-setting to Tommy, Tommy improved before any specific therapeutic intervention was made with him directly.

We can summarize the parallels in Tommy's development to his parents' difficulties: (1) the mother–child bond exhibits an anxious attachment, verging toward ambivalent detachment rather than a secure base, just as is the case with the sexual bond; (2) sex and aggression are confused at the core of both bonds, and in so being, trigger Tommy and Jack to strike out aggressively; (3) Emma's fear that sex will be her undoing is echoed by the fear that the child will be her undoing. In her guilt, Emma feels she deserves the 'punishment' Tommy gives her, thereby perpetuating the chain of hostile and retaliative bonds which her sexual relationship to Jack also represents.

Let us look now at another case.

I first saw Gordon Thompson at age 7. He was an appealing, well-related, articulate child, although he spoke in a babyish manner. When I saw him first it was in the family setting, with a teenaged step-brother who was in full rebellion and a step-sister who had been suicidal. I had seen Gordon's parents two years earlier for sexual dysfunction and they were now asking for help with a variety of family matters, including deterioration in their own relationship. Gordon's parents were also concerned with his difficulty, noting his immaturity, school difficulty, and trouble with peers. His teacher corroborated the immaturity in both learning capacity and peer relationships. He was easily distractable and focused on school work with difficulty. He cried frequently, and was the class scapegoat, taking teasing passively. His friends were younger girls whom he tried to protect. I thought he was also depressed and had a masochistic symbiosis with his mother and an impoverished identification with his father. He was constantly afraid of abandonment.

Let me turn to a brief picture of Mr and Mrs Thompson and then describe how Gordon embodied their issues. For both parents, this was a second marriage. Mr Thompson had originally come to us with secondary impotence at age 41. A transient impotence had been part of the Thompsons' early pre-marital sexual history nine years before, but it cleared up with Mrs Thompson's gentle understanding and support. It had next recurred four years ago sporadically at first, but gradually increasing. It was due to a combination of physically-based neuro-vascular erectile difficulty due to Mr Thompson's diabetes mellitus which he had had since the age of 21, and a difficult emotional situation between the Thompsons. He was a depressed, passive man. She was depressed too, but much more angry. She interpreted her husband's increasing impotence as a sign of diminished love for her. She thought his occasional masturbation might imply 'homosexuality.'

Mrs Thompson had been the youngest and favorite of five children. Between the ages of 6 and 8 she slept in the same bed with her father without any overt sexual activity. When she was 8, he developed cancer. She nursed him through the last two years of his lingering illness until he died when she was 12. At about the time of his death, Mrs Thompson guiltily discovered masturbation. She remembered thinking, 'My mother would kill me if she knew.' She gave it up a year later and had no sex beyond kissing until her first marriage at 19. Sex had been pleasant in that marriage, including her ability to have orgasms, but the marriage was generally unsatisfactory and she began an affair with Mr Thompson five years later, leading to her divorce and remarriage.

Mr Thompson was raised by his mother with whom he slept until the age of 11. He felt she had been controlling and overwhelming. His father was away 'in the Navy' during these years. When he returned when Mr Thompson was 14, he was alcoholic. Father became the family domestic while Mr Thompson's mother continued to work to support the family. Mr Thompson remembered an uncle fondling him when he was 8. At 12, he had his first ejaculation while engaged in mutual masturbation with an older boy. His first marriage was to an impulsive woman whose wish was for independence and whose values eventually led her away from him. Their sexual life had been satisfactory, but infrequent. He, too, was still

married when he began the affair with his second wife, but felt the
first marriage was essentially over.

The first sexual encounter between the Thompsons ended when
Mr Thompson experienced impotence. During three months in
which Mrs Thompson was caring and kind, he overcame the
impotence, which he felt was due to anxiety and guilt. Gordon was
conceived two years later, soon after their marriage. When Gordon
was 2, Mr Thompson began to experience impotence again on some
occasions. But he also began to withdraw emotionally, feeling now
that his wife's sexual initiatives were too aggressive. He became
depressed and obtained some brief psychotherapy. The sex became
less and less frequent. Mrs Thompson began to consider leaving her
husband over the sexual difficulty, but said that she had stayed
because 'my husband would kill himself if I left.' The Thompsons
asked for sex therapy when Gordon was 5. On the same day that
Mr Thompson wrote a letter to me asking for an appointment,
Gordon had a cystoscopy for enuresis.

The sex therapy for Mr and Mrs Thompson was successful
although tenuously so. Despite the diagnosis of impaired erectile
function secondary to the diabetes, Mr and Mrs Thompson worked
together to use the considerable function which was still preserved
to their shared benefit. But two years later things had deteriorated
seriously between them. Mrs Thompson was no longer willing to
be so patient and in addition there were problems with Mr
Thompson's older children and worries about Gordon as well. Let us
now return our focus to Gordon.

Gordon had a history of early daily separations from his mother
who was working. His clinging and generally anxious appearance
seemed to stem from this. In the family meetings in which I first
saw him, he was extremely empathetic for the suffering of his
step-brother. He was sad and frequently attempted to channel
parental anger onto himself, becoming the victim himself to spare a
parent or sibling. In the first session he drew a picture (plate 9)
which he titled 'A house is barning [sic].' Indeed, he felt it was
burning.

I saw him for an individual evaluation a few weeks later. He was
a sad little boy, but related well and talked easily. He exhibited
remarkable sexual confusion, unable to distinguish a toy bull from
a cow although he knew the cow's udder was a 'milk thing.' He said
a baby colt was 'a helpless lamb.' He told me a story about a monster

who was named after a little boy who scared the boy's family by invading their house. He then told me two 'King Kong' stories.

King Kong had a monster which he killed because he was mean to it. (It was unclear who was mean to whom.) However, the monster was also shot by men. A beautiful lady came to see King Kong. She was sent by the men and she did not see the men shoot the monster. King Kong got the lady but the men captured him because he had the lady. They brought him to town and showed him off. He was frightened. He broke his chains, climbed the building and was killed by the men.

In the second story (plate 10),

King Kong kills some *little* animals because he tries to be friends with them. He kills them because they are mean to him.

These stories illustrate the fear of aggression toward his objects and of their retaliation. He also fears the outcome of the oedipal situation. One experimental alternative is that he kills those he loves. The other is passive defeat for himself as the victimized monster.

In a picture he drew at my request (plate 11) Gordon amplifies the oedipal dilemma. Gordon and his father are together, and both have the bent 'penis-arm.' But Gordon also identifies with his mother who is a minor figure in the far corner (as indicated by the sharing of a color in the picture of himself and his mother). There is both the negative oedipal constellation in the tie to father, and a picture of sado-masochistic inadequacy as a positive oedipal solution. This second aspect is shown more clearly in the next pictures (plates 12 and 13), a school drawing presented to his mother on Mother's Day. The caption says:

My mother is good and lovedly and very very (mean) mad to me and you. I love my mother wen she is mad and I love her so much. My mother loves me too. Wen I play ball with her I cry. Because she crys. My mother is cry right now. At work.

It is worth noting that in the second picture, his mother has no arms, an indication of their shared helplessness to mitigate the depression.

Psychological testing elaborated further on Gordon's inadequate

integrative ego skills. There too he was preoccupied with his
relationship with his mother, with monsters, and with the threats
of being eaten. At one point he synthesized these themes about the
maternal introject when he said 'When you open a gate, a "*moster*"
[sic] comes out and it could kill you.' He was unable to defend
himself from the anger he saw in the frustrating mother/monster
object, and he had a preoccupying fear of being consumed by the
'moster' and by his own deflected rage at it.

Although Gordon's parents were themselves unable to regain
improvement in their relapsed sexual dysfunction, Gordon did
improve in individual therapy. Early in treatment he joined forces
with me in a male partnership (the negative oedipal tie) and moved
toward a more active, masculine identification. We were military
collaborators whose armies began by fighting against each other but
then joined forces. Then I was a helicopter pilot who refueled his
jet-pack for solo flight. As he became more independent, he could
explore his penchant for regression. On his eighth birthday, he
drew a life-line (plate 14) through which he told me that life was
good for babies, that it was best at 5 when he had friends, but
looked bad at 7, 8, and 9. Nevertheless his improvement continued.
In a later picture he drew a flowering of sexual functioning (plate
15) and toward the end of treatment (plate 16) a picture of 'Popis
Bay' (Porpoise Bay), a pair of islands representing both parents
with both sharks (a reference to my name and to me as dangerous)
and popises (loving fathers) in the water. This picture represents a
more active willingness to explore the badly split relationship
between his parents and his own relationship to each of them.

In this family, the parental sexual dysfunction represents the father's
passive, depressed response to anxiety and mother's feeling that she was
confirmed as a monster, a nurse whose charge is later to die. Gordon's
development incorporated the passive helplessness in identification with
his father. The castration anxiety is solved by a surrender to the
aggressive mother in a sado-masochistic symbiosis with her. Even the
phallic assertiveness of his enuresis formed a sado-masochistic bond
with her through her anger in changing his sheets. His growth embodied
the same kind of anxious attachment and defensive solutions as did the
failed sexuality of the parents. When he moved substantially toward a
more active masculine identification, his parents felt treatment should
end.

The final example is an adolescent whose issues with her parents and in her own development mirrored years of her parents' difficulty.

> Linda L, the youngest of five children of an admiral and his wife (described in chapter 7), was referred at age 15 by her parents because she seemed to be on the verge of plunging into sex. While not approving, they agreed that she needed some counseling on birth control. She was reluctant to discuss her situation but did say that she was indeed considering having sex with an older man who shared her interest in sailing. Her parents had indulged her nautical bent by buying her a boat, but she resented their wish that she would spend more time with them and less on the water. She went on to complain bitterly about her mother's nagging and depending so heavily on Linda that the girl felt she must get away. The social life around the yacht club offered the escape. Linda saw her father as better: 'He's lovely, but he's so busy. And he gets dragged down by my mother's depression and by her nagging him all the time.' Linda was depressed too, and wished to use sex as a solution to feeling pressured by her mother. Her turning to sex had nothing to do with enjoying it, as it was too conflictual for her. It had to do instead with giving a man something she thought was an inevitable part of the bargain. In addition, she began to toy with the thought of leaving Washington and going to school back in California where the family had been stationed until three years earlier, partly to return to a place she considered home and which the whole family missed, and partly to escape from her mother. Linda was an underachieving student, a self-indulgent, mildly self-destructive and depressed girl who tolerated talking to me, but did not like it much, and made that clear with a slight but persistent disdain.
>
> Her parents came for a consultation about how to deal with her, but within two meetings they divulged that Mrs L also felt chronically lonely and depressed, left alone while her husband had pursued his successful career. She and Linda had shared this depression for their first year in Washington. As Linda grew up and made friends, Mrs L was left even more alone. A discussion with the parents about sexuality in adolescence led Mrs L to say, reservedly at first, that their own sex life had never been good. Soon the story detailed in chapter 7 tumbled out. In brief she had married Admiral L despite having no sexual feelings for him, having spent such feelings on artistic teachers in her youth while she was resentfully under her

mother's eye, trapped into supporting her. Her mixed resentment for and loyalty to her mother had condensed into an ambivalence very like what Linda now felt toward her.

Admiral L, although successful and assertive in the military, had been sexually very shy, despite having libertine parents who lived in an active sexual threesome which included an old friend of his mother. His father had told him that 'adopting' one of his mother's friends into the family (to form the parental threesome) had deepened their sexual life. But there had been apparent strain too, as evidenced by his parents' guilty relief when the friend died. It was remarkable that, knowing these facts even as a boy, Admiral L was sexually so shy. He felt his wife loved him, and had therefore never complained about her lack of arousal, although he had always been aware of it. He had suffered both premature ejaculation, and in more recent years a progressive inability to ejaculate during intercourse.

For the Ls, the difficulty with the sexual aspect of their intimacy came into focus as Linda, the last child of their large family, began to think about leaving home. Mrs L began to face being alone with a husband who was chosen as a reliable caretaker but who was not a 'sensuous and emotional artist.' Her sexual reserve represented a compromise aimed at keeping her from being left as her mother had been, the fate of a woman who married for sensual love. But her resentment toward her mother then continued in the mixture of gratitude and resentment toward her husband. When she turned instead to her children for companionship and support, she again set the cycle of resentment in motion. Admiral L, despite his nautical air, staked his self-esteem on being gentle and caring at home. He was all too willing to forgo sexual satisfaction, perhaps because sex had so clearly strained his own mother. His chief sexual fantasy was of being tied and whipped by his wife, something she disliked hearing about. Picking a woman apparently like his mother he did not threaten her - except that a covert oedipal triangle was established with Linda who regarded her father more warmly than her mother did. It was this unconscious oedipal configuration which recreated the family constellation of 'a man and two women' in which both Admiral and Mrs L had grown up and from which both sought to escape.

Linda's wish to find a sexual relationship with a man when her parents had denied themselves an actively satisfying sexual life, represented the enactment through her of their own unconscious wishes for an active sexual life which they had projected onto her. But their reactions to her budding sexuality intensified their loneliness with each other. At the same time, it expressed Linda's wish to escape from being the source of both solace and discord for them. In this guilty bind Linda grew angrier at her mother, echoing her mother's unconscious anger and resentment at her own mother. This was finally clearly replayed in the mother's treatment transference outlined in chapter 7 when Mrs L turned angrily on the female co-therapist who was urging her to tolerate some discomfort in the service of cultivating buried sexual feelings and said, in effect, 'You are a hateful and insensitive woman who could never understand. I must get away from you.'

Therapy for this couple's sexual dysfunction began to fail most dramatically at the same time that Linda finally decided to go away to school, deserting her parents. They thought the move useful for her, but they unconsciously considered Linda to be a reincarnation of the parent-figures who had previously abandoned them. Linda's negativism left them battered and defeated, just as Mrs L's self-protective sexual negativism left their attempts at closeness defeated.

Linda illustrates something frequently seen in teenagers: the use of sexual acting out both to relive the family theme and at the same time to escape the family oppression. Her idealization of her father spurred the finding of an older man to care for her and extricate her. Her mother used the memory of the same kind of idealized relationship to denigrate the actual relationship with her husband, employing a memory to avoid an actual sexual relationship. Negativism, a prominent feature in Mrs L's sexual life and in much of her emotional life, became a major feature of Linda's life, including her refusals to share emotional issues with her mother, to work in school, and to be a patient in therapy. The frustrated search of each member of this family for love and caring left Linda trying to use sex to get what had escaped her parents for many years – a warm and mutual relationship which would compensate for earlier frustrations. Her bitterness about the family echoed her mother's despair about feeling alone. That sex was an area wherein this was particularly felt created a strong bond between daughter and mother. Unfortunately, it was a bond of rivalry about which of them would escape depression. The shared family assumption was that one person's escape from depression was always at her mother's expense. Linda was determined it would not be she who bore the expense, but it seems likely that when she herself becomes a mother, she also will struggle with the same internalized assumption.

Discussion

These three children, of widely different ages, all illustrate the way the child's difficulties in development echo the parental ambivalence which is also carried in the sexual disturbance. From the parents' side, the difficulty each person separately carried into the marriage is expressed both in the sexual difficulty and in his or her relationship to the child. There are many children who do relatively well, even normally, despite the parents' sexual difficulty. I have heard about children of patients in sex therapy who sound essentially normal. At least they do not present symptoms which their parents judge to require evaluation, even if they do have to struggle. Other children like these three are more affected by the parental difficulty, but the parents' denial does not allow evaluation or intervention. Having said that, let me list some theoretical points which are illustrated by the children who have been evaluated.

1   *The parental sexual dysfunction* per se *is not usually the cause of a given child's developmental pathology* except in those cases in which the parental boundaries and boundary-setting functions are so bad that there is actual sexual acting out – that is, real instead of symbolic incest. (See the examples and discussion in chapter 8.)

2   *The sexual failure may well be a cause of marital disruption which is the cause of family-wide and child-specific difficulty*, as in the cases of Gordon and Linda.

3   Even where there is no causal connection, *there is a striking similarity in these two central areas of*:
    (a) *the sexual interaction between the parents*; and
    (b) *the child's tie to his parents as illustrated during the course of his growth*. This occurs because *both the parents' sexual interaction and the development of their child bring to the light of the external world issues previously obscured in the shadows of the parents' inner world*.
    In these children, both express the same issue. Sometimes different parts of the parents' inner worlds are expressed by these two

vehicles, but more often, *there will be considerable overlap and sometimes even virtual congruence.* These will be the most symptomatic children in the families of dysfunctional parents. In these cases, the parents' genital form of intimacy becomes a 'screen' for the playing out of earlier abandonment and unmet dependency issues which have been carried forward. Genital sex is therefore taken over by pre-genital issues. In the same way, child caring and rearing is also subverted to these needs.

4 *The child's version of internal objects stems from and therefore parallels both his parents' attachment to each other and their individual relationships to him.* (This is the same point made in the chapter on the origin of the dysfunctions for the previous adult generation. How these two factors relate is, in practice, extremely complex, reflecting factors of multiple determination and over-determination.)[6]

The child struggles at times with the rift or tension between his parents, and at times with the tensions between one of them and himself, often at that moment buoyed up by a balance in which the other parent is supportive at that moment. Varying and rival forces in the family and in the phase of development at the moment emphasize some aspects more than others.

The family as a single psychic entity

The delinquency of adolescents speaks for hidden wishes and conflicts in a family which behaves

> as if it were a single psychic entity, with derivatives of drive and functions of superego dispersed among different family members.[7]

Tommy, Gordon, and Linda are chosen and self-selected to be bell-wether children for their parents' struggle, while other children in the families were sheltered from having to live out the anxieties. In these examples we can see with some specificity the parallels of symptom transmission into the parental sexual life and into the child's development.[8] It is not only, as Zinner and Shapiro note, that the child expresses otherwise silent drive and superego conflicts. *His symptomatology gains power and is sustained because the sexual issues are being expressed through it. In this way, the child's pathology is really a gratification of both sexual needs and dependency needs in the parents' interaction. A conflict may have been dead-ended in the parents' failure to achieve physical intimacy, but its force turns energetically to expression through the child's symptoms.* It is through the child's struggle that the parental block is expressed to the outside world. Both the sexual block and the child's behavior express the same wishes and frustrations, large components of which are not so much unconscious in themselves as unconsciously but consistently denied.

We can bring this aspect of the discussion full circle by returning to Erikson's discussion of Freud's Dora.[9] He pointed out that when Dora brought Freud her story, she asked of him acknowledgement of historical truth – a fidelity to reliability and accuracy, which would have contrasted to the multiple infidelities her family committed sexually as well as to her personally. Failing to get Freud to help her identify with a quality of *fidelity*, her identifications solidified and became the negativistic ones of 'a repulsive hysteric' and 'a famous patient.'[10] Linda's adolescent struggles, bitter and negativistic as they were, were not so different. A crucial point to be made about Dora is that Freud was not sufficiently aware of her early issues, *primarily with her mother*, which set the stage for the kind of interactions he saw in Dora's adolescence. By the time puberty set in, Dora had already had an early history with her mother which left her hungry for an attachment. She turned to the woman who was father's mistress to fill the void in mothering, feeling dislike for her own mother. This impoverished relationship with mother left her vulnerable for the family drama and the feelings of abuse and rejection she experienced in adolescence.

In the cases reported here, too, the children's symptoms and fears speak a faithful language of fears and worries, just as their parents' sexual symptoms – paradoxically even the sexual infidelities themselves – speak faithfully of a level of anxiety, fright, and sometimes terror about their own childhoods. A review of those anxieties which date from childhood is relevant to the cases discussed.

Developmental issues

Separation anxiety and the growth of attachment

Separation anxiety is a major factor in the issues shared between the parents' sexual life and the children's development. Bowlby's model of attachment and separation[11] is a useful tool for understanding the parallels. You will remember from chapter 3 that his continuum runs:

Secure attachment – the outcome of adequate early contact with mother.

Anxious attachment – the bond has been compromised by uncertainty, threats, or actual separations.

Detachment – the child has surrendered the tie to the primary object and now has difficulty attaching at all.

This series outlines the progressive decline of a trusting bond to mother and family in the first three to five years and in the continuation of the issues of attachment afterwards. Children with issues arising from the early stages of development grow up with trouble trusting the object, a problem at the foundation of the bond between parent and child and between parental partners. This may be caused by a strained or a synchronous mother–infant interaction, caused by a temperamental mismatch or overt medical complication. It may also be caused by distant, inconsistent, anxious, or otherwise troubled mothering. Tommy demonstrates this detachment graphically. He partly offers a temperamental, medically-based mismatch. But that was only part of the true picture. His mother's anxiety about separation from and invasion by her husband was the central theme in her sexual withholding as it was in her life with her parents, including the actual 'abandonment' by her parents when she was 5 (actually they sent her away). Tommy's clinging to his mother represents the anxious component of his attachment. In addition, under stress he moves toward detachment from her. When he does come back toward the attachment, it is often with anxiety and danger toward his objects. With the eventual steadying of the parental relationship, he is able to settle and to become more attached and less anxious.

Gordon represents a less severe example. Anxious as he is, he never moves toward emotional detachment. The bond with his mother is instead anxiously over-close. For all the aggressively-tinged symbiosis, he is a child who retains the capacity to relate warmly. Still, anxiety about harm and abandonment run through the early relationships to both parents, setting the stage for skewed oedipal development later as well.

Control of the object

Along with the separation and attachment anxiety, but differentiated from them, is the anxiety about controlling the love object, hoping and working to maneuver it into a position to satisfy needs both in fantasy and in reality. Mrs L and Mrs Thompson have invested heavily in controlling the other person to avoid both engulfment and the threat of abandonment. Mrs L keeps her husband at a sexual distance to keep from being controlled or submerged by the object, while trying to stay close to Linda for comfort. At the same time, the child's behavior is often controlling against the same threats. The quality of the controlling and the intensity of the dread behind it so closely parallels that of the parents that many of the children will be 'marked' to speak again for these characteristics in the next generation of the family.

The fate of aggression

Linda and her mother play out a new generational version of the same aggressive and competitive battle that the mother's sexual withholding represents in the marriage. Both use aggression in boundary-setting. Mrs L does so partly to shield her husband from her own assault and fury, here stemming from the fear of killing him off as her mother did her father. When Linda has a closer relationship to her own father than her mother does to him, the bitterness of the situation is not containable. Linda's struggle to cut herself off from her mother and to get rid of her exposes the two of them to the same aggression which Mrs L felt toward her own mother. This struggle had been quietly but definitely bound in the sex for years, only to escape and spring to life with Linda's adolescence, an example of the way the adolescent development of a child can revitalize a latent conflict in one or both parents. More will be said of this aspect in the next chapter.

Tommy, Gordon, and their mothers have bonds which are also the result of a sexualized aggression. The anger and lust between child and mother expresses the continuing fear that harm may come out of a primary bond. Eventually, aggression comes to form the foundation of the bond. This kind of case helps to explain the frequency of finding significant sado-masochistic elements in the relationships between children and their parents when the child's disturbance is related to a parental dysfunction.

The oedipal issues

Each of these children is an overt example of the child as a direct toxic threat to the ailing parental relationship, in Tommy's case even before he was himself old enough to be oedipal in the genital sense. The unresolved issues at the oedipal level may be rekindled for the parents by the fact that a rival appears on the scene even before a specific assault occurs. But just as Mr Thompson was displaced by Gordon's role in Mrs Thompson's life, Jack Smith was shut out by Tommy's birth. For such parents, the pre-oedipal displacement means that when the oedipal assault does come, it further stirs up troubled waters. The oedipal situation develops in the light of what has gone before. In the L family and the Thompson family, both parents used their child as a transference for an oedipal object of their own. Such a formulation emphasizes that oedipal issues are present almost from the beginning, even in 'oral' and 'anal' stages. While Melanie Klein described the early oedipal stages which are relevant here,[12] one can also refer to the more traditional position which acknowledges early forms of triangular issues which simply are not the focus as yet in pre-oedipal development.

The sexual life of the couple and the child's growth both give expression to the vicissitudes of the object relations life for each of the family members. The internalized object relations of the parents – central, libidinal, and anti-libidinal – are lived out in their sexual life as well as in their relation to the children. What was said in the beginning of this chapter bears restatement: For the child, *these parents are his internal objects in the making, as well as his current real objects. The central issues lived out in sex between them are also lived out inside him.* If conflict persists, the road to his further development has to travel through it. It thus becomes an internal landmark of his development. Whether he can safely find a route around and still progress as he should, or whether the obstacle constitutes a dead-end for him in one or another line of development will depend on complex factors.

For instance, mastery and ability to sublimate remained significantly blocked for each of these three children, even after intervention. The two younger children were referred because of these blocks. But the third child, Linda, also has a marked potential for a deficit in her own sexual and emotional life, just as her parents' sexual blockage continued to interfere with their lives together.

While the parents' sex and the child's growth are never completely congruent, there are enough parallels that we may often regard the child as giving graphic representation to the parents' sexual relationship in a continuing sense, extending from the moment of conception, to pervade much of the growth into adulthood. In fact, the influence often extends even from there, forming the context for the generations which follow.

A treatment predicament

Cases such as the ones presented in this chapter often provide the family-oriented therapist with a dilemma about where to intervene first or with most emphasis. It is not always possible to offer such a family everything it needs comprehensively. At times a decision to focus on the parents at one stage may provide some relief but not enough for the child, but a premature focus on the child would have provided a distraction from work with parents which seems to take precedence. These complex questions raised by the attempt to consider the child and adult sides of a reciprocal interaction are matters of more moment than passing intellectual curiosity. The answers to them have a central place in the development of a strategy of intervention. This aspect of the child–adult interrelationship will be addressed in the consideration of treatment issues in the next volume.

Chapter 15
The effects of the child's development on parental sexuality

Not only is a child's growth through life affected by his parents' sexual and marital relationship, but each stage of his development raises new issues for them. The fact of his own evolution places him in a dynamically changing relationship to his parents and to their sexuality. The child is acted upon by his parents, but equally they are acted upon by him, at first by a biological sequence of events, but increasingly by a more uniquely personal psychological interaction whose mode is determined both by the child's developmental stage and by the parents' unique adjustment to those issues during their own childhood. Therese Benedek has pointed out that even an infant is not acting only in imitation of his parents. They imitate him and are taught by him too.[1]

So it is throughout the duration of the child's growth. The child is reactive to his parents, and they are also reactive to him. The experience of living with their child changes them at each new stage. There are some generalizable characteristics of each stage, but it is equally true that some of the impact of the child is specific to his personality.[2] At each stage, some of the reactions will stem from surface phenomena, the physical and practical changes wrought by the new situation on the couple. And some will stem from psychological aspects, among the most important of which will be unconscious phenomena. The child's impact may be experienced chiefly by one of his parents or may be shared by both in a way which either disturbs or corrects a previous balance in object life.

The relationship of the child to the parents' sexual life begins in an obvious way before and during conception, when the child is only a hope (or fear) in the fantasies of the parents. Pregnancy is the first of many events which brings a couple into a developmental crisis. As they work through this, earlier crises and their solutions will be revived for reworking. This chapter will look at the way major landmarks in a child's normal growth act as stressors on the parental sexual relationship.

Conception and birth

The conception and birth of the child are well-documented object relations crises for the parents.[3] The decision or lack of one around conception represents one of the major turning points of adult life. Sexual life may be severely disrupted by a sense of urgency or a regimentation in attempting a speedy pregnancy in a couple who want a child. In a healthy marriage, however, there prevails a joyful sense of purpose in becoming generative. This, of course, can give added pleasure to the sexual life of a reasonably happy couple in a way which will be echoed later in the association between a loved child and their sexual life.

A couple, once they have knowingly conceived, can never go back to being fully non-parents, even if they never have a live child. Becoming a potential parent changes them in certain ways. For instance, ambivalence around conception or fear of having children taints sexual feeling. This occurs frequently in unplanned adolescent pregnancies, but it may occur even in planned adult ones if the idea of the child-to-be begins to haunt either of the parents.

> In the case of Emma Smith (chapters 7 and 14) her enjoyment of sex changed soon after conception. Although her pregnancy was planned and wanted, neither she nor her husband expected that the specter of her own painful position within her family of origin would be revived. After conceiving, the experience of being an only child who was blamed and felt responsible for her own parents' unloving marriage haunted her. Not that she made a conscious connection. She simply began to feel that her husband would stab her in intercourse. It was only in therapy that she uncovered the symbolic connection to her own family. Her husband's family experience of being an only child whose parents had an unloving marriage meant that he too shared her unspoken anxiety and unknowingly reinforced her position.

In this case it was the unconscious impact of conception which began to haunt the Smiths even during the earliest stages of pregnancy, before most physiological change occurred. In other cases, the symbolic meaning of the new child will be more immediately mixed with the hormonal and physiological changes of pregnancy.

The studies of Bibring and her co-workers[4] document the parental internal struggles during pregnancy. Noting that disequilibrium is normal, Wenner[5] found that pregnancy was not responded to as a crisis with regression by women who had achieved a state of mature independence. Jessner notes that at the time of the first pregnancy a transition from romantic to marital love becomes imperative, with the couple valuing the woman's motherliness and the father's self-realization in parenthood.[6] Psychologically, pregnancy initiates the parental process. The woman becomes a mother and her changes trigger the process in which the man becomes a father. The shifts in the relationship of the woman to her own internalized mother and to her actual mother will set the stage for her newly developing view of herself. Through the period of gestation the husband and wife will have to cope with a powerful mixture of physiological and psychological issues.

The woman has to cope with bodily changes which signal her movement toward being a mother. At first these are just sensations – nausea, fatigue, weepiness – that may make her feel a stranger to herself. Later, as more visible changes in body shape have to be assimilated, the woman moves from a view of herself as a sexually attractive, non-pregnant female to that of a pregnant female, possibly not attractive. At the same time, her husband has to shift his attachment to her to include a delight in her motherliness, sometimes difficult for him if he is reminded of rage and disgust at his own pregnant mother or if his wife is vehemently attacking her own new image. Her disgust may be based on a dislike of feeling fat, with depression at the loss of her figure. This may recall the loss of the boyish pre-pubescent figure as adolescent changes occurred, changes which were longed for but whose implications may have been feared.

Just so the pregnant state. These psychological difficulties add to the physical discomforts to produce a relative decrease in frequency or involvement in intercourse which tends to confirm the fear. Envy of the husband's continued strength and freedom can lead to hostility against him and against his offspring, which may be experienced as a fear of harming the baby by intercourse. At this point, some husbands withdraw emotionally or seek affairs.

At the same time, the wife may seem withdrawn from her husband as she becomes increasingly introspective, her focus drawn by the relationship to the foetus within her. Paradoxically, she is also reaching out and becoming more dependent on others, so it is now critical that he be able to stand by and support her, providing an envelope for her new preoccupation. The future mother must now adjust to the intrusion of another being in her body, learning to accept it as part of herself. After the foetal movements are felt, she then has to accept it as being another person, part of her that is yet separate from her. A physical representation of a love object becomes an internal object from which she has to separate, all in advance of the real relationship. Work done at this stage prepares the husband and wife to accept the 'intruder on their romantic bliss,' in Jessner's words, as a welcome addition to their married joy in having a family. As they move to their new identities as parents, the inner object relations with their own parents come up for review and reworking, a process that will continue constantly over the years as the children move through each developmental stage.

Masters and Johnson have outlined the physiologic changes in sexual response in pregnancy and the post-partum period.[7] Although there is a wide variety of responses to pregnancy, generally the frequency of sexual intercourse decreases.[8] One factor in this decrease is often the potential fear of causing miscarriage which a couple may feel, either if the husband is concerned about his own potential for being a harmful object, or if the couple has been left feeling that there is a medical potential for danger.[9]

The range of maternal contextual feelings may run the gamut in pregnancy from those of a woman who feels she has become much more creative or erotic to one who feels primarily burdened, limited, and shackled.[10] Similarly, the husband's feelings may range from a proudly enhanced potency and generativity to a feeling of being excluded from his wife's body and maternal care.

Irwin, a young man described previously (chapters 9, 10, and 12), had great ambivalence in moving toward marriage, afraid that he would relapse into depending on his wife to take care of him. Having successfully negotiated this decision, however, he and his wife attempted immediately to conceive. When they were successful, he initially was proud and confident, identifying with his own father as a potent husband. During the whole course of their relationship, the couple had had daily intercourse. But now as his wife became physically uncomfortable and gradually lost interest in sex late in the second trimester, Irwin felt increasingly excluded. In therapy he discovered that the deprivation revived memories of being excluded by his mother as she had other children and had less time for him. The foetus began to stand for a rival sibling and the decline in his wife's sexual interest was proof of his diminished importance.

With the many variations in physiological and psychological response, many couples may lose the ability to communicate about their mutual needs and frustrations. Because the impact of this period is so important, once off the track in this way, some couples may never recover.

The impact of the infant on the parents' sexual life

Masters and Johnson's study of post-partum sexual physiology of six women indicated a rapid return to normal (six to twelve weeks), even for women who nursed. However, many women may still be less available or comfortable sexually. Those who nurse for extended periods (six to nine months) usually experience lessened lubrication.[11] An episiotomy generally done on primiparous mothers may increase the wife's discomfort when coitus is first resumed. Many couples also experience the mother's preoccupation with the infant as a bond whose strength predominates temporarily over the couple's own bond. The baby who was a narcissistic extension of the mother within her body continues in that role in the earliest weeks. The realignment of forces as the mother falls in love with the baby in her state of 'primary maternal preoccupation,'[12] borrows against a margin of strength from the couple's prior bond.

In addition, some nursing mothers feel a sexual excitement during the nursing process. This may or may not satisfy the mother's own sexual interests and it may stir up jealousy in the husband, especially if he feels he has lost his wife's 'mothering' and in the process has been replaced as her sexual partner as well. Usually, however, the father is also caught up in an 'engrossment' of his own with the infant as he forms his own bond to it. In fact, some fathers become so preoccupied they tend to shut out their wives and function as if they were the mothers.[13]

There is nearly always also some sense of loss of the exclusivity of their previous dyadic attachment. Often there will be a sense of *some* grieving and anxiety even if the couple is predominantly glad to have a child. This is true because it is the nature of all 'psycho-social transitions' that an old familiar world must be partially lost in order to adjust to a new one.[14] As the old internal world is lost, some form of reaction to that loss occurs, whether or not it is consciously mourned. Despite a couple's perception of pregnancy as a happy occurrence, the successful mourning and grieving of the loss of the previously exclusive bond is a necessary prelude which allows the couple to move into a new world in which sharing mutual concern for the baby can potentially multiply the strength of their own attachment. This process once begun will help to shield them from some of the unexpected negative impact of the child's growth. Meanwhile, the husband's sense of displacement from the care of his wife has both a normal component and many exaggerated varieties. A history of early or prolonged separation will also contribute to an increased vulnerability in this area.

The hormonal and physiological shifts and sense of loss in the mother may also predispose her to post-partum depression which may linger as a more profound depression. Some new mothers are preoccupied with a sense of overwhelming responsibility in taking care of their infant. The late nights, the new duties, or the seemingly endless crying of a newborn overwhelm many a well-prepared young mother. If support is not available to help her past this stage or if ordinarily adequate amounts of support are not felt to be enough, she may seem to sink beneath the burden of her new role. In these cases, the sexual life of the couple will probably also atrophy.

The newborn also provides many opportunities for a couple, delivering the parents from their own childlessness into their new life as parents, beginning the process of bringing them up. In practical terms, the infant will interfere to some extent in any unfettered sexual life they had previously enjoyed, but beyond that the parents may use the child as an opportunity to externalize their sexual difficulty. Such a use of the infant for persistent sexual defense can begin a serious inroad on the strength of the marital bond. However, the infant does also offer an opportunity for multiplying the parents' joy as recreated in him.

Parenting during separation-individuation

The strain on the parents' sexual life during the early months comes during the formation of the symbiotic attachment between mother and child. But for the next two or three years, the child is progressively separating from the exclusiveness of that bond. Toilet training, night fright, wakings, wet beds, angling to get into the parents' bed, are all part of the landscape. Mothers may be longing for some relief at the end of the day, while fathers may seek to escape altogether. As we have seen, the predominant theme for the child through this period is control of access to the object and control of the relationship to it. The 'terrible twos' can leave a battered mother, while a judgmental father may feel his wife is not handling the child well. Control struggles between the parents over the child may now intervene, bringing into prominence elements of aggression and rejection.

> One mother was able to enjoy the first year with her first daughter,
> but when the girl began to say 'no' and fight for control, it revived
> the sense of battling for her own self-esteem against her own mother.
> Not only did the relationship deteriorate, but her husband's
> judgment of her for 'mistreating' her daughter invaded their previous
> sense of trust. Feeling that she had to defend herself against his
> accusations, she withdrew in many ways, including sexually.

The birth of a second child

For some mothers who have had poor relationships with their first children, the birth of a second child may restore a sense of well-being, both generally and sexually. Mothers who were still battling their first-born children felt an unexpected sense of relief and well-being at the births of the second. In one of these cases the second child was not planned, was ambivalently expected and was a daughter like the first child. Nevertheless, with this daughter's birth, everything in the family improved, including the mother's relationship to her first child *and* her sexual relationship to her husband. This is analogous to Harlow's finding with some of his 'motherless mother' rhesus monkeys. For some of these monkeys, although they were abusive and incompetent in the care of their first infants, they could adequately mother a second. The more abusive ones, however, continued the same abusive behavior.[15] In some instances, children seem to mature our patients.

The family of the oedipal child

Between the ages of 3 and 4, the child begins to show active sexual curiosity about his parents, attempting to intrude on them for specifically sexual purposes (see chapter 5). Most families feel somewhat assaulted by this stage but weather it by dint of the resilience of the parental bond and the reassurance this provides the battered parent. However, if a vulnerability exists in that relationship, it may well be exploited. The attack of the oedipal girl on her mother can be seen in the picture by a 5-year-old girl (plate 2) depicting a disguised 'elopment' with her father. The following example illustrates the family liability of the oedipal stage.

> Tamsen was 6 when I saw her because her mother felt they had a poor relationship. Father came along to say that his wife did not treat Tamsen fairly. The following typical nightly scene was described. Mother put Tamsen to bed at 7:30, hoping to spend some time with her husband. Tamsen then began to cry and summoned her father, detailing to him with tears in her eyes how mother had mistreated her by the early bedtime. Father then offered solace to Tamsen and subsequently berated mother, ending any chance for a sexual encounter during the evening. In this family, mother's experience in growing up was that she did replace her own depressed mother in her father's affection. Her fear that she would suffer the same fate was revived by Tamsen's oedipal assault. Helping this couple understand the nature of the developmental 'attack' let them unite to support Tamsen through it together, enabling Tamsen to move toward positive identification with her mother rather than the previously rivalrous one.

Latency, puberty, and adolescence

Ordinarily, the years between 7 and 11 or 12 offer some respite to the family as the child's development moves in the direction of the sublimation and channelling of sexual drives into the acquisition of skills. During this period the couple may experience a relative freeing of their energies, resulting in a swing of energy back to their investment in each other. However, in families where the child has not successfully negotiated oedipal development, the earlier forces will continue to be played out without respite. In any event, puberty and adolescence bring about a resurgence of oedipal and pre-oedipal matters more forcefully as the child is now more driven by sexualized energies, and being large, is more able to act on his impulses. Parents may attempt to live out their own denied sexual issues by projection onto their adolescent children. But they may also react enviously, berating the adolescent about increased sexual expression or waiting to pounce on the child who is then sure to falter. Much of the urgency of an adolescent's sexual life may stem from these unacknowledged family sources while the parents may feel an envious emptiness in comparison to the newly sexual child who stirs up previously successfully repressed aspects of the parents' adolescent sexual development. Linda L's family, discussed in the previous chapter, was one in which the parents' lack of satisfactory sexual life came to light as Linda became sexual, reviving old conflicts for the parents. The parents avoid their own sexual impulses because they cannot cope with the intolerable rage, longing, or guilt they arouse. Instead, they split them off from the central ego control and get rid of the difficult feelings by projecting them outside the self and onto the adolescent.

Finally, in the post-adolescent and young adult period, when the child 'deserts' them, the parents begin to face themselves again, relying on their own sexuality to help in refocusing their needs for intimacy back onto each other. The vicissitudes of this struggle are partly the focus of the next two chapters and we will examine them there.

A parental sexual dysfunction can present in conjunction with difficulties around their child's negotiation of a developmental crisis at any stage, just as a child's presenting symptoms may be precipitated by the parents' sexual tension. In reality, these variables interact and each influences the other. Distress in one area of the family may well bring an echo of distress in the other. But similarly, the bridging of a difficult passage in one area of family life may make healing more possible in related areas. When we see either a parental couple with sexual difficulty *or* a child who is having trouble with a particular stage of psychosexual development, it is important to keep in mind the interlocking of development of parent and child.

Chapter 16
Sex and the mid-life crisis

No one has described the mid-life crisis more poignantly than Dante in the opening lines of *The Inferno*.

> Midway in our life's journey, I went astray
> from the straight road and woke to find myself
> alone in a dark wood. How shall I say
> What wood that was! I never saw so drear
> so rank, so arduous a wilderness!
> Its very memory gives a shape to fear.*

In his paper, 'Death and the mid-life crisis,' Elliott Jacques describes this crisis as a psychosocial transition which occurs roughly in the years between 35 and 45.[1] It begins with a growing recognition that life is finite. The scope of life has shifted. Less remains ahead than behind and an increasing awareness of the inescapable fact of death gains a new immediacy. The re-evaluation that this realization promotes inevitably includes a painful sense of profound loss of opportunity. Along with the grief over lost potential comes the process of reassessing the worth of one's life in working and in loving. Jacques describes a return to the paranoid/schizoid tendency to split objects once again into good and bad. The good objects would offer comforting reassurance at mid-life; the bad would be the ones associated with death and worthlessness. When the crisis is resolved maturely, it is by a reattainment of the depressive position, an integrated acceptance of the limits and possibilities of the life situation.

In this transitional period there is an increased potential for change, whether for better or worse. In the realm of work life, careers may stop or start abruptly, people may become inspired or depressed. Artists may begin their careers, like Gauguin, or die like Mozart. Some like Shakespeare are able to incorporate the crisis as an opportunity for growth as demonstrated by his period of great tragedies, coming midway between the youthful comedies like *Twelfth Night* and the mature late-life parables which culminate in *The Tempest*.[2]

The same dilemmas are acted out in the realm of each person's family and sexual life. In many marriages, one or both people face the feeling they can no longer build for the future. The question arises whether the life they currently have will be enough to sustain them without the fantasized embellishment of an idealized future. Hopes can no longer be postponed to the indefinite future, for as never before, the future is the present and the past becomes larger than that future.

So too in sexual life. What is to come is measured by what the couple now have. If they do not now feel that when they are older and look back, sex will be felt to have been good enough for a lifetime, a sense of loss and depression sets in *now*. The notion of the future retrospective becomes part of the current review. The shock of a realization can produce panic, numbness, anger, or denial – all the components of grief reactions which become maladaptive if the couple cannot progress through to resolution. These incomplete transitions are often expressed by changes in sexual life, by suddenly turning to sex outside the marriage, or by a withering of sexual feeling.

Such sexual symptoms are predominantly sexual disjunctions rather than pure dysfunctions. As discussed earlier, these most often correspond clinically to the 'desire phase' disorders described by Kaplan.[3] They represent a disconnection of the person from his former self, from his good internal objects, and from the spouse he has previously felt to be a good object, while the sex becomes the focus of a projective mechanism which identifies the spouse with the frustrating internal objects.

The menopause and its vague male counterpart, the 'male climacteric' deserve comment at this point although menopause often does not occur until late in the age group we are considering or even afterwards. When it does occur, menopause represents a clear hormonal shift in the aging woman. The loss of hormonal support is certainly a stress in many women.

While the role of physiological changes in the etiology of sexual discomfort is unclear,[4] the shifts themselves interact with psychological issues, both those which were previously present and those triggered by advancing age. Some women may experience an overwhelming desire to become pregnant one final time during the pre-menopausal period.[5] Others experience actual menopause as signalling relief from fear of pregnancy and now allow a new sexual interest.

For the middle-aged man, the situation is far less abrupt. No sudden hormonal shift accompanies his aging process. In the absence of an actual disease process, his mid-life reactions are apt to be more purely triggered by the reactions to his awareness of advancing age.[6] Further aspects of this question will be taken up in the next chapter.

Superficial and profound disjunctions

A recent study of normal couples reveals that many well-adjusted couples complain of minor dissatisfactions with their sexual union – e.g., about the frequency of intercourse, the lack of synchronized sexual rhythms and preferences – but these are tolerated or compromised on as the couple rework their adjustment to each other.[7] In contrast to the relatively superficial disjunctional complaints of these couples, the more profound disjunctions are those which bear an intrinsic relationship to underlying difficulties between partners. In mid-life, defined here as the period between 35 and the early fifties, a *series* of developmental steps occur which are described by Levinson, Gould and others[8] as elaborations on Jacques's ideas about the mid-life crisis. The disjunctions of these years will stem from and interact with several factors which are illustrated in the examples that follow.

An 'uncomplicated' mid-life crisis

In the first example, sexual dissatisfaction is the presenting complaint in a case in which professional and personal dissatisfaction at mid-life was all blamed on dissatisfactions with marital sex.

> Mr Connel, age 37, brought in his wife, age 34, with the complaint that she was not a willing *enough* sexual partner. She was, he conceded, available for sex liberally, but her dislike of oral sex and new positions left him so dissatisfied that he thought he might feel compelled to leave the marriage, despite its being otherwise happy, built on a genuinely warm feeling between the two of them, and extending to children and mutual friends. When I first saw them, I

was extremely puzzled about what was really wrong. Mrs Connel
agreed to try harder, to push on her inhibitions, and indeed she
managed to try oral sex, but with obvious and indefatigable disgust.
Still, Mr Connel was not satisfied. Nor was I satisfied to think that
this was a true sexual dysfunction.

Within three weeks, the answer was out. Mr Connel was engaged
in an affair with a work colleague ten years younger than himself –
brilliant, blonde, and energetic – not weighted down by previous
commitments, children, or a history of twelve years of marriage.
The secret was uncovered when he erroneously thought his wife
overheard a phone conversation in which he told this woman he
loved her. He rushed to tell his wife about the affair.

What emerged behind this revelation was the story of his mid-life
crisis. Competent in his job, he felt he had nowhere further to go
in his career, at least not without risking or sacrificing stability and
material achievements, which he was reluctant to do. His failure to
obtain a law degree when a young man now stood between him and
career advancement, so that he felt at a dead-end. This left him
to turn to his personal and family life for an answer to the gnawing
dissatisfaction with the ultimate rewards of his life, and here he
reached out to a younger and symbolically revitalizing woman. The
symbolism of the sexual disjunction, apparently superficial, ran to
the roots of his infantile needs, as revived by the mid-life threat.
Oral sex and his other 'sexual needs' became invested with the
sense of excitement which he felt would assuage his depression,
and give him a sense of meaning. The wounded feeling of coming
up against the limitations of his life was defined by the approach of
death and its limitations. Although he was clearly feeling stung by
this inner confrontation, he was not willing to acknowledge it.

Of course, it was not the oral sex and the new positions which
were fundamentally in question. But the confrontation did have a
profound effect on Mrs Connel, facing her with issues in her own
developing life which were parallel to her husband's. Sexual
inhibition, mild as it was, had been her way of maintaining stability
through familiarity. It represented an unwillingness to give up a
stabler, known 'world' in favor of more richness, but also more risks
in life. Her fear of the future paralleled her husband's fears. Having
faced and shared this fear, she began to feel there was no reason for
not offering both him and herself increased experiences in life.
Partly, she rose to the challenge to her married stability by finding

new sexual resources to insure it. But she also experienced a kind of thaw which opened new avenues of exploration for her life in general. The apparently superficial sexual symptom had profound roots, not only in the life crisis of these two people, but in the way this crisis revived the needs of previous developmental times for bonding, love, nurturing, security, and flexibly responsive caring.

I did not have much information about the early history of either of the Connels. A similar picture was, however, present in a couple who gave a more complete history, that of Henry and Claire de F, previously described in chapter 7.

Henry de F became significantly depressed at 40. It was after his wife was able to become sexually responsive in sex therapy that he inexplicably lost most of his interest in sex. He began to talk about his career as meaningless compared to his peers despite what appeared to be a successful public service career. At the age of 5 his mother had left the man he thought was his father to live with and marry her lover. This man turned out to be Henry's actual father. From that time on, the mother was preoccupied by efforts to care for this narcissistic, depressed man, leaving Henry to feel abandoned by the loss of her and the caring father of his early years. The real father's disappointment with his career was part of what Henry identified with himself at 40.

Henry's wife, Claire, had also lost her father who died when she was 10. Her mother had then withdrawn from the children to the job she took to support the family. This parental loss experienced by both Mr and Mrs de F was carried forward as a shared fear of abandonment by the primary object. This fear was first contained in Mrs de F's lack of sexual interest. Our suspicion that she held the sexual disinterest for both of them was bolstered by Henry's initial selection of her as someone who was *not* very interested in sex. When she was able to give up this defense during treatment, Henry became severely depressed, feeling that life did not offer the security he sought. His mid-life crisis presented as a loss of sexual interest and resentment at his internal objects, followed by a severe depression.

This example makes clearer the role of early experience in setting the stage for mid-life difficulty. Henry de F's good adjustment until this period belied a tenuous relationship to his internal objects, one which was not sufficient to allow reacceptance of the anti-libidinal projections and to weather the assault of the mid-life recognition of his own limits.

Children and the mid-life crisis

In the previous chapter, we examined some of the ways in which the developmental stages of child and parent interlock. Many of the children of the mid-life couples are adolescents who reawaken in their parents aspects of sexuality which may have been long dormant. While keeping this in mind as a prominent factor, in this chapter we will focus on the parental side of the interlocking developmental crisis, the one which tends to occur when the parent is in mid-life and the urgency comes primarily or equally from the developmental transition of the parent. This was the case in the following example.

Mr and Mrs C, ages 42 and 40, were referred for problem pregnancy counselling. She was inadvertently pregnant after a birth control failure during apparently competent use of a diaphragm. She wanted to have the child, while Mr C argued that with the growth of their two children, ages 16 and 11, he had been looking forward to the increased intimacy of the coming years, freed from the shackles of the young children, even though he had enjoyed them. Mrs C was unable to agree with his view. But she had an abortion while remaining deeply resentful. The pregnancy had revived mothering feelings, and an interest in facing mid-life by returning to mothering. After the abortion, she pulled away from Mr C, became lackadaisical about sex, and invested much more in relationships with women. She particularly developed an extremely close relationship with a woman doctor in a new project in her work as a pediatric nurse. The new relationship may have been a lesbian one physically; Mr C certainly felt she had no sexual interest left for him.

Feeling rejected, Mr C in turn began to lose interest in sex with her. At the same time, he began to have fantasies about having affairs with younger women, which he refrained from acting on. In this case, the dissatisfaction, which was marked by the noteworthy mutual deinvestment of their sexual life, followed the loss of a 'rebirth' solution to mid-life crisis. Mrs C's grief and resentment that her husband had deprived her of a return to mothering as the way out of the losses of mid-life led to her unconscious determination to withhold from him not only sex in retaliation, but emotional investment as well. Part of her loss of sexual interest came in the wake of the painful abortion decision, so that the loss of the pregnancy also pushed her into an angry flight from sexual involvement.

In most cases, children provide a reconstructive link, helping their parents overcome losses at mid-life. Part of the difficulty in this case was set into action by the impending loss of a parenting role for Mrs C by the growth of her children. This is even more true in the next case in which the last of four children had recently left home. There is another similarity in the two cases: both women pull partially away from their husbands toward other women.

Selma, a 48-year-old artist, had ceased to enjoy sex over the last few years. She had been moderately responsive early in her marriage to Edwin, now 49, but lately had found him clinging and sex oppressive. Particularly, she had found his interest in her breasts repulsive. On his side, Edwin had been turning increasingly to her for life satisfaction, having made a somewhat bitter peace with his career after deciding it would not be greatly successful. He looked to his relationship with her to help him past this disappointment of his forties.

For Selma, however, this would have involved losses. She was wanting to invest more heavily in her artistic career as a solution to the loss of the four children. The youngest child had just left, while another, married with a 1-year-old child, was in a phase of rejecting his parents, and would not speak to Edwin or Selma. This rejection by one child, and the loss of the last, were prominent themes for Selma, and tied into her resentment of Edwin for being interested in 'getting something out of her.' Although she was able to reconstruct a fragile but functioning sexual responsiveness to him, she was unable to allow him access to her breasts, and bitterly resented his continued interest in them.

The withholding of the breast represented her wish to protect from further hurt her injured, rejected, and not-to-be-tampered-with sense of mothering. She split her feelings about the loss of her mothering into their angry and sad elements. The sadness was

expressed through her tears when her departing daughter was
mentioned. But only anger was evident when Edwin wished to
caress or kiss her breasts. When the 'nurturing breast' was not needed
by daughter, and rejected by son, it could not be available to husband
or to herself as a sexually gratifying part of her body. Instead, her
artistic interests led her to identify with Vita Sackville-West and
Virginia Woolf as women who had known so much about sensuality
in life. Her gynecophilic identification shielded her from the bad
object in men and protected the good mother – a defense against
feeling hurt by the rejection of her own children.

Here the disjunction was contained in a missing part of the sexual
response. The couple could share a modified intimacy, but the pain
around the breast taboo signified a shared sense that something vital
was still missing emotionally. The departing child had carried their
hopes for the future. Without them, Edwin and Selma were left
with the need to turn to each other for solace from losses and for
renewed intimacy. The sexual disjunction was a symptom of
difficulty in this task.

The effect of chronic disease

A group of sexual dysfunctions which present with increasing frequency
with advancing age are those associated with chronic diseases which
involve neurologic or cardiovascular deterioration. Where the emotional
bond is strong (or can be strengthened) these couples with dysfunctions
can be offered considerable help. In other cases, the medical difficulty
triggers a severe disjunction which offers a considerable obstacle. I
will give one example of this in mid-life here and another in the next
chapter on aging.

Mr Thompson, age 41 (see chapter 14) had a twenty-year history of
diabetes mellitus. In his relationship to Mrs Thompson, now 38, he
had had two prolonged episodes of impotence. The first occurred
several years earlier when they met, while he was still married to his
first wife. Mrs Thompson had been able to 'nurse' him through this
erectile difficulty with three months of patient, caring, and unde-
manding physical attention, and without therapeutic intervention.
Both assumed that the impotence had represented his guilt at
breaking up his marriage and leaving his children, although in

retrospect it also seemed to contain his reaction of withdrawing from Mrs Thompson's aggressive dominance in sexuality. The second episode involved neurological and small vessel changes attributable to his diabetes, but since he was still able to have some spontaneous erections, the dysfunction seemed to involve the resurgence of the disjunction as well now that the diabetes had decreased his physical tolerance to psychological stress.

The mid-life issues for Mr Thompson were complicated. Originally, he felt his first marriage a failure, an unsatisfactory base for a sustaining relationship even though the sex had been fully functional. His finding his second wife represented a solution to an earlier life crisis. The mid-life crisis also involved a decision to change his career from law into business. He came to be dominated by tenacious depression, and began a passive retreat from his wife in the face of her demand that he perform sexually. This mid-life sexual failure occurred when Gordon, the child of the second marriage, began to show difficulties. A renewed sense of defeat in life began to haunt him. Try as he might, erections in the shared situation became scarcer and scarcer. The sexual disjunction and the shared despair in this couple became so severe that they could consider neither the implantation of a penile prosthesis,[9] nor the development of adjunctive substitute methods of sexual satisfaction such as the use of mutual masturbation. (For comparison with a couple who were able to manage this in a similar situation, see the example of George and Ida Schneider in the following chapter.)

Extra-marital affairs

The subject of extra-marital sexuality is extensive enough to warrant separate consideration (chapter 18). Here I only want to indicate the special role at mid-life of the option to use a lover as a way to 'breathe new life' when the spouse seems to offer dead-ending engulfment, as in the cases of Mr Connel and Selma. We will take up this aspect of splitting objects in affairs more specifically later. Meanwhile, in the next example, the extra-marital affairs played the role of allowing sexual expression while preserving the marriage.

Mr and Mrs Z, at age 50, came because Mrs Z was considering separation. The major issue for her was her husband's lack of interest in her sexually. He was perfectly able to function, and when they did manage to have intercourse, she enjoyed it. He was willing on rare occasions to have intercourse for her, because, he said, he loved her and wished to stay married. But he simply did not feel aroused with her sexually. She was hurt by his rejection, attributing it to her mild obesity, but he said he found her attractive. Each had had a few extra-marital affairs through the years. Mrs Z's affairs had occurred with only two consistent men with a good deal of caring for each of them, while Mr Z said he had in general a low sex drive, and had only sporadic encounters on business trips, on which occasions he performed satisfactorily.

This disjunction had been present for years in embryo. The couple had had only an irregular sex life until about five years before when Mr Z retired from teaching to take another job. But now Mrs Z felt she had to re-evaluate her life and decide what the rest of it would be like, and she longed for more intimacy. Her children were grown and gone, and she felt there ought to be more to life. She preferred it be with her husband, but the sadness over the physical rejection, as well as his gruff irritability aimed at keeping bedtime from being friendly enough for sex to occur, left her feeling so depressed that she resolved she would be better off on her own. This resolution brought them to the psychiatric evaluation, and it forced Mr Z to consider the psychological content of his progressive sexual withdrawal.

The issues which came to the fore for him were those of anger and resentment of controlling women, stemming from the memories of a dominating mother and milk-toast father, and from a sense of his own inadequacy and failure. Indifferently successful in a college teaching career, he had retired after failing to achieve adequate promotion after 18 years, and entered a second career in business administration in which he also felt not particularly invested. This sense of failure threw him into a more dependency-prone relationship with his wife, and he recoiled from that, fearing his own dependent longings would trap him. Wishing deeply to be loved, understood, and cared for by her, he felt with increased urgency the sense of impending entrapment he had avoided for years by frequent travels. He managed this combination of fearing and wishing by retreating sexually. He begged her to tolerate the compromise.

In a final example, a couple who had had a distant relationship throughout their marriage fell apart in every way in their forties. The death of the wife's interest in sex was a signal in concert with her wish for the death of the relationship.

> Mr E, age 48, came asking if I could make his 47-year-old wife respond with more sexual interest, as she had recently when she received a trial course of testosterone injections. When Mrs E saw me, she at first seemed interested, but then let me know that while she did not mind sex with her husband, she did mind being with him. He had been alcoholic for ten years and she had encouraged his increasingly frequent business trips. Now she was in school acquiring computer-programming skills and she would be leaving him as soon as she was economically self-sufficient. Her lack of sexual arousal with him contrasted sharply with her feelings around other men, even though she had yet to sleep with any of them. Their last child had left home a year before and now Mrs E was determined to make more of the rest of her life than she felt she could have with her husband. She felt there was no room for turning back.

Not all mid-life crises result in the deterioration of relationships as in these examples. For many couples, even without active intervention, the time of mid-life offers an opportunity for maturation, for the repair of many of the hurts of immaturity, and for reconciliation to each other and to internal objects. For these couples, the sex will offer considerable opportunity for symbolic reparation and may be a force for renewal. That it has the power to do so underscores the importance of the treatment of sexual disorders in couples seeking help at mid-life.

Chapter 17
Aging, loss, and sexual development

The process of aging superimposes the process of life's continuing developmental stages upon the inexorable march of involution. In sexual life, the weight of physical losses due to illness and bodily decline may end functioning prematurely, but in the absence of specific illness, this need not be so. Masters and Johnson have established that the physical decline of sexual functioning unfettered by illness is extremely slow, not marked by the sudden loss of capacity for erection or lubrication. They state, 'There are only two basic needs for regularity of sexual expression in 70–80-year-old women. These necessities are a reasonably good state of general health and an interested and interesting partner.'[1] The same is true of the aging male. They note, 'Really the only factor that the aging male must understand is that loss of erective prowess is not a natural component of aging.'[2]

The gradual change of function in men and women, however, often triggers a husband, wife, or both to withdraw from sexuality, often out of a mistaken sense of deference to the other's wishes. The increased time and attention it takes for the male to achieve an erection sufficient for penetration, the prolonged time before ejaculation and the increase in refractory period all may cause him or his wife to feel something is wrong. On the woman's side, after the loss of internal hormonal support, the thinning and atrophy of vaginal mucosa or painful cramping of uterine contractions during orgasm may lead to physical irritability and dyspareunia, reversible by hormone replacement therapy.

The general physical complications of increasing age can seriously limit sexual capacity. The neurovascular changes of hypertension and diabetes, the side effects of medication or surgery (especially genito-urinary or gynecological surgery) and a growing potential for disability from stroke can impinge on both men and women. In the absence of specific causes of disability, there is virtually no age limit on the continued ability to engage sexually.[3]

Psychological impediments resulting from the increasing loss of security as the overall sense of loss mounts are a cause of sexual dysfunction whose frequency increases rapidly with age. The careful differential diagnosis of physical from psychological cause is as essential in this age group as in any other, but more frequently a mixture of physical and emotional threads is encountered in the etiology which have led to a deterioration in a previously satisfactory sexual adjustment. When this is true, the diminished sense of well-being often reawakens the powerful frustrations of the infantile psychosomatic partnership causing a major disruption in the couple's overall bond. This inability to withstand loss in old age will be taken up below. For other couples, the lessening of sex is mourned but accepted and the couple is buoyed by the strength of a more enduring partnership. Even so, the acceptance of this loss may not be required by physical circumstances. The fact that many of these couples would be glad to see the sex restored to their lives makes it important to help them in the many cases in which such help is possible.

Loss, mourning, and aging

Loss and mourning form the context of the aging process. Even without the loss of a spouse or the loss contained in a physical disability, the process of aging beyond mid-life involves relative loss of functioning when one is no longer in the 'prime of life.' The psychosocial transitions which introduce old age call on the capacity to mourn with a new intensity. Loss of parts of the self, the spouse, family (growing and departing children, for instance), and work all call on the capacity to bear depression and to reintegrate. The ability to do this relies on the previous achievements of maturity which in turn rest on the infantile achievement of the depressive position. The continued ability to maintain these gains is the hallmark of a sense of integrity, the achievement of which is the psychosocial challenge of aging.[4] Robert Butler has described the shift in sexual expression through mid-life which parallels Elliott Jacques's[5] description of the shift from the 'youthful hot fires of creativity' to the 'sculpted productions' of later life. Butler writes: 'When people are young . . ., their sexual activity tends to be urgent,

explosive, involved largely with physical pleasure and . . . the conception of children.' But in later years, he notes, they rely more on the
relationship the sex has formed, on the 'ability to recognize and share
feelings in words and actions and to achieve a mutual tenderness and
thoughtfulness between oneself and another person.' In this mode,
Butler concludes, there are 'bountiful possibilities for enough new
emotional experiences to last a lifetime. . . . The normal physiological
changes – the longer maintenance of an erection and the longer refractory period – can and should be capitalized upon: change does not
mean end.'[6]

Acquisition of the overall ability to accept such matured relationships
depends on the lifelong ability to accept loss, to mourn it, and to move
on to the new opportunities which therefore become available. It also
depends on the persistence of good, secure internal objects as proof
against an inner sense of abandonment. The developments of later life
are heavily dependent on the attainments of early life and on the
attempts throughout life to reconcile oneself to harsh internal objects.
This is not to say, however, that it is ever too late to help someone
overcome earlier deficits. There are always the patients who have lost
so much interpersonally because of a general defensiveness throughout
their lives that they are finally ready toward the end of life to give up
defense and enjoy the need only now unfettered by fear. They have
lost too much to fear loss further.

George Schneider was a 62-year-old corporate president, now retired
but still called on steadily for civic activities. He took pride in his
house and gardening. Ida Schneider was still busy at 64 as an active
patron of music and the arts. Within the marriage, however, George
was a crusty curmudgeon and Ida felt she only barely tolerated him
now and had for many years past. Since a pituitary ablation x-ray
procedure five years ago for a benign chromophobe adenoma,
George had been completely impotent. His personal physician had
suggested to him that the remnant of the tumor might even be
secreting an inhibitory hormone which interfered with his hormone
replacement regimen. George had had no erections for four years,
and he did not want a surgical prosthesis. The absence of any spontaneous nocturnal erections was further proof of the organic
etiology of his impotence.[7]

But the real problem was the lack of a warm relationship, physical
or emotional. Ida put up with George because 'the sun is setting

anyhow, Doctor.' But she resented his demandingness and bumptious rudeness to her and his abrupt shortness with their grown children which meant they could not be with them together. She wondered if he had suffered some personality change for the worse during the pituitary radiation, but noted that these were exaggerations of previous character elements. In any event, she had liked sex and missed it. But George was even more impossible than he had been before. They slept in separate rooms.

George felt if they could be physically warm, his life would be complete. He had everything else. He was oblivious to Ida's complaints, dismissing them summarily. He longed for her bodily warmth.

This was a difficult conjoint therapy. To summarize it, we were able to get George to govern his behavior in return for Ida's willingness to *consider* being closer physically. In one of those heart-warming developments which one hopes for but has no right to expect, he was able to give up yelling at his son and daughter and even stopped harassing waiters because he gradually understood his family could not tolerate it. As he met Ida halfway, she eventually found herself wanting him in her bedroom, liking him again, holding him, and fondling his limp penis while masturbating herself. They were delighted to have found each other. Neither wanted him to have a penile prosthesis, but they were in hopes that a research hormone antidote might reverse the impotence.

Here the lack of sex paralleled:

1   an inability to sustain and renew intimacy after disruption by ill health;
2   a bitterness about lost opportunity and about the future which soured past accomplishments as well; and
3   poor relationship with children which echoed the impoverishment of internal objects.

The restoration of 'good-enough' sex which followed other improvements, even though very incomplete, did in turn return reparative energies to some of the tangled 'psychological skeins,' meeting the pain of loss and providing the growth of intimacy as a bulwark against future losses. With the restoration of a feeling of integrity and sexuality, George and Ida were, they told us, happier than they had been in years.

In some cases, a complicated medical or psychological difficulty may have severely impinged on functioning, but a basically adequate relationship resurfaces with exploration.

Mr Q, aged 61, came with his wife, aged 59. He was a negativistic and combative opinionated man with a complex medical history. He said he had no use for his wife since a year earlier when he began on drugs for high blood pressure. His wife, however, was doggedly dedicated to him, although frustrated in her inability to help sexually and on the point of despair. Mr Q was mildly alcoholic. He had a lowered testosterone level, hypertension treated with aldomet, and mild Peyronies disease (plaques in the distal corpus of the penis). He had felt unable to have adequate erections since three years before. At that time, having taken their savings and started off to sail around the world, he and his wife were both hit by an automobile and were hospitalized for almost nine months in adjacent hospital beds. Afterwards, he bitterly returned to work, but was unable to achieve an erection adequate for intromission. He became even testier than usual and his wife withdrew in fear of his rages.

Despite his characterologic history, in a therapeutic setting he was able to limit his alcohol intake, change anti-hypertensive medication, begin testosterone replacement therapy and use therapy to reduce his demands on himself and his wife. Erectile competence was restored almost to the level of function prior to the accident and sex was said to be actually more enjoyable. Mr Q began to dream of starting out again to sail around the world and Mrs Q, although not enthusiastic, agreed that she would go if he did. 'It's all part of my sexual dream, Doctor,' he said. 'I dream of laying her down on a tropical beach and f . . . ing the hell out of her.'

This parting statement is partly proof of his readjustment and partly represents a return to his pre-accident view of sex as association with narcissistic vigor and power, a way of controlling the object instead of caring for it. However, this irascible and unpredictable man was fortunate enough to have found someone who would stick by him, truly 'for better or for worse.' Although it could never have been predicted, the fit between their internal object systems was obviously adequate to support a better sexual adjustment and they left just as 'happy as clams' – or at least as happy as they could be.

The next case presents the kind of internal circumstances in which substantial improvement is far less likely because of the lifelong pattern of undermining integrity and the despair the couple now felt.

Samuel and Prudence N were referred to me for Mr N's impotence. Samuel was 62, Prudence 61. His impotence had come on six years after Mrs N's successfully treated sexual dysfunction of non-arousal and primary non-orgasmic status. They had seen a number of other psychiatrists, some of whom they had managed to work well with and whom they idealized, but most of whom they stringently criticized as too authoritarian, intrusive, or uncaring. In the first interview, they idealized me, saying they felt I understood things even famous other physicians had not, but when they saw me again, this was broken by sharp criticisms about small details of my interaction with them. When I met with Mrs N, she told me of her anger at her mother for having openly disparaged her father for years, presumably, she thought, while denying him sex. She broke into tears over missing the opportunity to be closer to him herself. Mr N told me of his own dominating mother, and of the two images of his father: he could be critical, scathing, and uncaring; yet he was also idealized by Mr N as a model whose approval was constantly sought. Mr N had been remarkably successful in his career as an architect, but at several junctures his career had been marred by a falling-out with a much younger associate whom he had hoped would be a kind of 'son' to him in his professional life. These men always parted from him in bitter and somewhat unexplained circumstances. He had partially retired a year before seeing me, and the onset of his impotence dated from about the time of his retirement.

Mrs N decided soon thereafter that she could not tolerate any form of therapy which would 'dig up painful memories or feelings,' but Mr N, still trusting me tentatively, decided to proceed, particularly taken by my contention that his secret extra-marital affairs were part of the late-life despair that he had previously linked only with the loss of his career at retirement. He agreed that he was feeling in despair about himself and was having trouble facing his wife across the gap of inner and outer depression. The lifelong affairs had never been discussed by Mr and Mrs N, even during the previously successful sex therapy. He agreed that his secondary impotence symbolized a guilty withdrawal from his wife as a critical and unsatisfiable conscience, making her a derivative of both the severe disapproval of his father and the threatening mother. Soon afterwards, Mr N, who was an accomplished jazz musician, told me of a dream in which he went to a man named David Mender who best restored woodwinds, who could finally, he trusted in the dream, restore his clarinet to true and faithful pitch. The dream, he felt, was an indication of his hope that I could mend him.

And then he suddenly broke off treatment. I can only guess that our work on his ambivalence about me was threatening because of the marked ambivalence about his father and mother – the splitting of them into irreconcilable part-objects who could never be knit. Hate of mother and longing for an ideal father was an experience shared by both these people. Mr N's ability to idealize doctors and younger male work associates almost invariably ran into some insurmountable obstacle which he invariably imported into the experience. His anger at his father for being the unreachable and unsurpassable ideal made him feel finally belittled in each of these situations – open to attack from the younger men he longed to befriend.

This couple relived their childhood anger at parents in feeling criticized, deprived, and belittled by me transferentially. Mr N's tentative trust of me easily crumbled into his chronic mistrust, and like his wife, he turned his anger onto me in leaving. Having done little therapeutic work (and perhaps unable to do any), the Ns were left with only each other to focus the distrust and anger on when no transference substitute was available. The recurrence of sexual dysfunction, now in the husband, was probably a direct result of this pattern, seen here recreated briefly in the distrustful longing of the brief transference relationship. The demands of this life phase for a sense of integrity to offset the threat of despair are not met by this couple. The sexual difficulty and the return of a shared depression are an expression of this failure.

Other couples form less extreme pictures of the struggle for integrity and intimacy. Despite a prolonged pattern of affairs, they may be able to pull together.

Nick and Mabel U, he 60, she 56, had an open marriage for ten years before seeking help. Her conscious initiative in seeking lovers was aimed at finding one who made her feel lovable since her husband did not. It also recreated an oedipal pattern. Her father had openly had many affairs. Night after night, her mother would send her to him to ask him not to go out. She remembered feeling he would never have done this to her if she had been his wife. Now in her maturity, she identified with what her father had done, but in straying from the marriage and in flaunting her own affairs. Sexually, she felt Mr U had never been accomplished or interested enough as a lover to give her an assurance of being loved. That the source of her insecurity stemmed from her own history and not from his technique never occurred to her.

Mr U had come from a relatively stable and loving family, but he had left home early and lived with Mrs U's family as a lodger, fastening onto her as a substitute parent in his early adolescent break from home. Many years later, when she suggested an open marriage, he was reluctant, but did it 'to please her' until recently when he met a 24-year-old woman who was far more attentive and reassuring. He felt he had never been a great 'lover' and was always dissatisfied with himself, and it was this lack of self-confidence that led to his going along with his wife's swinging. But the new girlfriend opened his eyes to new possibilities. In contrast to his activity leading to professional competence and integrity, Mr U's covert passivity had led him into a sexual path which undermined his sense of personal integrity without confronting either his wife's inner lack of security nor his unaltered dependent attachment to her. The therapeutic work used sex therapy as a vehicle for exploring this lifelong pattern. In the end, Mrs U was able to let go of much of her insistence on sexual perfection and enjoy a gentle give-and-take. Mr U could expect less of himself while giving more, expressing his anger in more direct ways than through the previous sexual withholding. Still, he remained unsure of his commitment to Mrs U. She was his best friend, but he was still unable to decide whether his acceptance of her anti-libidinal context for years had undermined his sustained love for her. When they left us, with the sex itself now fully restored, he remained unsure about the answer to this question and it has remained an open question in the year since treatment ended.

For this couple, the sexual symptom had spoken for ambivalence about the central bond. When the sex was used to examine and treat the bond, the ambivalence was uncovered as itself touching on central problems. Sexually, ambivalence is normally tested in adolescence and is hopefully integrated by the time of mate selection. This couple had maintained their marriage by splitting and externalizing their shared ambivalence about internal objects. The repair of the physical sex only uncovered the underlying difficulty.[8]

Loss and remarriage

The sexual life of widows and widowers affects the bereaved family when a bereaved partner is young and remarriage occurs while he or she is still raising children, or when the grown children are in a position to react or influence the remarriage of an older parent.

The prototypical picture of grieving is seen in those who have lost a spouse. The reactions include denial, depression, tears, anger, focusing of thoughts on and searching for the dead spouse. Even when grief is tempered with relief, still the death of a spouse is a loss of security which is disruptive of life arrangements and may lead to personal disorganization.[9] Sexual urges may be disrupted during an acute grief, but are likely to return, especially in the younger population of widows and widowers.[10] After about a year, many are able to reintegrate a new sexual relationship and consider remarriage. Widowers have a marked advantage in these respects because there are fewer of them at any age and they therefore are in demand. They can admit sexual longings more easily and are able to negotiate loss and reattachment more readily. However, neither widows nor widowers assess satisfactory new relationships as primarily sexual in nature.[11]

The last example illustrates some of the restorative functions of sexual repair in a second marriage. In this case, the new wife had been widowed and the husband divorced.

Sean and Bridey O'Neil (ages 60 and 56) came for help in their second marriage. He had been married for 25 years to a woman who was uninterested in sex and gradually withdrew from the relationship. Reluctantly, as he was a devout Catholic, he had moved to separation ten years previously, but did not divorce until he met Bridey five years ago. Bridey had a 22-year marriage to a 'good man who thought of nothing but himself and running the family business. We had three children, Doctor, but that was about it for the sex.' When he died, she grieved but she was also relieved. Meeting Sean fifteen months later, she felt she had fallen in love for the first time. She did not mind his occasional impotence. Sex had never been important to her and she had never been orgasmic, although she treasured the physical closeness. But Sean felt he was letting her down in not providing her with the pleasure of intercourse or with an orgasm. His impotence became recurrent and finally almost complete.

Treatment went quickly and easily in this cooperative couple who were very much in love and whose anxiety and inexperience had interfered with their ability to give to each other sexually. They had an adolescent freshness and naivety when they came to us, although Sean was depressed about his failure to satisfy his wife. Even the superficial reassurances provided by the behavioral framework of the sex therapy were enough to lift their depression. In the absence of any significant interactional difficulty, inter-pretations were readily accepted and a successful outcome followed.

The challenges of aging are among the most formidable the individual meets in his life's progress; for not only does he face profound losses even more closely with each day, but the inheritance of scars from the past may press with an overwhelming quality. Sex may fall an easy victim to these processes, but that need not be so. For many couples, the strengths inherent in their past accomplishments will again serve them well here. Others, now with nothing to lose, may enjoy a new-found freedom. Treating the elderly couple can offer some of the most touching clinical rewards found anywhere.

Chapter 18
The dynamics of extra-marital sex

This chapter deals with the family and individual dynamics of extra-marital affairs. When sexuality occurs outside the boundaries of a marriage, its context is established by the existence of the marriage. When such marital partners bring their marriage to us seeking help, our therapeutic interest in the object relations of the couple has to widen to include the group which extends beyond the family to include the extra-marital partners. Finally, we are also interested in the effects of extra-marital sexuality on the children of the couple. This chapter will consider some theoretical issues and examples.

The cultural contribution

There are times in the history of a culture when sexuality, including extra-marital sex, is treated with more license than at other times. We are in a period which makes extra-marital sexuality more frequent and more likely to occur in a given marriage. Something difficult to assess statistically, but which could be called the 'amount of overall satisfaction with the marriage' also influences the likelihood of affairs.[1] Nevertheless, interpersonally and psychodynamically, the increase of sexual behavior which goes beyond the bounds of a marriage must be understood in the individual case in a way that is specific to the partners in that marriage.

From the standpoint of the variations within individual and cultural value systems, this is not always easy to accomplish. If one begins by taking 'married love' as the point of greatest maturity in a culture, then extra-marital relations would be said to represent lesser (and therefore regressive or defensive) forms of relationships, undertaken

199

by those individuals who are not the most mature. In other cultures where affairs are apparently more openly sanctioned, as perhaps in some social classes in France, we might speculate that this may not be true.

Even within a dominant culture which values marital fidelity, however, the circumstances of a given couple or individual's life may dictate a different value system or a compromise in behavior which does not necessarily represent less mature or defensive behavior. The case of a 50-year-old man married to a woman who was chronically institutionalized and had essentially no conscious mental functioning, illustrates this point in its extremity. When such a person seeks 'extra-marital' attachments which include sex, it would be difficult to call this behavior pathological, even though it could be seen to defend against a sense of loss and loneliness. Even in less extreme examples, such as marriages which have withered but are not over, it may be the staying together and the reluctance to separate, whether through affairs or more direct means, which represent the defensive position.

In what follows, however, the narrowest view of these matters is taken. It is the marriage which is 'the patient,' not the separate individuals — if the members of the couple define it that way and if they share an interest in its viability. Therefore, sexual relationships which go on outside that marriage are considered with reference to the ailment in the marriage.

If one remains true to such clinical orientation about marital and family therapy, then it can be said that *in those marriages which seek help*, extra-marital sexual activity will represent a failure in those marriages. By the definition of the couple who themselves seek help, that failure is a problem for them for which they would like assistance. Avoiding the debate about the morality of their situation, or of 'swinging' and 'open' marriages in general, this vantage point centers simply on the question of what kind of help the couple seeks. What is it about this which contributes to their marital and family difficulty? This perspective prompts an assessment of whether an affair is primarily 'benign' or 'malignant' — that is, whether it may offer an attempt to import love into a marriage when it is lacking, or is an attempt to destroy a bond felt to be oppressive.[2] What follows is said, then, completely within the context of the clinical situation.

The role of split-off objects

The splitting of the physical bond from the marital bond implies the inability of the individual to achieve an integration of his object life – that is, achieve the depressive position – within the marital context. A particular individual might have that capacity if the family situation were different *or* it may be that he would be unable to integrate his feelings toward any single central object regardless of his family context. While it may be difficult in some circumstances to know whether it is the person or his family that is lacking, in practice people often find objects who share their level of integration. As previously discussed, this is often accomplished in mate selection by finding someone with complementary functioning: a man who projects a split-off character trait may find a wife willing to accept that projection, while she assigns out a different complementary role onto him. For instance, a husband may deny weakness in himself by finding a dependent wife of whom he can take care. At the same time, she assigns the strength but perhaps also an unfeeling quality to him, while she takes over the function of 'sensitivity' for both of them. As the marriage progresses, these divisions of self and other may no longer 'stay put,' leading to renewed attempts to find people who can be recipients of the projections.

From its first appearance in infancy, splitting occurs in the service of issues at each level of development. Because each developmental stage rests on the foundation of previous stages, an early weakness in this integrative capacity runs through subsequent steps, taking on new meaning in each new stage. Thus, understood at the level of earliest attachment – that is, at the oral stage – splitting of objects, which takes the literal form of sexual affairs, may signify an overly close, symbiotic attachment which is fought against and/or it may speak of a detachment from the spouse as primary object. The difficulty of containing both good and bad objects within the single attachment may operate both to protect the object from aggression in the self and to protect the self from frustration and aggression at the hands of the object. At the next stage of separation and individuation, roughly corresponding to the level of anal development, rapprochement issues are handled by attempting to control the object. The person attempts to maintain access to the object by various maneuvers, splitting it into pieces (for instance through multiple affairs), dominating it, and controlling its access to the self without surrendering to domination by the object.

Aggression is again crucial here in the service of the control struggles, as it is at all levels of splitting. In the phallic–narcissistic phase, the person may employ the control of the object to maintain a flattering or reassuring reflection of himself and to avoid castration threats.

Herbert S. Strean has categorized the unconscious dynamics of the individual having an extra-marital affair into four overlapping groups that he feels contain the essentials of most affairs: (1) the spouse as an incestuous object with whom sex is therefore forbidden; (2) the spouse as embodiment of superego which is fought; (3) the affair as an expression of bisexuality, especially in multiple-person arrangements, and (4) the affair as a defense against a symbiotic relationship with the spouse.[3]

Strean's categories suggest some of the motivations which may be present when a person undertakes an affair. He can live out certain things with a new partner which he does not choose, or is unable to achieve with his spouse. Affairs usually have several unconscious meanings, some more obvious than others.

> Max and Ginger Wheeler came for sex therapy for her sexual
> aversion and non-orgasmic status. He was 37, she 27. Max was a
> wheeling and dealing character, a mid-level bureaucrat who had a
> lifelong history of premature ejaculation. In the evaluation it also
> emerged that he had a long history of extra-marital affairs. In his
> first marriage, these had begun shortly after the birth of his second
> child. His several affairs had included the one with Ginger. In the
> subsequent marriage to Ginger, he had again begun having affairs
> with several women while Ginger was pregnant with their first child.
> None of the affairs during this marriage had come to light, although
> Ginger knew of the ones during the first marriage.
>
> Max's mother was seen by him as a smothering, judgmental, and
> castrating woman, even though she idolized him. He felt she con-
> trolled and emasculated both of her husbands. He always feared she
> might turn on him, but he also loved the narcissistically rewarding
> attention she gave him.
>
> Their daughter not only competed with him for love from Ginger,
> but she also represented yet another woman coming to surround him
> and threaten him with demands and responsibilities. Fearing control
> and domination by women, he fled to the field to scatter and
> splinter his commitments among so many women that none could
> claim him. It was also behavior like his step-father's who, while

meekly badgered by mother at home, had been owner of a famous beauty salon, much adored by his women clients. Max's own father who died when Max was 5 had lent another part of this behaviour to him: wheeling and dealing. He had been a small-time financier and loan shark for whom life's interests were largely beyond the home. He had, it was rumored, died in the arms of another woman. Ginger's pregnancy and the child's arrival had, in sum, precipitated a combined crisis for this marriage which was met by Ginger's sexual loss of interest and Max's affairs.

Max's premature ejaculation *and* his many sexual affairs shared in expressing a number of elements. He feared domination by the maternal object, and withheld his penis from it by rapid ejaculation, and himself from it by the many affairs. In this sense, Ginger represented the bad object to be avoided while the other women were the exciting objects. The splitting was in the service of preserving his access to the good objects (other women) while preventing a bad maternal object (Ginger) from trapping him. He could thereby also *control* the various objects, keeping any of them from being in too powerful a position in regard to him. The affairs restarted just as he feared Ginger would become less available to him as she was occupied with their daughter.

However, in a paradoxical sense, the splitting (and splintering) of the object protected the good mother in Ginger from the aggression seen in his penis – both via the avoidance of penetration and by keeping the sex active with other women where it could not harm his central object. Thus, in regard to the attitude that Ginger might control and harm him, the splitting avoided her as a bad object and turned to others as exciting objects. In regard to the attitude that *he* was destructive, the splitting protected her as a good mother and protected access to her. In addition, the attention of many women was flattering and reassuring to Max who had many needs at the level of phallic-narcissism, stemming from the fear his own mother's idealization would be withdrawn from him. A final further illustration in Max's case is the unconscious identification with both fathers in having affairs.

Finally, when splitting serves issues of oedipal development, the focus will be on simultaneous avoidance and maintenance of the in-cestuous aspects of the sexual tie. All adult sexuality descends from the person's experience with the parents, but the undigested and unsublimated oedipal issues are often the leading edge of the issues which spur affairs. (On the other hand, the presence of an affair should not be assumed to indicate oedipal development.) The recreation of a triangular situation and the attempts to regain a missing balance between mother and father have so many versions that we cannot enumerate them here. We can say that the acting out of these oedipal issues in lieu of bringing them into a balanced flux within marriage is *usually* an immature or pathological solution. The penchant for acting out these splits instead of working them through within a relationship constitutes an early faultline which runs through all subsequent levels of growth.

> Alice was discovered in bed with her lover by her 3-year-old son. She had methodically chosen her husband as a stable but uninteresting businessman, but she tended to love men who were more creative and less reliable. Her lover was an artist, but too dependent and unrealistic a person for her to imagine marrying. Before her marriage, she had an extended relationship with a flamboyant military officer, a fatherly older man.
>
> Alice's early history involved the idealization of her father and the denigration of her mother. Father was a dapper, cheerful, confident man who was solicitous of Alice. Mother was seen as dour, depressed, and unattractive. Alice remembered fantasies of replacing her mother and living with father. At 16 she left home for art school and the first of a series of romantic attachments to older men.

Although this patient began in adolescence to choose older men as an embodiment of father, she made a marital choice based on choosing a safer man to avoid the threatening retaliation of the oedipal choice. She was then left still longing for the exciting oedipal object which she found through affairs with artistic men. The symbolic discovery of her affair by her oedipal-aged son who was also the recipient of her own oedipal feelings, added a note of irony to the situation.

While these four elements are present in many, and perhaps all, affairs, they are not sufficient explanation of the unconscious motives for affairs. They represent aspects of object relationships present normally and abnormally. What underlies each category when an affair occurs is the acting out of object-splitting to achieve a *particular* relationship to both the *libidinal and anti-libidinal object*. At the same time, the splitting protects both the libidinal part-objects and the ideal object from the aggression of the anti-libidinal ego.

The life stage of individuals

The life stage of each member of the family may also contribute to any family event. It may be that it is the sum of their individual forces which forms a final motivating cause for one person's going outside the family boundaries sexually. Mid-life crises or the dawning sexuality of an adolescent child are forces whose influence can be felt in extra-marital affairs as well as in other sexual symptomatology. For instance, in the example of Max Wheeler, the pregnancy of his wife was a significant threat to his sense of being able to rely on her as a symbiotic object. In addition, his own age became a threat to his ability to get reassurance from her. (See also the examples in the chapter on mid-life crises, chapter 16.)

The family dynamics of extra-marital sexuality

Robin Skynner has shown that we can think of some families as show-ing a shared deficit in integrative capacity in which the members collude in a family-wide process of splitting which augments the splitting by individuals.[4] This is one of many ways that extra-marital sexual activity can be said to express an aspect of a central issue on behalf of the couple or the whole family. In turn, the overall family will be affected in some way by the extra-marital sex *and* by the factors which triggered it in the first place. In this case, the family boundaries are enlarged to include the outside party psychologically within the family group.

As a group, the family may be expressing a mode of relating by symbiotic fusion from which one spouse attempts to escape for them all. Or the family may be expressing a shared sense that something is missing. Perhaps they may be unconsciously concerned by an aggres-sive force within their bounds which threatens the family with dis-solution. There may be a fear that a generative function is not possible in the family without the importation of something from the outside. The listing of these possibilities is meant to include a developmental range of family-group preoccupations or unconscious fantasies which would support extra-marital sex as a family-motivated event, whether one or both partners were actually engaged in it.

In each particular family, we will have to examine the situation to determine whether the balance of initiative is with the family or individual forces. If, however, family and individual are at too much psychological variance over a long enough period, then the family will no longer meet the needs of the individual and this incongruity will often lead to a threatened break from the family. The same forces will contribute to adolescent sexual acting out which may bear important resemblances to the adult sexual acting out. In some of these families, the same forces may spur sexual symptomatology in parent and adolescent.

> Harper Winchester's childhood was marked by the kind of high-level parental neglect in which a maid substituted for most parental functions, while his parents were largely absent working. The maid, a young, uneducated woman, used to invite him to her room for intercourse frequently in his pre-adolescent and early adolescent years. In adulthood, Harper had a continued pattern of multiple affairs from the time of his marriage to Sarah, but when his oldest daughter, Karen, reached adolescence, he began to feel squeezed out of his family. For the first time he developed a prolonged outside relationship which now came to light. Sarah threatened divorce if he could not give up the relationship. At the same time, the 15-year-old Karen began to flaunt a new sexuality, staying out all night and keeping company known for their sexual and drug involvement. Everyone in this family shared a fear that there was insufficient nurturance. When Karen developed a more undesirable sexuality, a cycle began in which her mother felt threatened and anxiously withdrew. Harper felt aroused by Karen as a reminder of the maid of his own childhood and turned more definitively outside the family as a defense against the arousal of incestuous feelings. And Karen, feeling the family stirrings and identifying with the sexualization of dependency needs, turned to sexual adolescent attachments.

Throughout this volume, it has been noted that the object relations life of the current family descends directly from the experience of each member of the couple with his own family of origin. The influence of those internalized families forms the internal 'culture' on which current activity is based. Both our understanding and our treatment strategies will need to focus on reintegration, therefore, not only of the current family's relationship and on the reacceptance of projective identifications by each of the individuals, but on these processes in regard to internally split objects as well – what Steirlin has called 'intergenerational reconciliation.'[5]

The role of the secret in the secret affair

Another important element in the extra-marital affair is its life as a 'secret.' Alfred Gross notes that the function of having secrets changes with the psychosexual stage of the person.[6] At the anal level, the need for a secret is the need for a possession to control and withhold from the object. As the child progresses, the conflict is manifested in the ambivalent urges to retain and surrender the secret to the object. At the phallic stage, the secret tends to be used in the service of narcissistic exhibitionism, and finally at the oedipal level, it is used as a means of initiating friendships, maintaining trust, and as an aid to wooing. In the oedipal period, the infantile neurosis may take on the quality of secrecy in that 'the child may identify the secret with the adult genitals and by this, or some other means, internalize the secret as a substitute for his oedipal wishes, and incorporate it into his ego.'[7]

If we extend Gross's insights into secrets to apply to affairs as the secret life of the marriage, we can see how they may express varying aspects of the relationship. The secrecy of the affair may be more important than the sex itself, expressing distance and withholding from the spouse. This may have the quality of anal control of the object – 'I won't give all of me to you because I'm in charge of me' – or of defense against earlier symbiotic fusion – 'My sexual intimacy is with another. Therefore, I am separate from you.' Or it may express an exhibitionism – 'See what I can do. I am more powerful than you will allow me to be.' Or it may reflect an oedipal relationship – 'I can have the other parent which you as my parent would not allow me to have if you knew.' In another view, the secret can be maintained in defiance of the anti-libidinal object as superego so as to maintain the attachment while affording the self-forbidden pleasure. Finally, the secret may be shared by both spouses, either consciously or unconsciously, in a false solution of oedipal issues and in an attempt to have an intimacy around the secret which they cannot have directly through the sex. In this paradoxically constructive motivation the shared secret may also be an attempt to import some physical love into a marriage in which it is felt to be lacking in order to maintain the marriage itself.

Of course, the alternate perspective is also important. What is the role of the secret held between the spouse and lover? The same dynamics apply here, so that it may be oedipal, symbiotic, or in the service of controlling aggression. For instance, the lovers may be sharing an intimacy whose secrecy is the shared oedipal victory and this victorious sharing constitutes the principal poignancy of their relationship. For others, however, the shared secret may operate to establish a symbiosis free from the threatening maternal object by proving that the bad object is not 'in the know' about the secret liaison.

The following example illustrates the attempt to exploit the secret aspect of sexual affairs.

Alexandra wished that her marriage had more passion and more sexual vitality in it. Her husband, she felt, was a steady and reliable person whose interest in sex was secondary to his interest in everything else. She embarked by plan on a series of affairs, feeling that her husband knew in a way that she was doing so. After sometime she then confronted him with the fact she had affairs, hoping it would mobilize him into a greater sexual interest. She had enjoyed sharing the secret life with other men (kept from her husband as an oedipal mother), but when that began to tire, she attempted to increase their intimacy by sharing the secret. She urged him to have an affair as well, hoping that another woman would stimulate his sexual interest and would help him appreciate her more. Instead, she found that he wanted to confide in Alexandra about his affairs, investing more energy in the discussion with her than in the pursuit of extra-marital sexuality.

The sexual disjunction in this case represented the substitution of interactions around early mothers for an oedipal relationship. When Alexandra attempted a manipulation of her 'secret life' to revitalize a more oedipal connection, she triggered her husband's version of an oedipal relationship: he preferred talking about sex with a safe maternal figure to treating Alexandra as a fitting oedipal object herself.

Sexual identification and affairs

The example of Max and Ginger Wheeler demonstrates one of the more frequent issues in the genesis of extra-marital affairs: identification with one or other parent. In that example, Max identified with the father of his early childhood who had real affairs, and the step-father of his later childhood who, in so far as Max knew, had only symbolic ones with the women who formed his clientele. The adult identification with parents which is enacted represents a return to the infantile identification with the parent in a fantasy constellation. The person may or may not be conscious of elements of such an identification.

Max's wife, Ginger, provides an example of this in her original 'affair' with him. Here she, a young and unmarried girl, begins an affair with an older man as an enactment of her oedipal fantasy. Then, later, her identification with the mother whom she defeated in the original fantasy now leads her to expect to be abandoned and, by withholding her sexual response, she unconsciously encourages Max to have affairs.

The understanding of extra-marital affairs as enactments of barriers to whole object relationships within marriage leads one to many issues which undermine this achievement. Sources from the early object history and developmental phases of each partner and of the whole family offer fresh attacks on the vulnerable marriage. In some instances, however, the extra-marital affair may be an attempt to inject love into a deprived marriage. And at times, it works: an unknowing spouse is jarred into a new awareness of what was missing (see the example of Mr Connel, chapter 16), and with or without further help, the couple reorganizes in a better way. However, it is also often not successful and the effort is either for naught or actually backfires.

The complications of these issues raise important questions about the clinical management of the extra-marital affair, which is such an extensive aspect of marital treatment in so many cases. Masters and Johnson, for instance, cite a number of cases in which sexual secrets, including the secret affair, blocked therapeutic work.[8] The task of therapy is to promote higher levels of integration of the person and of object relationships. By this definition of the therapeutic task, the affair will be seen as a fragmentation of the marriage, making it difficult or impossible for the couple to pull together even though it may serve common defensive purposes.

The integration of the split and scattered parts of the relationship emotionally and sexually is the task of therapeutic work in marriages whose difficulty is expressed in part by the extra-marital affair. A previous article has dealt with the value of the relevation of sexual secrets in the therapeutic setting.[9] This and other aspects of the treatment of extra-marital affairs will be discussed in the second volume of this work.

Chapter 19
Toward a framework for sexual maturity

What we call 'genital love' is a fusion of disagreeable elements:
of genital satisfaction and pregenital tenderness. The expression of
this fusion is genital identification, and the reward for bearing the
strain of this fusion is the possibility of regressing periodically for
some happy moments to a really infantile stage of *no* reality testing,
to the short-lived re-establishment of the complete union of micro-
and macrocosmos.

Michael Balint, 'On genital love'*

This book represents an attempt to take advantage of the opportunity
provided by new knowledge in the field of human sexuality to explore
the ways in which sexual life expresses the inner world of the individual
and thereby influences his relationships. This exploration has offered,
in turn, an opportunity to see how the sexual aspects of relationships
modify that inner world. This final chapter attempts to formulate what
it is that constitutes mature sexuality in the context of the link
between inner and outer worlds.

More than twenty years ago, Michael Balint suggested that mature
love was the result of a combination of pre-genital elements and genitality.[1] The pre-genital elements, brought into a sexual episode in fore-
play, integrate the tenderness of the successful infantile inheritance
with genital expression in an exchange between mature sexual partners.
All that comes early in development is included and gives harmonious
expression in such a union.

In a more recent discussion, Levay and Kagle outline a progression
toward sexual maturation by characterizing three levels of sexual
achievement: those of the ability to achieve (1) pleasure; (2) intimacy;
and (3) cooperation.[2] Sexual development can go astray at any of these

211

levels. *Pleasure* level difficulties refer to the developmental inability of the person to experience pleasure himself, for whatever reason. *Intimacy* difficulties refer to the inability to experience pleasure with another. And trouble in *cooperation* represents an inability to work together for sexual pleasure which can, however, be enjoyed if it occurs. What may appear to be the symptom may have roots at any of these levels. For instance, some non-orgasmic women have a lack of knowledge about how to enjoy sex (pleasure) but are able to be intimate and to cooperate. Others who can experience pleasure have a fear of intimacy or opening up to the other person. And for a third group, the inability is in working and playing together.

> An example in which a shared narcissistic preoccupation shattered intimacy and cooperation was illustrated by a couple who went into a restaurant and ordered one ice cream sundae to share. The sundae came with one cherry. The wife thought that if her husband loved her, he would give the cherry to her; he thought that if she loved him, she wouldn't want to take it from him.

My own conceptualization of sexual maturation begins with a one-person, two-person, three-person progression. It focuses not on the expression of the sexual drive or the quality of orgasm in sexual situations, but rather on sex as one example of play at the different levels of development.

The developmental levels of play

As the child moves from his first union with his mother into a separate, although attached, state in the relationship, his first object of play is mother's body. From her body he moves to the second 'toy,' his own body. He learns to play with himself as a direct result of her loving gaze and handling, later developing transitional objects as symbols of her and as a memorial to the lost closeness of the progressively attenuated exchanges between them. When he launches out on his own as a toddler, his first toys represent bodily functions and his play is egocentrically absorbed with himself, with the toy as a fused but separating part of himself.[3] With the later achievement of more separation, the play concerns his relationship to the mother-of-separation. Toys are now the transitional objects and the play is aimed at mastery, at doing it himself, without sharing, and at getting the other person to mirror his feelings and needs. He wants to be allowed to be in charge and to be supplied but to be separate. Finally, as the child enters oedipal development, his play becomes the lively, cooperative fantasy play we are so familiar with, the world of pretend, of fantasy elaboration and of trading roles with peers. It is a more mutual, sharing kind of play with which adults sympathetically identify. Latency represents the period of apparent desexualization of play and of first extending it to the wider world away from the family, while adolescence represents the merging of play with the reality of the world, a chance for the creative play of childhood to become a creative approach to those realities.[4]

Sexual maturity: A function of relationships

Sexual maturity is not a fixed quality, a permanent achievement to be attained only at a certain stage in one's life. It is rather the development of a capacity for the level of sexual exchange appropriate to each stage of life. There is, then, a sexual maturity for the infant, the child, the adolescent, the young adult, and the older adult, each different and each building on what has gone before. Nor does sexual maturity belong to the single individual. It exists in a relationship between two people, and in a larger sense in the family in which they live and relate.

A stage-appropriate definition of mature sexuality which occurs in relationships with others implies also that the individuals have the capacity to interact sexually so as to respond and reflect experience in a manner which gives the other person a sense of having a secure attachment and of being loved.

At each stage of development, the individual has the *potential* to offer a response to others which gives them this sense of well-being, and which therefore contributes to their own phase-appropriate satisfaction. For instance, when babies first 'sexually' play with the mother's breast or face and use her arms, hands, and breast to form their environment, there is infinite potential for giving pleasure to the mother. Later, when the baby's auto-erotism is centered on its own genitals, it recreates for itself a part of the physical relationship with her and reinforces an aspect of the object relationship to her.

Even the apparently solo practice of adolescent masturbation involves a *potential* for external relatedness. It is a way of consolidating the relationship of self to internal objects and thereby preparing for future skirmishes and encounters which will impinge on the inner world as the adolescent attempts new levels of external relatedness.

Finally, the mature adult sexual interchange values the mutuality of two people, each of whom has a relatively well-established inner world, allowing a trusting exchange with each other and thereby creating the possibility of growth in themselves and in their wider family.

Thus, at any given moment, the maturity of sexual relatedness is an achievement resting on the balance between the individual, his internal objects, and his external relationships.

A framework for sexual maturity

A framework for sexual maturity can now be constructed along guidelines which allow us to include elements of early object relationships in the assessment of later development.

I   The earliest level of maturation relates to *sexual interest stemming from an interest in one's own body as experienced with the mother of early attachment*. The other person is used as a masturbatory device and the only relationships which count are ones with the internal objects fused with the self. One's own pleasure is the sole measure of the success as it was originally in masturbation and as it was originally experienced with the 'good mother' who in the beginning asked very little for herself. It represents the wish to keep the object fused with and focused on the self, to avoid the risk of loss and separateness. This level only represents an aberration if it is the highest level of interactive pleasure which the individual achieves. It is also a normal *component* of more mature sexual interaction.

II The second level is that of *sexual interest stemming from an interest in the mother-of-separation as object*. Here intimacy is the goal of sexual activity, but primarily it is an intimacy focused on getting the object to provide a mirroring sense of security, safety and well-being, despite the separation which exists from the object. Mutual sexual satisfaction is not the principal aim, but only the securing of a safe, pleasurable attachment to the mother. Again, this is a normal component of higher level interactions, 'immature' only if it is the maximal achievement available to the individual or couple.

III It is only at the third level, *sexual interest stemming from oedipal relationships*, that cooperation and mutual sexual satisfaction are generally in mind, although this should allow for satisfaction which includes the earlier modes in a flexible interchange between partners. It is only at this level that the kind of sexual playfulness and interplay associated with 'genital sexuality' fully occurs, integrating pregenital tenderness and bodily genitality.[5]

IV Once this achievement is possible, a couple has a base on which to build toward the family achievements which stem from successful *latency* and *adolescent growth*: the sublimated investment in children, work, and the creative products of intimacy, cooperation and secure self-reliance.

This is partly a way of saying what John Bowlby[6] has said: the growth of self-reliance and of full adult productivity rests on secure attachment and the ability to be autonomous which flows from that security. In adult life, sexuality has the potential to revitalize the connection between the internal figures of our past and the current family, gathering together myriad aspects of physical and emotional growth, as it brings the problems and the reassurances of past relationships forward into our current lives. Sex forms the bodily link in this process. It acts at an unconscious level to maintain a loving attachment to primary objects despite life's many assaults on that attachment.

For those who have achieved a development which includes sexual maturity, a successful sexual interaction bonds together disparate elements from infancy to adulthood. In so doing, it renews the original psychosomatic partnership and bridges the gap between internal objects and external relationships. I hope this volume will contribute to the task of understanding the difficulties in achieving such integration, and that the second volume will contribute further to the treatment of these difficulties.

Appendix I
Object relations theory and the family

The theory which I have found most useful clinically in understanding sexuality and the life of couples is that of the British object relations school. This is a theory of object relations based on the converging views of independent thinkers, Michael Balint, Harry Guntrip, Donald Winnicott, and Ronald Fairbairn, the principal theorist. Their views grew out of a Freudian theoretical background and were heavily influenced by clinical contributions from Melanie Klein and her followers of the English school, although they did not subscribe to the Kleinian theoretical system.[1]

Appendix I sketches the contributions of Fairbairn and Klein, and then briefly outlines the application of object relations theory to understanding families, drawing on the 'group analytic' approach as explored by Henry Dicks and Robin Skynner.

1 The object relations theory of W.R.D. Fairbairn[2]

Fairbairn's model holds that the infant's psyche at birth consists of a unitary or pristine, undifferentiated ego in a helpless, dependent relation to the object of its attachment, the mother. To cope with the anxiety of this precarious situation of helplessness in the face of inevitable frustration when mother could not be perfectly depended upon, the ego defends itself from the helplessness by 'splitting off' and repressing *two aspects of the mother* – the need-exciting part and the need-denying part, called the *libidinal* and *anti-libidinal objects*, respectively. They are repressed along with the *part of the ego* that invested in them, namely, the *libidinal* and *anti-libidinal parts of the ego*, and with the *affects* which in each case characterize the relationship between the part of the ego and its object. The mental apparatus now includes a libidinal ego with its exciting (libidinal) object, a system characterized by the affects of excitement and longing; and an anti-libidinal ego and its rejecting (anti-libidinal) object, characterized by affects of frustration and aggression. These structures are split off from conscious experience by repression. What remains is the conscious part

216

of the infant psyche represented as the 'central ego' and the dependable, caring, not too frustrating or exciting part of the mother as experienced by the helpless infant, represented by what is called the 'ideal object.' Fairbairn also associated the central ego with more conscious function. The 'split-off' (or repressed) introjected objects tend to remain relatively unmodified and unmetabolized over time because they are subject to repression. They tend to retain their infantile, primitive quality regardless of the person's later experiences. It is because of the prevailing existence of these split-off systems that the excitement or frustration of intimate interactions (which activate them more easily) precipitate seemingly idiosyncratic, powerful, and abruptly changing experiences of the self and others, in spite of the current experience of the 'real' other with whom interaction is different from that of the internalized early object relationship.

Similarly, the repression ensures that the libidinal and anti-libidinal systems are the main contributors to transference phenomena in later life. Reference to the accompanying diagram (figure A.1) will show that they thereby 'deplete' the central ego in an economic sense, in an ongoing way.

One other factor described by Fairbairn which is of interest is the way in which the anti-libidinal ego, because of its attachment to the rejecting object, powerfully reinforces the repressions of the libidinal ego by the central ego (see figure A.1). To understand this, I should clarify that the anti-libidinal object is the frustrating 'bad object', the

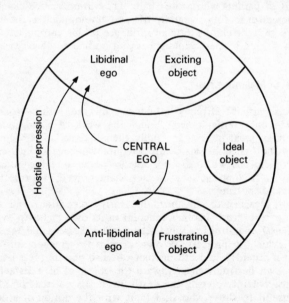

Figure A.1 Fairbairn's model of psychic organization

one against whom anger is felt for privation. The libidinal object is not, on the other hand, the really 'good object' any more than the anti-libidinal object represents the useful limit-setting aspect of parental privation. The anti-libidinal object is both the *actually* frustrating and the *fantasized* depriving aspects of the mother. Just so, the libidinal or exciting ego is the internalization of the needs left by a feeling of unrequited love and intolerable longing. The libidinal object is one that would in fantasy excite an intolerable, unsatisfiable need and compensate for the longing with an unsatisfying overindulgence. The libidinal ego attempts to induce such behavior.

To return to the interaction between the libidinal and anti-libidinal structures, we can now say that the rage over frustration tends to make the irrationality of the libidinal ego and object all the harder to get at. The sense of privation tends to drive the child to rationalize and feel entitled to the exciting object, and at the same time to defend all the more strongly against the pain of becoming aware of any sense of neediness. This makes the libidinal system difficult to uncover and analyze, offering an explanation why, for instance, a couple's longing for love from each other may be covered by hate and denial.

It is these two structures and the sense of the individual at war within himself which generate the transference phenomena in psycho-analytically based treatment. Patients act partly as if their therapists are reasonable cooperative helpers and partly as if they are parents who excite an unpleasant longing, or are the depriving, misunderstanding part of parents whom they hate. These transference elements are also a powerful factory in family life and development as the inner world of the growing child exerts an influence on his current external world and is shaped by new experiences in a mutual feedback system.

2　The work of Melanie Klein[3]

Fairbairn was initially strongly influenced by the earlier work of Melanie Klein on internal objects,[4] and the work of Klein and her group remains of great interest to family theoreticians.[5] The Kleinians hold that, in the first half year of life, the infant organizes experiences by mental operations which are not integrated because the infant is capable only of the primitive processes characterized by projection, introjection, and splitting.

The infant deals with the inevitable early frustrations and with the anxiety of the death instinct inherent in its own make-up by the primitive mental operations of what Klein called *the paranoid/schizoid position* in which it projects its own primitive aggression into the image of its mother. (The death instinct can also be interpreted to be the infant's own destructiveness toward the object of his satisfaction. While this way of interpreting the death instinct is not that of Klein, it may be useful to those who find fault with the notion of a death instinct.) Paranoid anxiety and splitting of the ego and object are characteristic of the paranoid/schizoid position. The use of the word 'position' was chosen to emphasize a configuration of object relations, anxieties and the defenses against them which begin here in the first three or four months and persist throughout the rest of life. The first position is never fully replaced by the second and continues as a potential mode of operation.

The infant cannot conceive of a whole mother in these months since its ability to process experience is fragmentary. To protect the good experiences with mother, it projects the rage into an image of the breast and various other parts including the penis. These are then re-introjected into the infant to form the beginning of the infant's internal world. The frustrating or absent breast is felt to be the '*bad*' or '*persecuting object*' because the infant has projected his anger into it and it now is felt as attacking. It forms the prototype of the bad object, but because the infant can only conceive of a fragment of the mother at this stage, it is termed a *part-object*. Another image of the breast and other parts of the mother are experienced as loving and giving during feeding and comforting. The infant's own good feelings are projected onto this part of the mother (partly to keep them safe from its rage and frustration) and re-introjected from this image of her to form the '*ideal object*.' Klein's use of the term 'ideal object' is different from that of Fairbairn. For Klein, the ideal object is the recipient of the investment of the libidinal drive, and the bad object is the recipient of the death instinct. Thus, the original object is divided into two basic components: ideal and persecuting. For Fairbairn, there are three objects: Ideal (the object of the central ego); Exciting (the libidinal system); and Rejecting (the anti-libidinal system). No effort is made at this point to reconcile this usage. It should simply be kept in mind that the use made of the term 'ideal object' in this section follows Klein's use of it as a part-object. For her, the true 'good object' is a whole object which only comes into existence as a result of the intergrating developments of the depressive position.

In the first months, ideal and bad part-objects are experienced as separated, and the infant's internal world is fragmented. However, the infant is also seen as having an active mental role in 'splitting' the ideal objects from bad, keeping them separate in order to maintain the sense and internal experience of goodness (satisfaction, love). It tends to project the bad out onto objects viewed as external in order to keep the sense of goodness inside. Such mechanisms as splitting and projection are the basis for later mental sorting and for the establishment of the boundaries of the self as distinguished from the mother, but they also leave a legacy of tendencies to treat other people and the self as all good (ideal) or all bad. Even when the infant first sees mother as a whole person, she is two different people – an 'ideal object' fairy godmother when she is present or providing and a 'bad object' witch when she is absent or depriving. Because the infant attributes all good experiences to the ideal object, he wants it to be a part of him so he is never without it. Longing to possess and identify with the ideal, he attacks it enviously. The destructive rages of envy form some of the earliest attacks on sources of goodness and of life.

In summary, these earliest months of the paranoid/schizoid position are characterized by the mental processes of splitting, projection, and introjection, part-object relationships and a confused experience of disintegration.

In the second half of the first year, the *depressive position* begins when the infant begins to recognize mother as a *whole object*, and experiences ambivalence toward her rather than splitting her into separate part-objects. His experience is now progressively that of attacking an ambivalently loved mother, losing her as an external and internal object. The good object and part-object is the loving and giving mother and her parts, but it is not 'ideal' in that its bad parts are recognized and tenuously tolerated. Depressive anxieties include the pain of guilt, loss, and depression, as the good object is felt to be vulnerable to attacks. But the depressive anxieties also lead to the capacity to mourn and to pine for the good object and to make reparation. When the infant in the depressive position feels he has lost the good object through his own destructiveness, he experiences despair. Although he may regress painfully to paranoid mechanisms in defense against this despair and guilt, if all goes well he will gradually develop the capacity to tolerate depression and guilt and to make reparation.[6] Reparation is aimed at restoring the loved but injured object. While true reparation stems from this wish and involves a making up to the injured object in order to restore the lost happiness of a harmonious internal world, the use of 'manic defenses' shortcuts the process by restoring to 'triumph, control, and contempt' in object relationships. These are an expression of omnipotent denial of depressive anxieties.

Another word is in order about Klein's view of the father and the combined parents. The infant is seen as longing for the father's penis from a time very shortly after his perception of the breast. Before father and mother are fully differentiated, he constructs a fantasy figure of the parents combined in intercourse. The father's penis is then felt to be part of the mother's body. Klein envisaged an early form of the oedipus complex (the rivalry with one parent for possession of the other) from the beginning of the depressive position, experienced in pre-genital terms. Under the sway of early fantasies of the parents united together, the infant feels acutely deprived, jealous, and envious since the parents are seen as gratifying each other in an intense coupling from which he is excluded.

Many of the ideas of the Kleinian group are controversial, especially their use of the death instinct as the source of aggression, the early dating of the first appearance of complex mental phenomena, and their nearly exclusive emphasis on the infant's contribution to his own growth to the exclusion of the parents and the real world. However, the insights of this group can usefully inform us about mental functioning in later life. For instance, most relevant to a theory of marital life are the concepts of introjective and projective identification.

Introjective identification 'is the result when the object is introjected into the ego which then identifies with some or all of its characteristics.' Conversely, *projective identification* 'is the result of the projection of parts of the self into an object. It may result in the object being perceived as having acquired the characteristics of the projected part of the self but it can also result in the self becoming identified with the object of its projection.' *Pathological projective identification* 'is the result of minute disintegration of the self or parts of the self which are then projected into the object and disintegrated.'[7] Projective identification has varying aims: to avoid separation from the ideal object; to gain control of the source of danger in the bad object; to get rid of bad parts of the self by putting them into the object and then attacking it; to put the good self outside to protect it from the badness in the self; or 'to improve the external object through a kind of primitive projective reparation.'[8]

While Klein's concepts extend our ability to see the role of introjective and projective processes, of envy, guilt, manic defenses, and repair, they give less help in conceptualizing the role of the parents or of the early mother. But with Fairbairn's formulation, which does not view the infant's fantasy life in isolation, we have the opportunity to consider the contribution of both the actual experience with the mother *and* the effect the child has in interpreting, interacting with, digesting, and contributing to his environment. The combination of the two views can help construct a useful tool for the understanding of reciprocal and interactive processes.

3 An object relations view of family development

The family is an institution which has a course of development of its own. Its basic task is to provide stable attachment figures for each of its members while simultaneously promoting their individualized development. In turn each individual triggers changes in the family group in response to his or her characteristics, both those which are unique to him as a person, and those generally expected at this stage of development.

There are some broadly similar characteristics of families consisting of couples without children, which are distinct from families with infants, which are different yet again from families with adolescents. For each of these groupings we could list some general issues and developmental tasks triggered by the constellation of developmental phases represented by the family members. For instance, the nursing infant makes a demand on the mother which may precipitate certain issues for her, especially if she is depressed or fearful of the experience for her own reasons. But even if she is willing and responsive, new developments in her are triggered by the interaction with the baby. She *becomes* a mother because of the infant. In this sense, the infant gives birth to its mother as a mother. In turn, her interaction with her

husband changes and their previous relationship must alter to accom-
modate the new person, so that the overall family constellation under-
goes major alterations. In the language of infant–mother research,
instead of one reciprocal relationship now being negotiated, the mother
now adapts to two cue–affect–behavior synchronies, one with the
infant and one with her mate. To a lesser degree, the father does the
same. Thus, the adult developmental phase of parents is both cued by
and exerts influence upon the development of the child.

In these interlocking aspects of family development the child takes
in its experience of the parents at any one stage as data about the
'internalized object' and the 'ego' or part of himself corresponding
to the experience of that object at that developmental time. Since
the repressed libidinal and anti-libidinal systems are relatively unmodified over time, they are carried forward as parts of the self which
do not mature. At the level of their *central egos*, that is, in the main
stream of growth, parent and child continue to evolve and their
relationship represents 'real' interaction. But the aspects of the parent
taken into the repressed internal object systems tend not to evolve
and the child acts partly as if the real parent who had changed with
him is or ought to be the old 'internal object' parent of previous experience, subject to the action of the child's repressed libidinal and anti-
libidinal egos. Partly, of course, the actual parent also does act in the
same way as he did previously, and it is this similarity of parental experience over a prolonged period which tends to strengthen an internal
constellation. To the extent the parent continues to act in the old way,
the introjected model is reinforced and that part of the child's inner
world becomes more fixed and more resistant to change. Those things
formed first in life tend to be the models which persist – both because
inner and outer worlds are closer in experience and because they often
are reinforced by parental consistency.[9] Partly, however, the inner
model of experience can and does change with new experience – but
with an inertia that tends to conserve the known in the face of fresh
experience. The reason that psychotherapy takes so long is that this
conservation of old models permits change only slowly, and even then
each internal alteration involves a loss of the known internal world
which must be mourned before a new internal model can replace it.[10]

So at any one moment, a growing child *tends* to be using his parent
partly in a transferential way, partly with the illusion that he is in the
same place and has the same parent of the earlier experience, perhaps of
many years before, despite the fact that the same child is also sending
signals that he needs a parent appropriate to his current level of
development. The parent will often feel this inconsistency, as he also
wishes to respond to the current needs of the older child but is being
treated as though he were the parent of the younger one. Of course,
frequently the parent himself is being drawn to being the way he was
at the earlier time, or alternatively he may shun a role which is ordinarily required by a stage of the child's development because of the
reactivation of his own old conflicts.

The final interaction between parent and child transpires not only between central egos and real external objects. It is also a 'conversation' between repressed unconscious parts of child and parent. For instance, during a transaction with its parent the child's libidinal ego may unconsciously seek something in the parent which corresponds to the child's exciting object. But if the parent fails to respond, the child may meet what he takes to be an anti-libidinal object instead. This situation is represented in figure A.2. The child now experiences the parent as a rejecting object, reactivating the anti-libidinal system. Meanwhile, the parent is often also searching for a lost and cherished libidinal object in the child and may equally feel that he finds a frustrating, angry object who reminds him of his own anti-libidinal parents. Such a mutually frustrating situation often develops between adolescents and their parents. This situation also frequently pertains to marital partners where central ego functioning is compromised because of sexual dysfunction and they are increasingly thrown back on anti-libidinal interaction.

Figure A.3 sums up the above theoretical example between this child expressing a transferential earlier need and a frustrated parent, *or* between any two people in an interaction in which each seeks the libidinal object while feeling they each meet the anti-libidinal one.

In each case, in so far as the interaction between any two people is satisfying to their 'central egos,' the main aims of each to establish and maintain a loving attachment are met. In the security of this mutual interdependence, the central egos may dare to express the repressed libidinal and anti-libidinal systems with relative safety about the threat to destroy the attachment. What gives these interactions the power they have to be repeated again and again is firstly the unending need we all have to be attached to others throughout life, even though which specific people we are most closely attached to and the ways we express the attachments must change with development; and secondly, the hope for tolerance of the repressed systems so that they can be restored to personality in a way which is then more freely available to the relationship.

Each of us, then, grows up carrying an assortment of internalized objects, good and bad ones, that constitute the way past family interactions with father, mother, and siblings, are remembered. And we have varying bits of ourselves which correspond to those inner objects. This constitutes the 'internal family' and it stays with us throughout our lives. These internal objects 'look over our shoulders' in present reality interactions and influence them. And in turn we, in our interactions with our children, even when we are still influenced by our internal figures, become the stuff of their internal family.

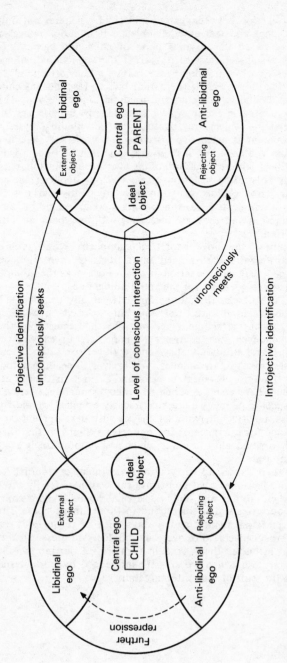

Figure A.2. The mechanism here is the interaction of the child's projective and introjective identifications with the parent as the child meets frustration, unrequited yearning, or trauma. The diagram depicts the child longing to have his needs met and identifying with similar trends in the parent via projective identification. If he meets with rejection, he identifies with the frustration of the parent's own anti-libidinal system via introjective identification. In an internal reaction to the frustration, the libidinal system is further repressed by the renewed force of the child's anti-libidinal system.

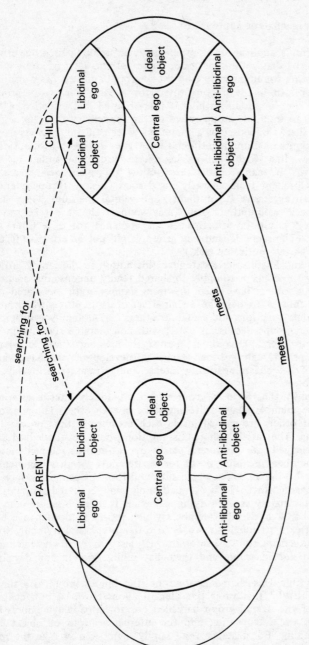

Figure A.3. The unconscious levels of interaction of a parent and child in a mutually frustrating exchange.

4 The group-analytic approach to families

Wilfred Bion's application of psychoanalytic thinking to group life[11] has taught us that within any group there are two sorts of group mentality existing simultaneously: the 'work group' and the 'basic assumption group.' In a group constituted for a task, the 'work group' embodies the functioning which is task-oriented and effective, while the 'basic assumption' group refers to the tendency for group action based on shared unconscious assumptions which fit unconscious needs of the members. Bion identified three types of basic assumptions: dependency, fight–flight, and pairing. Pierre Turquet has added 'fusion' to the list.[12] We can see how these follow the psychosocial stages of child development from an early fused stage (fusion) through dependent (oral), aggressive (fight–flight), and genital (pairing) stages. The hidden 'basic assumption' group may support the task (the way a dependency group is effective as an audience for a lecturer) or subvert it. (The same dependency group would not be effective in the conduct of a self-motivated task.)

Zinner and Shapiro have extended this notion to the family group, modifying the concept to apply to shared family unconscious assumptions, while others have used the term 'family myth' or shared unconscious fantasy to describe a shared set of assumptions which may support some functions and undercut others.[13] The family is different from other groups because it exists with considerable stability in its membership over a long time, because its members share long-term relationships through a broad range of developmental phases, and because of the characteristically intense and intimate relationship to internal objects.

The family thus forms a group which is uniquely interpenetrating, and whose members have a lifelong stake in each other. The relationships with others are carried inside each member as the context for daily living. The family's shared assumptions, both acknowledged and unacknowledged, are fashioned partly by the real attachment needs of each member (including needs for separateness within attachments) and partly by the anxieties which surround those attachments, such as real or imagined loss. The well-functioning family's shared assumption life operates mainly as a steadying influence. It offers a secure core of identity shared by family members which resists sudden change but which is flexible enough to evolve in different phases of family life. The shared unconscious assumptions may also express fears which are felt to be unmanageable and they may inhibit growth and development.

It is within this shared context of 'the family group as a single psychic entity'[14] that projective identifications are lived out, characteristics of the overall group parcelled out to individual members by projection and introjection, and the interpenetrations of object life given meaning. For instance, one family member may take the role of expressing all the family's disappointments while another expresses all its optimisms; one its strength and another its weakness.

The understanding of families in terms of the myths, shared interfering preoccupations, and task functioning is further enhanced by the work of Cooklin and Skynner.[15] Family members are seen as sharing a 'central group preoccupation' which Cooklin has linked to 'a shared avoidance of true internalization and separation.' In this view, the family's concentration is focused on shared defenses and concerns, the most important parts of which are unconscious. Shared parts of the repressed libidinal and anti-libidinal systems are in effect pooled and family interaction now operates to avoid acknowledgement of the shared family preoccupations, and to hide aspects of attachment and separation which represent vulnerabilities. Each family member will carry some specific aspect of the shared vulnerability, and is depleted in his outward capacity to function to the extent this is so, although some family members may overfunction in response to their unconscious role. The whole of the preoccupation can only be understood by a knowledge of its parts.

Applying group analytic understanding to the practical treatment of families draws most directly on the group-analytic approach developed by Foulkes. He viewed a therapy group as having a unified life.[16] The components of the overall group reside in various individuals and interpretive understanding focuses on both the whole and on the parts. Changes in the group of necessity change the individual and vice versa.

In the family-interpretive approach derived from this method, the family is seen as possessing the constructive potentials for understanding and for the facilitation of members' growth.[17] Although the therapist has a leadership position in this regard, the contributions of family members are a crucial positive factor and the work cannot be done without them. Henry Dicks's 1967 book *Marital Tensions* paved the way for the application of the analytic approach to the interaction of pairs in marriages.[18] Extending his work with Skynner's application of the ideas derived from the group-analytic method allows an approach to families. This approach has also recently been summarized by Shapiro in application to adolescent families.[19]

Appendix II
Sex therapy treatment model

Much of the clinical material reported in the main body of the book has been observed during the conduct of sex therapy with adult couples. The brief summary on the following pages is given to provide a frame of reference for the observations drawn. It should also serve as an introduction to the model of sex therapy employed by the author and his colleagues. It does not focus on the technique of applying sex therapy to the treatment of the disorders of sexual interactions, nor on the application of topics discussed in this book to other therapies. These will be the subject of the next volume.

Masters and Johnson's original model of sex therapy requires couples to stay in St Louis for two weeks of intensive work in isolation from their home environment.[1] After an initial medical, psychological, and sexual evaluation, sexual interactive exercises are prescribed for the couples to perform in privacy. The graded series much like that described below begins by removing the genitalia and woman's breasts from the interaction and also restricting verbal communication. Over the two-week period, physical components of the sexual relationship are added back. The *de facto* 'dissection' of sexual interaction allows the couple and the co-therapists to examine where sexual and interactive mistakes occur and to confront old attitudes and defensive reactions as well as to provide instruction and education. (This is done in a verbal review session after the couple conducts the assigned exercise privately.) A male and female co-therapy team are always used because of Masters and Johnson's view that understanding is fostered if each member of the couple has someone of the same sex 'in his (and her) corner.'

The essentials of the modification used by the author have been well described by Helen Singer Kaplan in *The New Sex Therapy*.[2] This method relies on a behavioral interactive framework derived from Masters and Johnson, but psychoanalytically derived interpretations are used whenever appropriate. Thus, therapists experienced in psychoanalytically-orientated therapy and in marital therapy can use these skills as applied to the sexual disorder. In practice, many modifications of technique, frequency of therapy sessions, and use of co-therapists

228

are employed by different workers. The reader may wish to refer to the work of Kaplan, Masters and Johnson, or to other references to survey the variety of technical approaches, some more psychodynamic, some more behavioral.[3]

Our current procedures are as follows. When a couple seeks help for a sexual disorder, or when one seems to play a prominent role in the symptomatology of marital disharmony, an evaluation is done, usually involving medical, urological, and gynecological examinations, and a psychological, interactive evaluation by a male–female co-therapy team (a single therapist may be used). After an initial meeting of the therapists and couple, separate interviews are conducted, the male therapist with husband and female therapist with wife, until general medical, sexual, and marital history is covered, usually two to three hours over one to three sessions. The therapists then exchange information, examine a sexual questionnaire each member of the couple has filled out by himself, and then conduct 'cross-over' interviews in which the male therapist meets with the wife and female therapist with the husband. Following final therapist consultation, the therapists meet with the couple for an interpretive session in which recommendations are made. Medical and physical findings, as well as psychological causes, are discussed. Assuming no medical/physical cause underlies the difficulty or is not the major cause, the recommendations for therapy range broadly to include formal sex therapy, marital therapy without a specific sexual focus, individual psychotherapy or psychoanalysis of one or both partners, group treatment (if, for instance, orgasmic failure in the woman is the major or only deficit), to *no* treatment at this time.[4] (This last recommendation ought to be made if the couple is on the verge of breaking up with more anger than commitment, or in some other circumstances in which the therapists feel that nothing useful can be offered under the present circumstances; e.g. on-going sexual affairs.[5]) Diagnostic categories are relevant, of course, to recommendations. For instance, a finding of a disorder predominantly deriving from the 'desire phase'[6] often requires individual psychotherapy or psychoanalysis, while other disorders such as situational dysfunction more often suggest conjoint treatment.

The author follows the classification of sexual disorders described by Kaplan.[7] She differentiates between 'proximal anxiety' caused by superficial or immediate factors in the sexual situation and more distant anxiety caused by underlying factors such as anger, depression, disinterest, etc. Further, disorders are divided by categories representing the phases of a triphasic model of sexual response, namely: (1) desire; (2) excitement; and (3) orgasm (see table A.1).

Assuming the recommendation for sex therapy is made and accepted, the couple is assigned the first of the series of graded home exercises which have the aim of reducing their sexual interaction to a non-threatening, non-genital level and then, as they master each step, adding a new component. Meetings, usually twice a week, are used for a detailed reporting and for study by couple and therapists. When any

Table A.1 Classification of sexual disorders (modified from Kaplan, 1979)

	Phase			Disorder
I	Desire	(1)	♂ & ♀	Low or absolute lack of interest
		(2)	♂ & ♀	Phobic avoidance of arousal or coitus (not clearly phase related)
		(3)	♂ & ♀	Unconsummated marriages
II	Excitement	(4)	♂	Impotence (or erectile dysfunction). Total or partial, absolute or situational
		(5)	♀	General sexual dysfunction in women (lack of enjoyment with or without desire)
		(6)	♀	Vaginismus
III	Orgasm	(7)	♂	Premature ejaculation (inadequate ejaculatory control)
		(8)	♂ & ♀	Total anorgasmia (far more frequent in women)
		(9)	♂	Retarded or absent ejaculation with a partner (usually in coitus)
		(10)	♀	Situational anorgasmia with partner and/or in coitus
		(11)	♂ & ♀	Dyspareunia associated with genital muscle spasm

level of exercise does not succeed, it is repeated. Additional components are not added until the current level is mastered. Much is learned from such failures and the couple is urged not to be discouraged. Here encouragement, support, and direct advice are blended with an interpretive approach which focuses both in depth and on phenomena relatively close to the current experience, such as 'spectator anxiety' in which a partner is essentially outside himself and watching over his own shoulder.[8] The in-depth interpretive work which is more emphasized in this task relies on less conscious material. The derivatives of the couple's interaction stemming from childhood, from experiences with parents and significant others, and from the long-standing patterns transferred from early experience to the spouse. This aspect of the work draws on verbal exchange, free association, dreams as understood by both the dreamer and the spouse, and the transference/countertransference techniques. It is the lessons and applications of this last group which are represented in this book. The techniques specific to them and derived from them are the subject of a second volume.

For purposes of reference, the rough sequence of exercises is listed in table A.2. Only the early assignments are standardized. The later ones are tailored to the couple and their specific difficulty. While many therapists may often omit the early exercises in their treatment modification, the author's group always begins with them because it is believed they invoke the early experiences of safety and reciprocity between the child and his parents. This point is clarified by chapters 3 and 4.

Table A.2 Series of exercises

	Title	Method	Communication
1	Non-genital sensate focus	Massage or 'pleasuring' of whole body in turns with oil or lotion *except* that contact with genitals and breasts is not allowed.	No verbal or non-verbal exchange except in case of pain. Focus is on a more self-directed experience, giving pleasure to self.
2	Genital sensate focus I	Genitals and breasts included *in passing* in pleasuring, arousal not to exceed a mild state.	Verbal and non-verbal (hand guiding) feedback by recipient about what is more or less pleasurable. Focus on getting pleasure from the other.
3	'Clinical' examination of genitalia and breasts	Couple gives a detailed examination of self and other. Speculum, instruction manual, and educational material provided.	Full informational cooperation and exchange is encouraged. Sexual arousal is not encouraged in this exercise.
4	Self-pleasuring and masturbation. (This may run concurrently with other exercises.)	Each partner, in private, pleasures himself and masturbates.	Communication with self, increased understanding of own body as preparation for communication to other.
5	Genital sensate focus II	Pleasuring focuses on genitals and breasts while still including whole body. Sexual arousal, while not required, is allowed to moderate degree but not to orgasm.	Broad communication encouraged verbally and non-verbally. Talking not encouraged beyond what is required, however.

Here the exercises diverge according to specific dysfunctions. Slow progression toward intercourse is the general method. Some or all of the following will be employed depending on the couple's situation.

	Title	Method	Communication
6a	For vaginismus	Insertion of progressively larger dilators during woman's self-pleasuring exercise.	Tolerance of own anxiety prior to shared situation.
6b	For premature ejaculation	The squeeze technique.[9] The woman stimulates the man to arousal, then uses thumb and first finger to squeeze just below the coronal ridge. This is repeated. or The Semans stop–start technique[10] in which the woman stimulates the man to near climax. At his signal, she stops until arousal diminishes. The procedure is repeated several times.	Communication about the man's increased knowledge of ejaculatory precursors and control.
6c	For impotence	Woman stimulates man's genitals and then moves to other areas, whether or not erection occurs, returning in several sequences to stimulate him.	Non-demand pleasuring reduces man's anxiety in interactive setting and reduces wife's demand.
6d	Absence or diminuation of female arousal, dyspareunia with predominantly psychological etiology, absence of female orgasm in shared setting.	Male alternately stimulates genitals and moves away in a non-demand format. Lessons from the woman's solo exercises are used for pleasurable approaches.	Non-demand pleasuring reduces the interference from woman's anxiety, learning transferred from solo to shared setting.

The next step is shared by all formats:

	Title	Method	Communication
7	Containment without movement	Woman (seated astride man) inserts penis and remains immobile. Man is passive throughout this step.	Mutual experience of reassurance in previously anxiety-provoking situation.
8	Containment with increasing movement	Slow movement is added with limit on arousal levels.	Mutuality of control and non-demand.

The following is again optional:

	Title	Method	Communication
9	For ejaculatory and orgasmic disorders: manual stimulation by woman of man, or man of woman, and/or either of self (the 'bridge technique')[11]	Woman may stimulate own clitoris during containment, man stimulates penis before entry or either use modifications of position to stimulate each other during containment.	Communication of patience and cooperation in place of demand.

Additionally, couples are encouraged to try new positions after the sequence of exercises with overt discussion about likes and dislikes. Orgasm is allowed during containment or in mutual masturbation depending on which anxieties interfere.

Typically, a final phase of sex therapy resembles termination of any therapy. Anxiety about stopping may trigger the brief return of symptomatology, offering a chance for review and fresh interpretation. Visits are usually tapered off to support the couple's progress in reintegrating new lessons into their on-going life without frequent contact with therapists. The usual time for this work is between three and five months, but may be somewhat shorter or longer.

It is important to note that in approximately one-third to one-half of our couples, further treatment of some sort is requested by one or both partners, either because the sex therapy reached an impasse or because its success demonstrated other areas of work still to be done which were previously covered from view by the couple's focus on the sexual disorder. Psychotherapy afterwards has ranged from a few sessions to psychoanalysis.

Outcome studies of sex therapy have recently become more controversial. Masters and Johnson's original report of 80 per cent overall success with only 5 per cent relapse in their five-year follow-up[12] remains impressive but has recently come under attack.[13] Levine, for instance, has reported that scrutiny of apparent successes yields a much lower rate of success than that reported by Masters and Johnson.[14]

The results obtained by the author and his colleagues seem to confirm these later views. Although a formal follow-up study has not been done to date, our results are clearly more moderate. Sex therapy is a valuable tool, but it is not the miracle it seemed it might have been. Our patients are complex and their marriages are complex. Success in one area, such as sexual satisfaction, is often blocked until other areas are approached. Sex therapy itself can work and for many couples is all that is needed. But for many others, it is one part of a longer path. Much of the material in the main text of this volume is an attempt to understand how and why this is so. So that the reader can assess the relative difficulty of the disorders mentioned in the text, Kaplan's estimates of prognosis are listed in table A.3.[15]

Table A.3 Helen S. Kaplan's estimates of treatment outcome of sexual disorders

Phase and/or type of disorder	Rate of treatment success in relieving sexual symptoms in brief sex therapy
Orgasm phase (anorgastic disorders ♂ & ♀ premature ejaculation)	90%
Retarded ejaculation	Variable with severity (good success if mild; little success if severe)
Excitement phase: Impotence	60% (50–80% depending on type and severity)
Excitement phase: General dysfunction in women	Variable (depending on relationship to partner and underlying causes)
Inhibited sexual desire	10–15%
Vaginismus (physical aspect only)	100%
Vaginismus with underlying phobia	Variable

Notes

Chapter 1 Introduction

1 J. Breuer and S. Freud, *Studies on Hysteria*, in *The Standard Edition of the Complete Psychological Works of Sigmund Freud*, vol. 2, J. Strachey (ed.) (London: The Hogarth Press, 1955); and S. Freud, 'Three essays on the theory of sexuality,' 1905, in *The Standard Edition of the Complete Psychological Works of Sigmund Freud*, vol. 7, J. Strachey (ed.) (London: The Hogarth Press, 1953), pp. 125–245.
2 A. Freud, *The Psychoanalytical Treatment of Children* (New York: International Universities Press, 1959). M. Klein, *The Psycho-Analysis of Children* (London: The Hogarth Press, 1932).
3 W.H. Masters and V.E. Johnson, *Human Sexual Response* (Boston: Little, Brown, 1966).
4 W.H. Masters and V.E. Johnson, *Human Sexual Inadequacy* (Boston: Little, Brown, 1970). H.S. Kaplan, *The New Sex Therapy: Active Treatment of Sexual Dysfunctions* (New York: Brunner/Mazel, 1974). H.S. Kaplan, *Disorders of Sexual Desire and Other New Concepts and Techniques in Sex Therapy* (New York: Brunner/Mazel, 1979).
5 J.D. Sutherland, 'Object-relations theory and the conceptual model of psychoanalysis,' *British Journal of Medical Psychology* 36 (1963): 109–24.
6 Kaplan, op. cit., 1974.

Chapter 2 The sexual relationship

* S. Freud, 'Three essays on the theory of sexuality,' 1905, in *The Standard Edition of the Complete Psychological Works of Sigmund Freud*, vol. 7, J. Strachey (ed.) (London: The Hogarth Press, 1953), pp. 125–245. See esp. p. 222.
1 D.W. Winnicott, 'The theory of the parent–infant relationship,' *International Journal of Psycho-Analysis* 41 (1960): 585–95. The

term 'psycho-somatic partnership' appears in D.W. Winnicott's *Playing and Reality* (London: Tavistock, 1971).

2 The approach I have taken is different from that of an earlier psychoanalytic attempt by Handelsman to relate early object experience to adult sexuality (I. Handelsman, 'The effects of early object relationships on sexual development: Autistic and symbiotic modes of adaptation,' *Psychoanalytic Study of the Child* 20 (1965): 367-83.) He attempts to describe the origin of 'healthy' and 'unhealthy' orgasms on the basis of defects in the autistic, symbiotic, and separation-individuation phases of development as described by Mahler. I agree with him that the vicissitudes of these phases are crucial in the growth of object relationships and the development of the sexual aspect of them, and that aspects of these phases will be important in the etiology of sexual difficulty for many of our patients. However, these difficulties will often not be about the 'health of the orgasm' alone. In any event, the maturity of the orgasm has been focused on by psychoanalysis to the exclusion of the total context of sexual relationship. We can now delineate sexual difficulties more specifically than we could in years past, and can trace their origins to describable interactions with primary objects. The earliest of these interactions take place in the context of the psychosomatic partnership of mother and child. Those interactions occurring later in childhood still influence the inheritance of this early partnership. The exploration of these matters is the subject of the ensuing chapters on child development and the origin of sexual disorders.

3 T.B. Brazleton and H. Als, 'Four early stages in the development of mother-infant interaction,' *Psychoanalytic Study of the Child* 34 (1979): 349-69.

4 I am indebted to Dr Jean Yacoubian for first calling this to my attention.

5 Freud, op. cit.

6 In this group are included Spitz, Bowlby, Winnicott, and Mahler, as well as others. See for instance R. Spitz, *The First Year of Life: A Psychoanalytic Study of Normal and Deviant Object Relations* (New York: International Universities Press, 1965); J. Bowlby, *Attachment and Loss*, vol. I, *Attachment* (1969); vol. II, *Separation: Anxiety and Anger* (1973); vol. III, *Loss: Sadness and Depression* (1980) (London: The Hogarth Press; and New York: Basic Books); D.W. Winnicott, *The Maturational Process and the Facilitating Environment: Studies on the Theory of Emotional Development* (London: The Hogarth Press, 1972); and M. Mahler, F. Pine, and A. Bergman, *The Psychological Birth of the Human Infant: Symbiosis and Individuation* (New York: Basic Books, 1975).

7 J.D. Sutherland has recently reviewed the history and contributions of this group. The reader not familiar with it should consult appendix I for a brief outline. 'The British object relations theorists:

Balint, Winnicott, Fairbairn, Guntrip,' *Journal of the American Psychoanalytic Association* 28, 4 (1980): 829–60.

8   H.V. Dicks, *Marital Tensions: Clinical Studies Towards a Psychological Theory of Interaction* (London: Routledge & Kegan Paul, 1967); A.C.R. Skynner, *Systems of Family and Marital Psychotherapy* (New York: Brunner/Mazel, 1976).

9   See appendix I for a detailed discussion of these concepts which are those of W.R.D. Fairbairn. See also his *Psychoanalytic Studies of the Personality* (London: Routledge & Kegan Paul, 1952), published in the United States as *An Object-Relations Theory of the Personality* (New York: Basic Books, 1954).

10   It is not my intent to summarize these biological underpinnings here but the reader may want to refer to the work of Money and Ehrhardt, Tanner, Kaplan, and Masters and Johnson, Sadock *et al.* as sources of information about the development and function of sexuality and sexual response. Sexual development from the psychological and interactional perspectives is discussed in the later chapters of this book which take up various life phases. References about sources at various life stages include: J. Tanner, 'Sequence, tempo and individual variation in the growth and development of boys and girls aged twelve to sixteen,' *Daedalus* 100 (1971): 907–30; J. Money and A. Ehrhardt, *Man and Woman, Boy and Girl: Differentiation and Dimorphism of Gender Identity* (Baltimore, MD: Johns Hopkins University Press, 1972); H.S. Kaplan, *The New Sex Therapy: Active Treatment of Sexual Dysfunction* (New York: Brunner/Mazel, 1974): W.H. Masters and V.E. Johnson, *Human Sexual Response* (Boston: Little, Brown, 1966). A compendium of briefer articles is contained in B.J. Sadock, H.I. Kaplan, and A.M. Freedman, *The Sexual Experience* (Baltimore, MD: Williams & Wilkins, 1976).

11   Hanna Segal has described the process of symbol formation as developing from the process of renunciation, a reliving of giving up the breast. The giving up of an object or instinctual aim is then successful if the object is assimilated within the ego by the process of loss and internal restoration. She suggests that such an object becomes a symbol within the ego, and that every aspect of the object and situation that is mourned gives rise to symbol formation.

> In this view symbol formation is the outcome of loss, it is a creative work involving pain and the whole work of mourning. If psychic reality is experienced and differentiated from external reality, the symbol is differentiated from the object; it is felt to be created by the self and can be freely used by the self (Hanna Segal, 'A psychoanalytic contribution to aesthetics,' *International Journal of Psycho-Analysis* 33 (1952): 196–207, and 'Notes on symbol formation,' *International Journal of Psycho-Analysis* 38 (1957): 391–7).

12   D.W. Winnicott, *Collected Papers: Through Paediatrics to Psycho-Analysis* (London: Tavistock, 1958).
13   M. Klein, 'Notes on some schizoid mechanisms,' *International Journal of Psycho-Analysis* 27, 3 (1946): 99–110. Also published in *Envy and Gratitude and Others Works, 1946–1963* (London: The Hogarth Press, 1975).
14   See appendix II for an outline of the techniques of sex therapy.

Chapter 3 The relevance of infancy for sexuality I: The child's attachment to its mother

*   H. Lichtenstein, 'Identity and sexuality', *Journal of the American Psychoanalytic Association* 9 (1961): 207.
1   R. Spitz, 'Hospitalism: An inquiry into the genesis of psychiatric conditions in early childhood,' *Psychoanalytic Study of the Child* 1 (1945): 53–74; and 'Hospitalism: A follow-up report,' *Psychoanalytic Study of the Child* 2 (1946): 113–17.
2   I owe much of my understanding of this area to extensive conversations with Charles Schwarzbeck. Some of this material is outlined in his paper, 'Identification of infants at risk for child neglect: Observations and inferences in the examination of the mother-infant dyad,' in G. Williams and J. Money, eds., *Traumatic Abuse and Neglect of Children at Home* (Baltimore, MD: Johns Hopkins University Press, 1978), pp. 240–6. See also T.B. Brazleton and H. Als, 'Four early stages in the development of mother-infant interaction,' *Psychoanalytic Study of the Child* 34 (1979): 349–69.
3   S. Fraiberg, E. Adelson, and V. Shapiro, 'Ghosts in the nursery: A psychoanalytic approach to the problems of impaired mother-infant relationships,' *Journal of the American Academy of Child Psychiatry* 14, 3 (1975): 387–421. See also S. Fraiberg, ed., *Clinical Studies on Infant Mental Health: The First Year of Life* (New York: Basic Books, 1980).
4   Other infant-mother therapists have emphasized that the baby often also has a role in the mismatch with its mother. Accordingly, they also provide an innovative form of therapy to the baby by offering a therapist substitute mother to provide remedial interactions. These are designed to make the baby more available to the mother as soon as she can respond. (S. Greenspan, 1981, personal communication.)
5   J. Bowlby, *Attachment and Loss*, vol. I, *Attachment* (London: The Hogarth Press, 1969), esp. chapter 13, 'A control systems approach to attachment behaviour.'
6   J. Bowlby, *Attachment and Loss*, vols. I, II and III (London: The Hogarth Press, 1969, 1973, 1980).
7   J. Bowlby, op. cit., 1973, p. 366 (in the 1975 Penguin edition).
8   Ibid., esp. p. 247 in the Penguin edition.

9 C. Schwarzbeck, 1981, personal communication.

10 H.F. Harlow and R.R. Zimmerman, 'Affectional responses in infant monkeys,' *Science* 130 (1959): 421-32; H.F. Harlow, J.L. McGaugh, and R.F. Thompson, *Psychology* (San Francisco: Albion, 1971); W.T. McKinney, 'Psychoanalysis revisited in terms of experimental primatology,' in E.T. Adelson (ed.) *Sexuality and Psychoanalysis* (New York: Brunner/Mazel, 1975).

11 W.T. McKinney, op. cit., 1975, p. 78.

12 E. Tronick, H. Als, L. Adamson, S. Wise, and T.B. Brazelton, 'The infant's response to entrapment between contradictory messages in face-to-face interaction,' *Journal of the American Academy of Child Psychiatry*, 17, 1 (1978): 1-13; K. Robson, 'The role of eye-to-eye contact in maternal infant attachment,' *Journal of Child Psychiatry and Psychology* 8 (1967): 13-25.

13 C. Schwarzbeck, 1981, personal communication.

14 H. Massie, 'The early natural history of childhood psychosis,' *Journal of the American Academy of Child Psychiatry* 14, 4 (1975): 683-707; H. Massie, 'The early natural history of childhood psychosis: Ten cases studied by analysis of family home movies of the infancies of the children,' *Journal of the American Academy of Child Psychiatry* 17, 1 (1978): 29-45.

15 D. Burlingham, 'Some notes on the development of the blind,' *Psychoanalytic Study of the Child* 16 (1961): 121-45; Selma Fraiberg, *Insights from the Blind* (New York: Basic Books, 1977); H. Als, E. Tronick, and T. Brazelton, 'Affective reciprocity and the development of autonomy: The study of a blind infant,' *Journal of the American Academy of Child Psychiatry* 19, 1 (1980): 22-40.

16 D.W. Winnicott, *Playing and Reality* (London: Tavistock, 1971). I am not here referring to Kohut's (1971) use of mirroring in the transference situation because I am trying to describe an actual developmental phase and function. (H. Kohut's *The Analysis of the Self*, New York: International Universities Press, 1971). I think there is no doubt that Kohut's use of mirroring draws on derivatives of this phenomenon. So does Lacan (J. Lacan, 'The mirror as formative of the function of the "I",' *Ecrits, A Selection*, translated by A. Sheridan, New York: Norton, 1977, chapter 1, pp. 1-7), who influenced Winnicott. The transferential use I also want to make of 'mirroring' in adult sexual life shares much with the observations of Kohut and Lacan, but derives more directly from Winnicott.

17 W.R. Bion, *Attention and Interpretation: A Scientific Approach to Insight in Psycho-Analysis and Groups* (London: Tavistock, 1970); H. Loewald, 'On the therapeutic action of psycho-analysis,' *International Journal of Psycho-Analysis* 41 (1960): 16-33.

18 H. Lichtenstein, 'Identity and sexuality: A study of their interrelationship in man,' *Journal of the American Psychoanalytic Association* 9 (1961): 179-260. Quotation is from pp. 206-7.

19 D.W. Winnicott, 'Ego distortion in terms of true and false self,' in *The Maturational Process and the Facilitating Environment: Studies in the Theory of Emotional Development* (London: The Hogarth Press, 1965), pp. 140–52.

Chapter 4 The relevance of infancy for sexuality II: Separation and individuation

1 M. Mahler, F. Pine, and A. Bergman, *The Psychological Birth of the Human Infant: Symbiosis and Individuation* (New York: Basic Books, 1975).

2 T.B. Brazleton, *et al.*, 'Presentation of infant–father, infant–mother and infant–stranger interactions.' Annual meeting of the American Academy of Child Psychiatry, Toronto, 1976.

3 It is also similar to interactions with inanimate objects like toys, suggesting the use of the father as a quasi-transitional phenomenon. (C. Schwarzbeck, 1981, personal communication.)

4 D.W. Winnicott, 'The theory of the parent–infant relationship,' *International Journal of Psycho-Analysis* 41 (1960): 585–95. Reprinted in *The Maturational Process and the Facilitating Environment* (London: The Hogarth Press, 1965).

5 Mahler, *et al.*, op. cit.

6 J. Bowlby, *Attachment and Loss*, vol. II, *Separation, Anxiety and Anger* (London: The Hogarth Press, 1973).

7 J. Robertson and J. Bowlby, 'Responses of young children to separation from their mothers,' *Courier du Centre International de l'Enfant* 2 (1952): 131–42; and J. Bowlby, op. cit., 1973.

8 J. Bowlby, op cit., 1973; *Attachment and Loss*, vol. III, *Loss, Sadness and Depression* (London: The Hogarth Press, 1980). Bowlby's 1960 paper 'Grief and mourning in infancy and early childhood' (*The Psychoanalytic Study of the Child* 15 (1960): 9–52) led to considerable controversy. A. Freud, M. Schur, and R. Spitz discussed the development and theoretical problems in the same volume (*The Psychoanalytic Study of the Child* 15 (1960): 53–94). The model of adult mourning, however, has been supported by repeated observers. See, for instance, E. Lindemann, 'Symptomatology and management of acute grief,' *American Journal of Psychiatry* 101 (1944): 141–9; and E. Furman, *A Child's Parent Dies: Studies in Childhood Bereavement* (London and New York: Yale University Press, 1974).

9 J. Bowlby, op. cit., 1980.

10 C.M. Parkes, 'Psycho-social transitions: A field of study,' *Social Science and Medicine* 5 (1971): 101–15.

11 D.W. Winnicott, 'Transitional objects and transitional phenomena,' in *Collected Papers: Through Paediatrics to Psycho-Analysis* (London: The Hogarth Press, 1958).

12 M. Mahler, *et al.*, op. cit., p. 100.

13 D.W. Winnicott, 'The location of cultural experience' chapter 7 of *Playing and Reality* (London: Tavistock, 1971), pp. 95–103. This is the same phenomenon Segal is discussing in locating symbol formation in the area of loss of the breast and the subsequent loss of objects. See H. Segal, *Introduction to the Work of Melanie Klein* (London: The Hogarth Press, 2nd edn., 1973).

14 H. Loewald, 'The therapeutic action of psycho-analysis,' *International Journal of Psycho-Analysis* 41 (1960): 16–33.

15 A. Freud, 'The role of bodily illness in the mental life of the child,' *Psychoanalytic Study of the Child* 7 (1952): 69–81.

Chapter 5 The beginnings of sexual relatedness in infancy and childhood

*   S. Freud, 'Three essays on the theory of sexuality,' 1905, addendum 1915, in *The Standard Edition of the Complete Psychological Works of Sigmund Freud*, vol. 7, J. Strachey (ed.) (London: The Hogarth Press, 1953), pp. 125–245. See esp. p. 182.

1 Ibid.

2 See the two articles by J. Kleeman: 'Genital self-discovery during a boy's second year,' *Psychoanalytic Study of the Child* 21 (1966): 358–92; and 'Genital self-stimulation in infant and toddler girls,' in *Masturbation: From Infancy to Senescence*, I. Marcus and J. Francis (eds.) (New York: International Universities Press, 1977), pp. 77–106.

3 R. Spitz and K..Wolf, 'Autoerotism: Some empirical findings and hypotheses on three of its manifestations in the first year of life,' *Psychoanalytic Study of the Child* 3/4 (1949): 85–119. See also R. Spitz, 'Autoerotism re-examined: The role of early sexual behavior patterns in personality formation,' *Psychoanalytic Study of the Child* 17 (1962): 283–315.

4 J. Nemiah, 1964, personal communication.

5 R. Edgcumbe and M. Burgner, 'The phallic–narcissistic phase: A differentiation between preoedipal and oedipal aspects of phallic development,' *Psychoanalytic Study of the Child* 30 (1975): 161–80.

6 H. Segal, *Introduction to the Work of Melanie Klein*, revised edition (London: The Hogarth Press, 1973).

7 H.J. Goldings, 'Jump-rope rhymes and the rhythm of latency development in girls,' *Psychoanalytic Study of the Child* 29 (1974): 431–50.

8 C. Sarnoff, *Latency* (New York: Jason Aronson, 1976).

Chapter 6 Sexual symptomatology in childhood and adolescence

1 Johnson coined the term 'superego lacunae' for the syndrome

described earlier by Szurek. Later she applied these findings to sexual behavior disorders and other behavior syndromes. For the progression of this work, see the following: S.A. Szurek, 'Genesis of psychopathic personality traits,' *Psychiatry* 5 (1942): 1–6; A.M. Johnson, 'Sanctions for superego lacunae of adolescents,' in K.R. Eissler (ed.) *Searchlights on Delinquency* (New York: International Universities Press, 1949), pp. 225–34; A.M. Johnson and S.A. Szurek, 'The genesis of antisocial acting out in children and adults,' *Psychoanalytic Quarterly* 21 (1952): 313–43; E.M. Litin, M.E. Giffin, and A.M. Johnson, 'Parental influences in unusual sexual behavior in children,' *Psychoanalytic Quarterly* 25 (1956): 37–55.

Chapter 7 The childhood origins of sexual difficulty I: The effect of early experiences with parents

*   S. Freud, 'Fragment of an analysis of a case of hysteria,' in *The Standard Edition of the Complete Psychological Works of Sigmund Freud*, vol. 17, J. Strachey (ed.) (London: The Hogarth Press, 1953), p. 56.

1   W.E. Masters and V.E. Johnson, *Human Sexual Inadequacy* (Boston: Little, Brown, 1970), pp. 139–40.

2   ibid., p. 175.

3   H.S. Kaplan, *The New Sex Therapy, Active Treatment of Sexual Dysfunctions* (New York: Brunner/Mazel, 1974).

4   R. Edgcumbe and M. Burgner, 'The phallic–narcissistic phase: A differentiation between preoedipal and oedipal aspects of phallic development,' *Psychoanalytic Study of the Child* 30 (1975): 161–80.

5   Freud had described the origins of the oedipus complex in the 1905 'Three essays' in the straightforward positive form. In 'From the History of an Infantile Neurosis' he referred to the oedipus complex of the Wolfman as 'an inverted one.' He did not link bisexuality to the oedipus complex until 1923 in 'The Ego and the Id'. There he clearly identifies the positive and negative aspects of the complete oedipus complex as due to the inherent bisexuality in children. Late in his life, in discussions with Ruth Mack Brunswick, he confirmed that the negative oedipus was the normal route in girls preceding this positive oedipal situation, but that any marked degree of negative oedipal development in boys was abnormal. (See Humberto Nagera's monograph *Female Sexuality and the Oedipus Complex* (New York: Jason Aronson, 1975) for a fuller consideration of Freud's development. This footnote draws on his discussion.) S. Freud, 'Three essays on the theory of sexuality,' 1905, in *The Standard Edition of the Complete Psychological Works of Sigmund Freud*, vol. 7, J. Strachey (ed.) (London: The Hogarth Press, 1953), pp. 125–245; S. Freud, 'From the history of an infantile neurosis,' 1918, in *The Standard Edition of*

the Complete Psychological Works of Sigmund Freud, vol. 17, J. Strachey (ed.) (London: The Hogarth Press, 1955), pp. 7–122; S. Freud, 'The ego and the id,' 1923, in *The Standard Edition of the Complete Psychological Works of Sigmund Freud*, vol. 19, J. Strachey (ed.) (London: The Hogarth Press, 1961), pp. 3–66; R.M. Brunswick, 'The preoedipal phase of ego development,' *Psychoanalytic Quarterly* 9 (1940): 293–319.

6   Brunswick, op. cit.; Edgcumbe and Burgner, op. cit.; R. Edgcumbe with S. Lundberg, R. Markowitz, and F. Salo, 'Some comments on the concept of the negative oedipal phase in girls,' *Psychoanalytic Study of the Child* 31 (1976): 35–61.

7   S. Freud, 'Three essays on a theory of sexuality,' op. cit.: Brunswick, op. cit.; J. Lampl-de Groot, 'The evolution of the oedipus complex in women,' 1927, in *The Psychoanalytic Reader*, R. Fliess (ed.) (New York: International Universities Press, 1948).

8   H. Nagera, *Female Sexuality and the Oedipus Complex*, op. cit. See esp. pp. 9–17.

9   Edgcumbe and Burgner, op. cit.

10   Brunswick, op. cit.; Nagera, op. cit.

11   Edgcumbe and her co-workers (op. cit., 1976) examined the Hampstead Psychoanalytic Index in 27 cases of girls who were analyzed. Their ages at the beginning of analysis ranged from 2:8 to 16:5. Only 8 had any evidence of significant negative oedipal material.

12   We would wonder if her husband is the 'father' of the inverted first stage in which she is a boy (figure 7.2, box E). The simpler explanation, however, seems more useful clinically since her clear primary sexual identification is as a woman and the unconscious bisexuality is only involved as a fall-back position.

13   See the previous note which also applies here.

14   W.R.D. Fairbairn, *Psychoanalytic Studies of the Personality* (American title: *An Object-Relations Theory of the Personality*) (London: Routledge & Kegan Paul, 1952; New York: Basic Books, 1954).

15   Freud, 'Fragment of an analysis of a case of hysteria,' pp. 79–80.

16   Freud, 'Three essays on a theory of sexuality,' p. 196.

17   M. Klein, 'Early stages of the oedipus conflict,' 1928, in *Love, Guilt and Reparation and Other Works, 1921–1945* (London: The Hogarth Press, reissued 1975). See appendix I for a brief summary of Kleinian theory.

18   Klein, op. cit.; H. Segal, *Introduction to the Work of Melanie Klein*, rev. edn (London: The Hogarth Press, 1973).

Chapter 8 The childhood origins of sexual difficulty II: The adequacy of the parents' functioning as parents

*   S. Freud, 'Three essays on the theory of sexuality,' 1905, in *The Standard Edition of the Complete Psychological Works of Sigmund*

Freud, vol. 7, J. Strachey (ed.) (London: The Hogarth Press, 1953), p. 225.

1 A. Freud, 'The role of bodily illness in the mental life of the child,' *Psychoanalytic Study of the Child* 7 (1952): 69–81.

2 See D.J. Henderson, 'Incest,' in *The Comprehensive Textbook of Psychiatry*, 2nd edn., A.M. Freedman, H.I. Kaplan, and B.J. Sadock (eds.) (Baltimore, MD: Williams & Wilkins, 1975), pp. 530–58; D. Meers, 'Precocious heterosexuality and masturbation: Sexuality and the ghetto,' in *Masturbation: From Infancy to Senescence*, I.M. Marcus and J.J. Francis (eds.) (New York: International Universities Press, 1975), pp. 411–38.

3 L.S. McGuire and N.N. Wagner, 'Sexual dysfunction in women who were molested as children: One response pattern and suggestions for treatment,' *Journal of Sex and Marital Therapy* 4, 1 (1978): 11–15.

4 See Henderson, op. cit.

5 J. Sandler, 'The background of safety,' *International Journal of Psycho-Analysis* 41 (1960): 352–6.

6 I. Kaufman, A.L. Peck, and C.K. Tagiuri, 'The family constellation and overt incestuous relations between father and daughter,' *American Journal of Orthopsychiatry* 24 (1954): 266–79; N. Lustig, J. Dresser, S. Spellman, and T. Murray, 'Incest: A family group survival pattern,' *Archives of General Psychiatry* 14 (Jan. 1966): 31–40.

7 M.M.R. Kahn, 'The concept of cumulative trauma,' *Psychoanalytic Study of the Child* 18 (1963): 286–306.

8 Henderson, op. cit. and Kaufman *et al.*, op. cit.

9 This conception is in accord, I believe, with O. Kernberg's formulation of mental structure in borderline personality development. For a thorough exploration of the psychogenesis of borderline personality, see 'Borderline personality organization,' *Journal of the American Psychoanalytic Association* 15 (1967): 641–85. This and other papers appear in *Borderline Conditions and Pathological Narcissism* (New York: Jason Aronson, 1975).

10 Kahn, op. cit. Fairbairn also held that it is not a defect at a single particular early moment but the prolonged exposure through later childhood to a constellation of object relationships which produces distortions of development. See *Psychoanalytic Studies of the Personality* (American title: *An Object-Relations Theory of the Personality*) (London: Routledge & Kegan Paul, 1952; New York: Basic Books, 1954).

Chapter 9 The parents' function as parents: Problems in sexual identity

* Heinz Lichtenstein, 'Identity and sexuality: A study of their interrelationship in man,' *Journal of the American Psychoanalytic Association* 9 (1961): 208.

1 Freud wrote that 'neurotic symptoms . . . give expression (by conversion) to instincts which would be described as *perverse* in the widest sense of the word if they could be expressed directly in phantasy and action without being diverted from consciousness. Thus, symptoms are formed in part at the cost of *abnormal* sexuality; *neuroses are, so to say, the negative of perversions.*' 'Three essays on the theory of sexuality,' 1905, in *The Standard Edition of the Complete Psychological Works of Sigmund Freud*, vol. 7, J. Strachey (ed.) (London: The Hogarth Press, 1953), p. 165. He held that the perversions were the expression in action of the same elements of infantile sexuality that the neurotic dammed up and only expressed in a disguised way.

2 H. Sachs, 'On the genesis of sexual perversion,' *Internationale Zeitschrift für Psychoanalyse* 9 (1923): 172–82, translation by H.F. Bernays, 1964, New York Psychoanalytic Institute Library, as quoted in C.W. Socarides, 'Homosexuality,' chapter 14, in *The American Handbook of Psychiatry*, vol. 3, 2nd rev. edn., S. Arieti and E.B. Brody (eds.) (New York: Basic Books, 1974), pp. 291-315.

3 O. Kernberg, 'Normal and pathological narcissism,' chapter 10, in *Borderline Conditions and Pathological Narcissism* (New York: Jason Aronson, 1975), pp. 328-31; C.W. Socarides has elaborated on Kernberg's ideas in his book *Homosexuality* (New York: Jason Aronson, 1978). He summarizes this formulation in chart form on pp. 489-96.

4 Socarides, op. cit., 1978, pp. 489-96.

5 I. Bieber, H. Dain, O. Dince, M. Drellich, H. Gand, R. Gundlack, M. Kremer, A. Rifkin, C. Wilbur, and T. Bieber, *Homosexuality: A Psychoanalytic Study* (New York: Basic Books, 1962).

6 Socarides, op. cit., 1974. It should also be noted that other explanations have been proposed including alternative family constellations, and the concept of multi-determined psychodynamic, sociocultural, biological, and situational factors. These include neuro-hormonal and constitutional causes and are reviewed by J. Marmor in 'Homosexuality and sexual orientation disturbances,' in *The Sexual Experience*, B. Sadock, H. Kaplan, and A. Freedman (eds.) (Baltimore, MD: Williams & Wilkins, 1976), pp. 374-91.

7 Socarides, op. cit., 1974.

8 L. Kolb and A. Johnson, 'Etiology and therapy of overt homosexuality,' *Psychoanalytic Quarterly* 24 (1955): 506-15.

9 M.T. Saghir and E. Robins, *Male and Female Homosexuality* (Baltimore, MD: Williams & Wilkins, 1973). This summary is taken from Marmor's summary of their work. See Marmor, op. cit.

10 Socarides, op. cit., 1974, pp. 306-7.

11 V. Volkan, 'Transsexualism: As examined from the viewpoint of internalized object relations,' in *The New Sexuality and Contemporary Psychiatry*, T.B. Karasu and C.W. Socarides (eds.) (New York: International Universities Press, 1979), pp. 189-221; J.K. Meyer, 'Clinical variants among sex reassignment applicants,'

Archives of Sexual Behavior 3 (1974): 527–58; and T.N. Wise and J.K. Meyer, 'Transvestism: Previous findings and new areas for inquiry,' *Journal of Sex and Marital Therapy* 6, 2 (Summer 1980): 116–28.

12   R. Stoller, *Sex and Gender* (New York: Science House, 1968).

13   Meyer, op. cit., 1974, and Volkan, op. cit.

14   Stoller, op. cit.; Volkan, op. cit.

15   See R. Stoller (1968), and his articles 'Boyhood gender aberrations: Treatment issues,' *Journal of the American Psychoanalytic Association* 26, 3 (1978): 541–58; and 'Fathers of transsexual children,' *Journal of the American Psychoanalytic Association* 27, 4 (1979): 837–66.

16   This patient was evaluated and classified as an 'aging transvestite' by Dr. Jon Meyer, to differentiate him from the true transsexuals described by Stoller (1974). Although these patients are like the transsexuals in claiming to feel they are women, the onset of this feeling is much later (as in this case) and has its origin in later issues than those of 'core gender identity.' See Meyer's 1974 article, op. cit., for a discussion of the differential diagnosis of these patients.

17   Stoller, op. cit., 1968, 1978, 1979.

Chapter 10 Adolescent precursors of sexual relationships: The move from self to object

*   Sigmund Freud, 'Three essays on the theory of sexuality,' 1905, in *The Standard Edition of the Complete Psychological Works of Sigmund Freud*, vol. 7, J. Strachey (ed.) (London: The Hogarth Press, 1953), p. 207.

1   P. Blos, *On Adolescence: A Psychoanalytic Interpretation* (New York: Free Press of Glencoe, 1962); P. Blos, 'The split parental image in adolescent social relations: An inquiry into group psychology,' *Psychoanalytic Study of the Child* 31 (1976): 7–33. B. Inhelder and J. Piaget, *The Growth of Logical Thinking from Childhood to Adolescence* (New York: Basic Books, 1958), A. Parsons and S. Milgram, translators.

2   M. Laufer, 'The central masturbation fantasy, the final sexual organization, and adolescence,' *Psychoanalytic Study of the Child* 31 (1976): 297–316.

3   V.L. Clower, 'Significance of masturbation in female sexual development and function,' in *Masturbation, from Infancy to Senescence*, I.M. Marcus and J.J. Francis (eds.) (New York: International Universities Press, 1975), pp. 107–43.

4   M.G. Kalogerakis, 'The effect on ego development of sexual experience in early adolescence,' in *Sexuality and Psychoanalysis*, E.T. Adelson (ed.) (New York: Brunner/Mazel, 1975), pp. 242–50.

5   D.R. Meers, 'Precocious heterosexuality and masturbation: sexuality

and the ghetto,' in *Masturbation: from Infancy to Senescence*, op. cit., pp. 411–38.

6 C.J. Kestenbaum, 'Some effects of the "sexual revolution" on the mid-adolescent girl,' in *Sexuality and Psychoanalysis* (1975), pp. 251–9. E. Hornick, 'Sexuality in adolescents: A plea for celibacy,' in *Sexuality and Psychoanalysis* (1975) pp. 238–41.

7 Laufer, op. cit.

8 P. Blos, 'The initial stage of male adolescence,' *Psychoanalytic Study of the Child* 20 (1965): 145–64.

9 P. Blos calls these stages 'Early adolescence, adolescence proper, and late adolescence,' op. cit., 1962.

10 M. Zelnik and J.F. Kantner, 'Sexual activity, contraceptive use and pregnancy among metropolitan-area teenagers: 1971–1979,' *Family Planning Perspectives* 12, 5 (Sept./Oct. 1980): 230–7; A.C. Kinsey, W. Pomeroy, and C. Martin, *Sexual Behavior in the Human Male* (Philadelphia: W.B. Saunders, 1948); A.C. Kinsey, W. Pomeroy, W. Martin, and P. Gebhard, *Sexual Behavior in the Human Female* (Philadelphia: W.B. Saunders, 1953); R.C. Sorenson, *Adolescent Sexuality in Contemporary America: Personal Values and Sexual Behavior, Ages 13 to 19* (New York: World Publishers, 1973).

11 Hornick, op. cit.

12 D.E. Scharff, T. Silber, G. Tripp, E. McGee, S. Bowie, and R. Emerson, 'The use of a sex rap group in an adolescent medical clinic,' *Adolescence* 15 (Winter 1980): 751–62.

13 E.J. Anthony, 'The reactions of adults to adolescents and their behavior,' in *Adolescence: Psychosocial Perspectives*, G. Caplan and S. Lebovici (eds.) (New York/London: Basic Books, 1969), pp. 54–78.

14 A.M. Johnson, 'Sanctions for superego lacunae of adolescents,' in *Searchlights on Delinquency*, K.R. Eissler (ed.) (New York: International Universities Press, 1949), pp. 225–34; E.M. Litin, M.E. Giffin, and A.M. Johnson, 'Parental influences in unusual sexual behavior in children,' *Psychoanalytic Quarterly* 25 (1956): 37–55.

15 J. Toolan, 'Sexual behavior in high school and college students,' in *Sexuality and Psychoanalysis* (1975) pp. 260–6.

16 Sorenson, op. cit.; Kantner and Zelnik, op. cit.

Chapter 11 Breaking in: Bodily aspects of bonding in courtship and marriage

1 E. Jacques has pointed out (*The Measurement of Responsibility*, London: Tavistock, 1956), that it is only while one is learning or teaching a job that a worker is explicitly aware of the parameters and anxieties which are involved in its exercise. With experience, the aspects of the job which require the most skilled judgments become essentially unconscious.

2   W.R.D. Fairbairn, 'The repression and return of bad objects (with special reference to the "War neurosis" (1943),' in *Psychonalytic Studies of the Personality* (American title: *An Object-Relations Theory of the Personality*) (London: Routledge & Kegan Paul, 1952; New York: Basic Books, 1954), pp. 59–81.

3   The term 'environment mother' was first used, as far as I know, by D.W. Winnicott in a 1963 paper, 'On communication,' published in *The Maturational Process and the Facilitating Environment* (London: The Hogarth Press, 1965). However, it is discussed and amplified helpfully in *Playing and Reality* (London: Tavistock, 1971).

4   S. Freud, 'Three essays on the theory of sexuality,' 1905, in *The Standard Edition of the Complete Psychological Works of Sigmund Freud*, vol. 7, J. Strachey (ed.) (London: The Hogarth Press, 1953). This quotation is from a 1915 addition, p. 222.

5   W. Goodrich postulates that a final phase of courtship is the testing of defenses. (Personal communication, 1981.)

6   The use of the term 'libidinal' here is not quite accurate in Fairbairn's terms (see appendix I). The attraction is formed partly to the ego-ideal and partly to the exciting (libidinal) object, and it is these combined forces which tend to temporarily suspend and deny the anti-libidinal forces, which return at a later date, sometime after the bond is made. If they return too strongly earlier, they may disrupt the bond and the couple fails to contract for a permanent relationship.

7   I am not intending to quarrel with the notion of primary narcissism or of a separate line of development for narcissism, as H. Kohut has argued (*The Analysis of the Self* (1971), and *The Restoration of the Self* (1977) (New York: International Universities Press) and H. Kohut and E.S. Wolf, 'The disorders of the self and their treatment: An outline,' *International Journal of Psycho-Analysis* 59 (1978): 413–25.) The argument does not change if we assume that it is the infant's primary love of himself which must be mirrored back to him in the mother's loving eyes. Obviously, I am more inclined to the object relations view that loving attachment to mother is a prerequisite to self-love which is born in the shared situation I have described. See D.W. Winnicott's discussion of the conditions required for 'The search for the self,' in *Playing and Reality*, pp. 54–6.

8   S. Freud, 'Observations on transference-love (further recommendations on the technique of psycho-analysis) III' (1915), in *The Complete Psychological Works of Sigmund Freud*, vol. 12, J. Strachey (ed.) (London: The Hogarth Press, 1958). For a clearer statement, see Freud's 'Beyond the Pleasure Principle', part III (1920): pp. 18–23, vol. 18, of *The Complete Psychological Works of Sigmund Freud*, 1955.

9   O. Kernberg, 'Mature love, prerequisites and characteristics,' in *Object-Relations Theory and Clinical Psychoanalysis* (New York:

Jason Aronson, 1976), pp. 215–39.

10 This pattern was first described by Freud in 'Some neurotic mechanisms in jealousy, paranoia and homosexuality (1922),' *The Standard Edition of the Complete Psychological Works of Sigmund Freud*, vol. 18, J. Strachey (ed.) (London: The Hogarth Press, 1955).

11 A second volume will consider the indications and problems of this form of treatment and of the triangular transference which is set in motion.

12 H.V. Dicks, *Marital Tensions: Clinical Studies Towards a Pyschological Theory of Interaction* (London: Routledge & Kegan Paul, 1967), pp. 129–33.

Chapter 12 The power of sex to sustain or disrupt marriage

1 L. Derogatis, J. Meyer, and B. Gallant, reporting on research at the John Hopkins Sexual Behavior Consultation Unit ('Distinctions between male and female invested partners in sexual disorders,' *American Journal of Psychiatry* 134, 4 (1977): 385–90) found that non-dysfunctional husbands of sexually dysfunctional wives showed as much psychological upset as if they were sexually dysfunctional themselves. In contrast, non-dysfunctional wives with dysfunctional husbands were not significantly different from a non-patient group. The male 'invested partners' (as they called them) showed elevations in anxious and depressive symptoms, higher levels of a paranoid style of thinking, and reported feeling worthless, frustrated, alienated, and blamed. With no firm explanation available for the difference in these findings, they suggest it may well be due to gender-specific role expectations for men which do not plague women. Regardless of the explanation, the potential for personal disruption by a sexual disorder is clearly demonstrated.

2 D.W. Winnicott, 'Ego distortions in terms of true and false self,' in *The Maturational Process and the Facilitating Environment: Studies on the Theory of Emotional Development* (London: The Hogarth Press, 1965), pp. 145–6.

3 Fairbairn suggests that the superego 'is really a complex structure comprising (a) the ideal object (or ego-ideal); (b) the anti-libidinal ego; and (c) the rejecting (or anti-libidinal) object.' See 'Synopsis of an object-relations theory of the personality,' *International Journal of Psycho-Analysis* 44 (1963): 224–5.

4 See appendix II for description of this stage.

5 L. Friedman, *Virgin Wives: A Study of Unconsummated Marriages* (London: Tavistock, 1962; Philadelphia: J.B. Lippencott, 1962). See also a review by V.J. Sadock, 'The unconsummated marriage,' in *The Sexual Experience*, B. Sadock, H. Kaplan, and A. Freedman (eds.) (Baltimore, MD: Williams & Wilkins, 1976), pp. 411–14.

Friedman's work reports on work done with groups of general practitioners under the sponsorship of Michael Balint in London, one of the original object-relations theorists.

6 This diagnostic category was established by Masters and Johnson as follows: 'For clinical purposes the primarily impotent man *arbitrarily* has been defined as a male never able to achieve and/or maintain an erection of quality sufficient to accomplish coital connection.' W.H. Masters and V.E. Johnson, *Human Sexual Inadequacy* (Boston: Little, Brown, 1970), p. 137.

7 The rationale for the treatment of the secret affair is alluded to in chapter 18 and will be considered extensively in the second volume. It is also discussed in D. Scharff, 'Truth and consequences in sex and marital therapy: The revelation of secrets in the therapeutic setting,' *Journal of Sex and Marital Therapy* 4, 1 (1978): 35–49. The somewhat magical outcome in this case is sometimes seen as an early response to this intervention. Most couples will need further help, but I do not have a further follow-up on this case.

8 See appendix I for discussion of the paranoid/schizoid and depressive positions.

Chapter 13 Facing the brink: Sex and separation

* J. Bowlby, *Attachment and Loss*, vol. II, *Separation, Anxiety and Anger* (London: The Hogarth Press, 1973).

1 J. Bowlby, *Attachment and Loss*, vol. III, *Loss, Sadness and Depression* (London: The Hogarth Press, 1980).

2 R. Weiss, *Marital Separation* (New York: Basic Books, 1975).

3 J. Wallerstein and J. Kelly, *Surviving the Break-Up: How Children and Parents Cope with Divorce* (New York: Basic Books, 1980).

Chapter 14 Children of parents with sexual dysfunction

* S. Freud, 'Three essays on the theory of sexuality,' 1905, in *The Standard Edition of the Complete Psychological Works of Sigmund Freud*, vol. 7, J. Strachey (ed.) (London: The Hogarth Press, 1953), p. 228.

1 S. Freud, 'Fragment of an analysis of a case of hysteria,' 1905, in *The Standard Edition of the Complete Psychological Works of Sigmund Freud*, vol. 7, J. Strachey (ed.) (London: The Hogarth Press, 1953), pp. 7–122.

2 F. Deutsch, 'A footnote to Freud's "Fragment of an analysis of a case of hysteria",' *Psychoanalytic Quarterly* 26 (1957): 159–67.

3 E.H. Erikson, 'Reality and actuality,' *Journal of the American Psychoanalytic Association* 10 (1962): 454–61.

4   This was the finding of family therapists from the beginning. See
    N.W. Ackerman, *The Psychodynamics of Family Life: Diagnosis
    and Treatment of Family Relationships* (New York: Basic Books,
    1958; reissue, Harper Torch Books, 1972). He discusses, for ex-
    ample, the rejection of a child by father secondary to sexual frus-
    tration (p. 185). But a more graphic illustration is given in his
    Treating the Troubled Family (New York: Basic Books, 1966), in
    which the first chapter gives a verbatim transcript of a case in
    which parental sexual discord underlies the children's symptoma-
    tology. See also S.A. Szurek, 'Concerning the sexual disorders of
    parents and their children,' *Journal of Nervous and Mental Dis-
    eases* 120 (1974): 369–78; and A.C.R. Skynner, *Systems of Family
    and Marital Psychotherapy* (New York: Brunner/Mazel, 1976).
5   Again, the names and circumstances of all cases have been thor-
    oughly altered.
6   R. Waelder, 'The principle of multiple function: Observations on
    over-determination,' translated by M.H. Milde, *Psychoanalytic
    Quarterly* 5 (1936): 45–62.
7   J. Zinner and R. Shapiro, 'The family as a single psychic entity:
    Implications for acting out in adolescence,' *International Review of
    Psycho-Analysis* 1, 1 (1974): 179–86.
8   See also A.M. Johnson, 'Sanctions for super-ego lacunae of adoles-
    cents,' in K.R. Eissler (ed.) *Searchlights on Delinquency* (New
    York: International Universities Press, 1949), pp. 225–34; A.M.
    Johnson and S.A. Szurek, 'The genesis of anti-social acting out in
    children and adults,' *Psychoanalytic Quarterly* 21 (1952): 313–43;
    and E.M. Litin, M.E. Giffin, and A.M. Johnson, 'Parental influ-
    ences in unusual sexual behavior,' *Psychoanalytic Quarterly* 25
    (1956): 37–55.
9   Erikson, op. cit.
10 Deutsch, op. cit.
11 J. Bowlby, *Attachment and Loss*, vol. I, *Attachment* (London:
    The Hogarth Press, 1969).
12 See appendix I for the discussion of early oedipal development.
    Also see: M. Klein, 'Early stages of the oedipus conflict,' in *Love,
    Guilt and Reparation and Other Works, 1921–1945* (London: The
    Hogarth Press, 1973), pp. 196–98. For a brief and readable summary
    of Klein's views, see H. Segal's *Introduction to the Work of Melanie
    Klein*, rev. edn. (London: The Hogarth Press, 1973).

Chapter 15 The effects of the child's development on parental sexuality

1   T. Benedek, 'Parenthood as a developmental phase: A contribution
    to the libido theory,' *Journal of the American Psychoanalytic Asso-
    ciation* 7 (1959) 389–417; also, 'The family as a psychologic field,'
    in *Parenthood, Its Psychology and Psychopathology*, E.J. Anthony
    and T. Benedek (eds.) (Boston: Little, Brown, 1970), pp. 109–36.

2   The book *Parenthood*, op. cit., provides a wealth of contributions in this area.

3   L. Jessner, 'On becoming a mother,' in R. Griffith (ed.) *Conditio Humana* (Berlin: Springer, 1966); L. Jessner, E. Weigert, and J. Foy, 'The development of parental attitudes during pregnancy,' 1970, in *Parenthood*, op. cit., pp. 209–44.

4   G.L. Bibring, T.F. Dwyer, D.S. Huntington, and A.F. Valenstein, 'A study of the psychological processes in pregnancy and of the earliest mother–child relationship: I. Some propositions and comments, II. Methodological considerations,' *Psychoanalytic Study of the Child* 16 (1961): 9–72.

5   N.K. Wenner, 'Dependency patterns in pregnancy,' in J.H. Masserman (ed.) *Science and Psychoanalysis* 10 (New York: Grune and Stratton, 1966), pp. 94–104.

6   Jessner, op. cit., 1966; and Jessner *et al.*, op. cit., 1970.

7   W.H. Masters and V.E. Johnson, *Human Sexual Response* (Boston: Little, Brown, 1966), pp. 146–68.

8   A. Tolor, in a commentary on 'The impact of pregnancy in marriage,' by P. Brenner and M. Greenberg, *Medical Aspects of Human Sexuality* 11, 7 (July 1977): 21–2, summarized findings that 47 per cent of his sample of women reported a decreased desire for intercourse during pregnancy, but 16 per cent actually reported a heightened desire. He found median weekly frequencies of intercourse to be: first trimester, 2.25; second trimester, 2.39; and third trimester, 1.08; while post-partum women reported a median weekly frequency of 2.65. He does not indicate how much of the decrease in frequency during pregnancy was felt to be secondary to physiological factors, but his findings seem to contradict Masters and Johnson's findings of increased eroticism and lubrication early in pregnancy. In late pregnancy, they note that physiological changes do offer an impediment (*Human Sexual Response*, 1966).

9   P. Brenner and M. Greenberg, 'The impact of pregnancy in marriage,' *Medical Aspects of Human Sexuality* 11, 7 (July 1977): 15–21.

10 Masters and Johnson, op. cit.

11 M. Greenberg and P. Brenner, 'The newborn's impact on parents' marital and sexual relationship,' *Medical Aspects of Human Sexuality* 11, 8 (August 1977): 16–28.

12 D.W. Winnicott, 'The theory of the parent–infant relationship,' *International Journal of Psycho-Analysis* 41 (1960): 585–95; reprinted in *The Maturational Process and the Facilitating Environment: Studies on the Theory of Emotional Development* (London: The Hogarth Press, 1965), pp. 37–55.

13 M. Greenberg and P. Brenner, op. cit., August 1977.

14 C.M. Parkes, 'Psycho-social transitions: A field for study,' in *Social Science and Medicine* 5 (1971): 101–15.

15 W.T. McKinney, 'Psychoanalysis revisited in terms of experimental primatology,' in *Sexuality and Psychoanalysis*, E.T. Adelson (ed.) (New York: Brunner/Mazel, 1975), pp. 67–93.

Chapter 16 Sex and the mid-life crisis

* Dante Alighieri, *The Inferno*, John Ciardi, translator (New York: Times Mirror, New American Library; London: New English Library, 1954), Canto I, lines 1–6, p. 28. I have followed Elliott Jacques in using this passage as an introduction to the discussion of the mid-life crisis. See E. Jacques, 'Death and the mid-life crisis,' *International Journal of Psycho-Analysis* 46, 4 (1965): 502–41.

1 E. Jacques, op. cit.

2 ibid.

3 H.S. Kaplan, *Disorders of Sexual Desire, and Other New Concepts and Techniques in Sex Therapy* (New York: Brunner/Mazel, 1979).

4 W.H. Masters and V.E. Johnson, *Human Sexual Response* (Boston: Little, Brown, 1966), p. 243.

5 H. Deutsch, *The Psychology of Women*, vols. 1 and 2 (New York: Grune & Stratton, 1945).

6 Masters and Johnson, op. cit.

7 E. Frank, C. Anderson, and D. Rubenstein, 'Frequency of sexual dysfunction in "normal" couples,': paper presented at Annual Meeting of the Eastern Association for Sex Therapy, New York City, March 3, 1977.

8 R. Gould, 'The phases of adult life: A study in developmental psychology,' *American Journal of Psychiatry* 129 (1972): 521–31; D.J. Levinson, *The Seasons of a Man's Life* (New York: Knopf, 1978); G.E. Vaillant and E. Milofsky, 'Natural history of male psychological health: IX, Empirical evidence for Erikson's model of the life cycle,' *American Journal of Psychiatry* 137, 11 (1980): 1348–59.

9 W.M. Sotile, 'The penile prothesis: A review,' *Journal of Sex and Marital Therapy* 5, 2 (Summer 1979): 90–102.

Chapter 17 Aging, loss, and sexual development

1 W.H. Masters and V.E. Johnson, *Human Sexual Inadequacy* (Boston: Little, Brown, 1970), p. 350.

2 ibid.

3 W.H. Masters and V.E. Johnson, op. cit.; H.S. Kaplan, *The New Sex Therapy: Active Treatment of Sexual Dysfunctions* (New York: Brunner/Mazel, 1974); R.N. Butler and M. Lewis, *Sex After Sixty* (New York: Harper & Row, 1976).

4 E.H. Erikson, *Childhood and Society* (New York: Norton, 1950; rev. paperback edn., 1963), pp. 268–9.

5 E. Jacques, 'Death and the mid-life crisis,' *International Journal of Psycho-Analysis* 46, 4 (1965): 502–41.

6 R.N. Butler, 'Sexual advice to the aging male,' *Medical Aspects of Human Sexuality* 9, 9 (Sept. 1975): 155–6; see also Butler and Lewis, *Sex After Sixty*, op. cit.

7 This is a finding which can be confirmed in the laboratory by sleeping measurement of spontaneous nocturnal penile tumescence. See C. Fisher, C.R. Schiavi, A. Edwards, D. David, M. Reitman, and J. Fine, 'Evaluation of nocturnal penile tumescence in the differential diagnosis of sexual impotence: A quantitative study,' *Archives of General Psychiatry* 36 (1979): 432-7.

8 The sexual expression of ambivalence itself can be thought of as having a line of development which derives from the early splitting of the object and is normally largely resolved in adolescence. See D. Scharff, 'Expressions of ambivalence in sexual relationships,' *Medical Aspects of Human Sexuality* 11, 3 (March 1977): 59-78.

9 J. Bowlby, *Attachment and Loss*, vol. III, *Loss, Sadness and Depression* (London: The Hogarth Press, 1980); R. Weiss, *Marital Separation* (New York: Basic Books, 1975); and R. Weiss, 'Commentary,' in *Medical Aspects of Human Sexuality* 10, 9 (1976): 48-51. See also C.M. Parkes, *Bereavement: Studies of Grief in Adult Life* (London: Tavistock; New York: International Universities Press, 1972), and L. Pincus, *Death and the Family: The Importance of Mourning* (London: Faber & Faber, 1976).

10 P.J. Clayton and P.E. Barnstein, 'Widows and widowers,' *Medical Aspects of Human Sexuality* 10, 9 (Sept. 1976): 27-48.

11 R. Weiss, commentary on Clayton & Barnstein, op. cit., 1976.

Chapter 18 The dynamics of extra-marital sex

1 J.N. Edwards, 'Extramarital involvement: Fact and theory,' *Journal of Sex Research* 9, 3 (August 1973): 210-24.

2 H.V. Dicks, *Marital Tensions: Clinical Studies Towards a Psychological Theory of Interaction* (London: Routledge & Kegan Paul, 1967).

3 H.S. Strean, 'The extramarital affair: A psychoanalytic view,' *The Psychoanalytic Review* 63, 1 (1976): 101-13; H.S. Strean, *The Extramarital Affair* (New York and London: The Free Press, 1980).

4 A.C.R. Skynner, *Systems of Family and Marital Psychotherapy* (New York: Brunner/Mazel, 1976).

5 H. Steirlin, *Psychoanalysis and Family Therapy* (New York: Jason Aronson, 1977).

6 A. Gross, 'The secret,' *Bulletin of the Menninger Clinic* 15, 2 (March 1951): 37-44.

7 ibid., p. 44.

8 W.H. Masters and V.E. Johnson, *Human Sexual Inadequacy* (Boston: Little, Brown, 1970).

9 D.E. Scharff, 'Truth and consequences in sex and marital therapy: The revelation of secrets in the therapeutic setting,' *Journal of Sex and Marital Therapy* 4, 1 (Spring 1978): 35-49.

Chapter 19 Toward a framework for sexual maturity

* Michael Balint, 'On genital love,' *International Journal of Psycho-Analysis* 29 (1948): 34-40; reprinted in *Primary Love and Psycho-analytic Technique*, rev. edn. (London: Tavistock, 1965), p. 117.

1 ibid.

2 A.N. Levay and A. Kagle, 'Ego deficiencies in the areas of pleasure, intimacy, and cooperation: Guidelines in the diagnosis and treatment of sexual dysfunctions,' *Journal of Sex and Marital Therapy* 3, 1 (Spring 1977): 10-18.

3 L.E. Peller, 'Libidinal phases, ego development and play,' *Psychoanalytic Study of the Child* 9 (1954): 178-98; D.W. Winnicott, *Playing and Reality* (London: Tavistock, 1971).

4 J.M.M. Hill, 'The child's changing perception of work from the age of seven,' in D.E. Scharff and J.M.M. Hill, *Between Two Worlds: Aspects of the Transition from School to Work* (London: Careers Consultants, 1976).

5 Balint, op. cit.

6 J. Bowlby, *Attachment and Loss*, vol. II, *Separation, Anxiety and Anger* (London: The Hogarth Press, 1973).

Appendix I Object relations theory and the family

1 Sutherland has recently summarized the theories and relationship of the object relations group. See J.D. Sutherland, 'The British object-relations theorists: Balint, Winnicott, Fairbairn, Guntrip,' *Journal of American Psychoanalytic Association* 28, 4 (1980): 829-60.

2 W.R.D. Fairbairn, *Psychoanalytic Studies of the Personality* (American title: *An Object-Relations Theory of the Personality*) (London: Routledge & Kegan Paul, 1952; New York: Basic Books, 1954); W.R.D. Fairbairn, 'Observations on the nature of hysterical states,' *British Journal of Medical Psychology* 27, 3 (1954): 105-25; W.R.D. Fairbairn, 'Synopsis of the object-relations theory of the personality,' *International Journal of Psycho-Analysis* 44 (1963): 224-5; J.D. Sutherland, 'Object-relations theory and the conceptual model of psychoanalysis,' *British Journal of Medical Psychology* 36 (1963): 109-24; and J.D. Sutherland, op. cit., 1980. Sutherland's articles give the best available overview of Fairbairn's theory and its amplifications by others in this group.

3 The following discussion draws extensively on H. Segal's *Introduction to the Work of Melanie Klein*, rev. edn. (London: The Hogarth Press, 1973). This and her more recent exposition are invaluable sources for understanding Klein's work. See also her *Klein* (Glasgow: Harvester Press and Fontana/Collins, 1979).

4 Sutherland op. cit., 1980.

5 M. Klein, *Love, Guilt and Reparation and Other Works, 1921-1945*

and *Envy and Gratitude and Other Works, 1946–1963* (London: The Hogarth Press, 1975). Helpful papers include 'Notes on some schizoid mechanisms,' presented in 1946, a particularly clear paper, and 'Our adult world and its roots in infancy,' first published in 1959.

6 E. Zetzel, *The Capacity for Emotional Growth* (London: The Hogarth Press, 1970).

7 H. Segal, op. cit., 1973, pp. 126–7.

8 ibid., pp. 27–8.

9 J. Bowlby, *Attachment and Loss*, vol. I, *Attachment* (London: The Hogarth Press, 1969); see also Fairbairn, op. cit., 1952.

10 C.M. Parkes, 'Psycho-social transitions: A field for study,' *Social Science and Medicine* 5 (1971): 101–15; and C.M. Parkes, 'What becomes of redundant world models? A contribution to the study of adaptation to change,' *British Journal of Medical Psychology* 48 (1975): 131–7.

11 W. Bion, *Experiences in Groups* (London: Tavistock, 1961). Margaret Rioch has summarized Bion's contribution in an easily comprehensible way. See M. Rioch, 'The work of Wilfred Bion on Groups,' *Psychiatry* 33, 1 (1970): 56–66. Reprinted in *Progress in Group and Family Therapy*, C. Sager and H. Kaplan (eds.) (New York: Brunner/Mazel, 1972), pp. 18–32.

12 P. Turquet, presentation at the School of Family and Community Psychiatry (London: Tavistock Institute of Human Relations, 1973).

13 J. Zinner and R. Shapiro, 'The family group as a single psychic entity: Implications for acting out in adolescence,' *International Review of Psycho-Analysis* 1, 1 (1974): 179–86; R. Shapiro, 'Family dynamics and object-relations theory: An analytic, group-interpretive approach to family therapy,' in *Adolescent Psychiatry*, vol. 7, S. Feinstein and P. Giovacchini (eds.) (Chicago: University of Chicago Press, 1979), pp. 118–35; A.J. Ferreira, 'Family myth and homeostasis,' *Archives of General Psychiatry* 9 (Nov. 1963): 457–63; J. Byng-Hall, 'Family myths used as a defense in conjoint family therapy,' *British Journal of Medical Psychology* 46 (1973): 239–50.

14 Zinner and Shapiro, op. cit., 1974.

15 A. Cooklin, 'A psychoanalytic framework for a systemic approach to family therapy,' *Journal of Family Therapy* 1 (1979): 153–65; A.C.R. Skynner, *Systems of Family and Marital Psychotherapy* (British title: *One Flesh, Separate Persons: Principles of Family and Marital Psychotherapy.*) (New York: Brunner/Mazel, 1976).

16 S.H. Foulkes, *Introduction to Group-Analytic Psychotherapy* (London: Heinemann, 1948), *Therapeutic Group Analysis* (London: Allen and Unwin, 1964); S.H. Foulkes and E.J. Anthony, *Group Psychotherapy: The Psychoanalytic Approach*, 2nd edn. (Harmondsworth: Penguin, 1965); A.C.R. Skynner, op. cit., 1976.

17   A.C.R. Skynner, op. cit., 1976.
18   H.V. Dicks, *Marital Tensions: Clinical Studies Towards a Psychological Theory of Interaction* (London: Routledge & Kegan Paul, 1967).
19   Shapiro, op. cit., 1979.

Appendix II Sex therapy treatment model

1   W.H. Masters and V.E. Johnson, *Human Sexual Inadequacy* (Boston: Little, Brown, 1970).
2   H.S. Kaplan, *The New Sex Therapy: Active Treatment of Sexual Dysfunctions* (New York: Brunner/Mazel, 1974). See also her second volume for later developments and modifications in what Kaplan has aptly termed 'psychosexual therapy.' H.S. Kaplan, *Disorders of Sexual Desire and Other New Concepts and Techniques in Sex Therapy* (New York: Brunner/Mazel, 1979).
3   For instance, Hartman and Fithian, and LoPiccolo and LoPiccolo are more behavioral, while Kaplan's two volumes are the most psychodynamic. See also the articles on the psychodynamic approach by Jon Meyer in the volume he has edited and a recent compendium by Lieblum and Perrin. *The Journal of Sex and Marital Therapy* has published a wide variety of contributions to sex therapy. Treatment of the late adolescent and young adult population specifically is discussed by Lorna and Philip Sarrel. W.E. Hartman and M.A. Fithian, *Treatment of Sexual Dysfunctions: A Bio-Psycho-Social Approach* (Long Beach, CA: Center for Marital and Sexual Studies, 1972); S.R. Lieblum and L.E. Pervin (eds.) *Principles and Practice of Sex Therapy* (New York: Guilford, 1980); J. LoPiccolo and L. LoPiccolo (eds.) *Handbook of Sex Therapy* (New York and London: Plenum Press, 1978); J.K. Meyer (ed.) *Clinical Management of Sexual Disorders* (Baltimore, MD: Williams & Wilkins, 1976); L.J. Sarrel and P.M. Sarrel, *Sexual Unfolding: Sexual Development and Sex Therapies in Late Adolescence* (Boston: Little, Brown, 1979).
4   For the group treatment of female orgasmic disorders, see one book for the lay audience and two technical articles: L.G. Barbach, *For Yourself, The Fulfillment of Female Sexuality* (Garden City: Anchor Press/Doubleday, 1976) and L.G. Barbach, 'Group treatment of preorgasmic women,' *Journal of Sex and Marital Therapy* 1, 2 (1974): 139–46; and L.G. Barbach and M. Flaherty, 'Group treatment of situationally orgasmic women,' *Journal of Sex and Marital Therapy* 6, 1 (1980): 19–29.
5   See chapter 18 of this volume for a discussion of the psychic and interpersonal dynamics of affairs. A major element of management is discussed in: D.E. Scharff, 'Truth and consequences in sex and marital theory: The revelation of secrets in the therapeutic setting,' *Journal of Sex and Marital Therapy* 4, 1 (1978): 35–49.

The overall clinical management of extra-marital affairs will be considered extensively in the next volume.

6 Kaplan, op. cit., 1979.
7 Kaplan, op. cit., 1974, 1979.
8 Masters and Johnson, op. cit., 1970, p. 11.
9 Masters and Johnson, op. cit., 1970, pp. 102–6.
10 J. Semans, 'Premature ejaculation: A new approach,' *Southern Medical Journal* 49 (1956): 353–8; Kaplan, op. cit., 1974, also extensively discusses this technique which she feels to be superior to the 'squeeze' method. In practice, we have found both to be of use in different patients.
11 Kaplan, op. cit., 1974.
12 Masters and Johnson, op. cit., 1970.
13 B. Zilbergeld and M. Evans, 'The inadequacy of Masters and Johnson,' *Psychology Today* 14, 3 (Aug. 1980): 29–43.
14 S.B. Levine and D. Agle, 'The effectiveness of sex therapy for chronic secondary psychological impotence,' *Journal of Sex and Marital Therapy* 4, 4 (1978): 235–58.
15 Kaplan, op. cit., 1974, 1979.

Index

264 *Index*

Index of cases